Building Your
Multi-
Million-
Dollar
PRACTICE

"It's refreshing to read a book that combines the Vesseneses' insights from different fields. They provide keen observations from a broad perspective, distilling their financial and management thinking into practical, specific advice. Katherine and Peter have done the hard work necessary to put together a book that is both helpful and interesting."

KATHY KOLBE
Chairwoman, Kolbe Corporation
Author of *Powered by Instinct*

"Regardless of where you are in your financial advisory career, you will prosper from the smart business development and operational techniques shared in this book. Learn them, implement them, and design your business to fully work for you!"

SHERYL GARRETT, CFP®
Founder of The Garrett Planning Network, Inc.
Author of *Garrett's Guide to Financial Planning, Just Give Me the Answer$*,
and *Money Without Matrimony*

"The greatest threat to the development of financial planning as a profession is the lack of a sufficient number of multiprofessional firms that can accommodate the growing number of graduates from financial planning degree programs. *Building Your Multi-Million-Dollar Practice* directly addresses many of the concepts and strategies that can take this profession from the "lone wolf, one-person shops" of yesterday, to the vibrant, collegial, professional environments that will thrive and survive over future generations."

FREDRICK E. ADKINS III, CFP®, MBA, ChFC, CLU

"If you want to transform your business into a high profile, high performance financial advisory practice, then *Building Your Multi-Million-Dollar Practice* is mandatory reading. Peter and Katherine Vessenes have translated decades of experience into a book so full of great ideas and concepts that you will want to read it several times. Whatever you do, keep this book away from your competitors!"

STEWART H. WELCH III, CFP®, AEP
Coauthor of *J.K. Lasser's New Rules for Estate and Tax Planning*
and *The Complete Idiot's Guide to Getting Rich*

"Katherine and Peter Vessenes have written a book every financial advisor should not just read, but study and implement. It's about running a financial advice *business*. You can be the best possible financial advisor, but if you can't budget, plan, promote, hire, and train, not very many people will know about it."

BILL GOOD
Chairman, Bill Good Marketing, Inc.

Building Your Multi-Million-Dollar PRACTICE

········➤ (8) SUCCESS STRATEGIES

OF TOP PRODUCING ADVISORS

Peter Vessenes, RFC
Katherine Vessenes, JD, CFP®, RFC

Dearborn™
Trade Publishing
A **Kaplan Professional** Company

This publication is designed to provide accurate and authoritative information in regard to the subject matter covered. It is sold with the understanding
that the publisher is not engaged in rendering legal, accounting, or other
professional service. If legal advice or other expert assistance is required, the
services of a competent professional should be sought.

President, Dearborn Publishing: Roy Lipner
Vice President and Publisher: Cynthia A. Zigmund
Senior Acquisitions Editor: Mary B. Good
Preliminary Editor: Connie Anderson
Development Editor: Karen Murphy
Senior Project Editor: Trey Thoelcke
Interior Design: Lucy Jenkins
Cover Design: Scott Rattray, Rattray Design
Typesetting: the dotted i

Published by Dearborn Trade Publishing
A Kaplan Professional Company

Printed in the United States of America

05   06   07   10   9   8   7   6   5   4   3   2   1

Library of Congress Cataloging-in-Publication Data

Vessenes, Peter.
    Building your multi-million-dollar practice : 8 success strategies of top
    producing advisors / Peter Vessenes and Katherine Vessenes.
        p.   cm.
    Includes index.
    ISBN 1-4195-1505-5
    1. Financial planners.   2. Investment advisors.   I. Vessenes,
Katherine.   II. Title.
    HG179.5.V474 2005
    332.024′0068′4—dc22
                                                                2005005517

Dearborn Trade books are available at special quantity discounts to use for
sales promotions, employee premiums, or educational purposes. Please call
our Special Sales Department to order or for more information at 800-621-
9621 ext. 4444, e-mail trade@dearborn.com, or write to Dearborn Trade Publishing, 30 South Wacker Drive, Suite 2500, Chicago, IL 60606-7481.

This book is dedicated to the entrepreneurs who use their business to bring prosperity and blessings to those they serve.

C o n t e n t s

In December of 2001, I launched into the biggest challenge of my career: remaking a broker/dealer from the inside out. After having an opportunity to discuss the challenges of my new position with my wife, I made the next call to Katherine and Peter Vessenes.

I had known Katherine for several years and had even tried to hire her as my chief marketing officer at the ING broker/dealer network. Peter was not as familiar to me, but I knew of his great reputation for fixing unfixable businesses.

Over the Christmas holidays, I flew to Minneapolis to meet with them about the challenges I would face in my new company. During those few hours, we laid out a plan for changing the entire underlying business premise of the firm. The goal was to create a client-centered and client-responsive organization that made the selling and relationship management process both simpler and more effective than our old way of doing business.

What I learned from my experiences and in working with Peter and Katherine will, I believe, help you to succeed, whether you are a financial advisor or an executive in a large financial services firm. The summary looks like this:

1. Step one is to get the right people "on the bus" and in the right seats—and to get the wrong people off the bus. Not everyone is going to agree with your vision of the future of your company. If they cannot, or chose not to work hand-in-hand with you on your vision, everyone would be better off if they worked for another company. It is always about the people.

2. Secondly, you must stay focused on the vision. It is frighteningly simple to lose sight of the "end-state" you desire while in the midst of a fierce battle and facing myriad distractions. The continual articulation of and focus on the vision of creating a consultative "no-sell" sales process for every advisor in the firm is always the most important element in the execution of the strategy. Everyone must be focused on the same pole star.

3. Nobody can do this alone. Business is a team sport and requires the accumulated skills and capabilities of the group working in concert to advance the cause. And it always pays to invest in quality people, training, and coaches who can get you and your company to the next level. Momentum is a powerful driving force, and you need a greater force to change the direction of that momentum.

In a complex world, the simple answers are usually those most successfully implemented. During the past few years Peter, Katherine, and I have been through some exhilarating times and some very dark times. Through the successes and the heartaches we have become great friends and I have come to respect them even more. The best thing I can say about them is this: their ideas work.

Brian Nygaard, Former President,
ING Broker Dealer Network

BUILDING YOUR
MULTI-MILLION-DOLLAR PRACTICE

If you are wondering if this book is for you, take this test to see if you need the information in this book.

	Yes	No
1. Are you a financial advisor who is earning more money but enjoying it less?		
2. Is worrying about your business keeping you up at night?		
3. Is it a constant struggle to bring new prospects in the door?		
4. Do you have a hard time hiring the right staff person?		
5. Has there been a lot of turnover in your office?		
6. Has work been stressing you out?		
7. Are you working hard, but not taking home as much money as you should?		
8. Are you looking to sell your practice in a few years and want to get maximum value?		
9. Are you a new financial advisor who wants to get started right and jump-start your business?		
10. Are you a midlevel financial advisor who has dreams of becoming a superstar?		
11. Are you in management at a broker/dealer or product sponsor and concerned about how to help your financial advisors be more productive?		
12. Are you in management at a broker/dealer and looking for ways to recruit new advisors?		

If you checked yes in even one of these boxes, there is information in this book that will help you make your life more profitable, less stressed, and a whole lot more fun.

By practicing the principles of this book, in three years you should

- not only increase your income 50 percent, 100 percent, or even more, but also double or triple your profits;
- reduce your stress level about work;
- have more free time;
- work within your natural abilities where you can get extraordinary results just being who you are;
- reduce your marketing expenses by increasing word-of-mouth advertising about your firm and getting a steady source of new referrals;
- reduce turnover in your office and increase staff morale;
- receive more enjoyment out of your work life;
- gain a greater sense of purpose and confidence about the future; and
- increase the valuation of your practice.

How is this possible? Vestment Advisors has achieved these great results time and time again with dozens of financial advisors and numerous entrepreneurs. The same techniques we created to help financial advisors of all levels break through the barriers that were keeping them back can help you, too. You can start using these ideas today to create the business of your dreams.

OUR BACKGROUND

Vestment Advisors is a hands-on organization that helps financial service companies of all sizes transform their business in trying times. Financial advisors help their clients achieve clarity and focus about the future, build the life of their dreams, and make more money. We help advisors become better advisors by bringing clarity and focus about the future, building the business of their dreams, and making more money. If you want to find out more about us, please visit us at http://www.vestmentadvisors .com.

For over 20 years we have had clients from numerous industries, and in the past several years we have focused primarily on financial services. During that time we have worked with dozens of what we call "superstars." A superstar is a financial advisor who is making a million dollars or more a year in fees and commissions.

We are careful about the kind of clients with which we work. It is true that all of our clients are in a bit of pain and need help managing their businesses, but we are looking for something special. Our ideal clients not only have a burning desire to get their businesses to the next level, they already have a substantial level of success. They also need to have integrity, honesty, and strive for excellence—in short, match our values.

Finally, they need a strong dose of humility because it is not easy to listen to outside people explain the shortcomings of your business. Our clients have a true longing to succeed, and they are willing to park their egos at the door to learn what they need to become a superstar. They are willing to do whatever it takes to get their business to the next level.

As we describe our clients and some of the things we have been able to help them accomplish, keep in mind that as an organization we often work undercover; sometimes employees of the companies who hire us do not know the real reason we are on the team. Frequently our clients want to remain anonymous. However, all the information in this book is about real businesses and real clients that we have served. However, to protect them, we have changed their names and some of the facts about their business.

Basketball versus Football

We think the business of being a financial advisor is like a game. Every financial advisor starts out playing basketball. In basketball, five sweaty athletes do their best to get the ball down the court and into the hoop. It is a game where defined positions may not mean much because the entire goal is to get a person in the right place to make a shot. If one person cannot do it, the ball is passed, sometimes many times, until finally someone else is in the right spot to make a shot.

At the beginning, every firm is playing basketball. All the employees and staff are scurrying around just trying to help make the shots (close the sales). Their jobs are not fully defined, their roles are fluid and their tasks overlap with everyone else's. The shot, or bringing in more income, is their primary focus.

Sooner or later, the superstars must transfer their practice from basketball to playing football. Football is a much more role-defined game. In basketball, players are in free-form motion, trying to get close to the hoop and be open to take a shot. In football, you have 11 players, each having a defined role with each play. Every player must, in their individual roles, be working in harmony in order to score a touchdown. The left offensive tackle may be required to move four steps back and two to the right in order to protect the quarterback. If the tackle decides that on this particular play he does not feel like doing that and would rather move three steps forward and two steps to the left, he will not protect the quarterback, who then gets sacked. Scoring becomes impossible.

As companies get larger, usually more than eight employees, they have to stop playing basketball and start moving toward playing football. If they do not, chaos follows. Later in the book we will talk about the systems, strategies, and techniques we use to help transition these firms from playing basketball to football.

Maybe you can see yourself described in some of our actual case studies. We've changed the names and identified them with an asterisk (*) to protect our clients' privacy. We use the term financial advisor to cover all people in this industry including: financial planners, wealth managers, investment advisors, insurance agents, stock brokers, and other financial consultants.

Case Study No. 1

High Plains Financial Planners,* a Kansas-based practice founded by Steve Smithson,* was one of the highest producers at his independent broker/dealer. High Plains was particularly effective at using innovative tax-reduction strategies for wealthy business owners. Although he always ranked in the top five financial advisors of his broker/dealer, Smithson had remained at approximately the same production level for many years and was frustrated. He had not been able to get his production to the levels he desired. Highly competitive, Smithson not only wanted to become number one in the company, he wanted to stay number one.

For High Plains Financial Planners, we helped them:

- Create the first-ever employee incentive program. It not only dramatically improved the corporate culture, in the first six months it also tripled profits.
- Realign staff in the first year to provide greater support for the other financial advisors in his office. This allowed those other financial advisors to increase production by 30 percent.
- Leverage strategic partnerships during the first year that resulted in a 20 percent increase in revenue from those sources.
- Build a strategic plan that resulted in Smithson's broker/dealer providing significant concessions from the home office, including a personal liaison in the broker/dealer to manage any problems he might encounter with the home office staff.

- Create their brand identity, logo, and all of their marketing materials as a part of a customized marketing plan.
- Increase commissions from $4,000 on average per case to $8,000 per case.

Result: Over a 350 percent increase in revenue over three years.

Case Study No. 2

Sunshine Investments, Inc.,* a large regional financial planning organization located in the southeast, had outgrown the management skills of the principals and their ability to manage its growth. We helped them:

- Utilize the Kolbe System™ for restructuring their teams and reporting structures to make the firm far more efficient and productive.
- Create an entire new business entity that within the first year generated 26 percent of the total company revenue.
- Launch a system for top producers that increased their new client referrals from 11 percent of their total new prospects to 44 percent in just 90 days.
- Reduce their dependency on a single source of leads from 85 percent to 57 percent.
- Tighten their compliance procedures to reduce lawsuits and customer complaints.
- Create a new brand, an image, and client-focused marketing materials.
- Develop new seminars and events that paid for themselves immediately.
- Expand their client base into a higher investor category. Investments went from an average of $450,000 to $670,000 per client in one year.

- Increase average commissions from $4,500 up to $6,700 per case.
- Leverage a midsized accounting firm's relationship with the practice to increase cross-selling opportunities.

Result: While industry revenues were down 40 percent during this time period, Sunshine's revenues were up 13 percent, a 52 percent swing in the right direction. The firm's valuation nearly tripled in two years, based on an evaluation by a national accounting firm.

Case Study No. 3

North Star Tax and Financial Advisors, a 1,500 rep broker/ dealer, had acquired a national brokerage company during the peak of the market and had been unable to effectively transition the organization during the two years since the acquisition. Working with the president and senior management team, we were able to:

- Design a strategy to migrate the division from a transactional brokerage firm to an advice-based financial planning firm.
- Create the framework and content of the division's three-year strategic plan.
- Define the positioning and strategic advantage of the organization.
- Write the sales strategy and talking points for assisting clients.
- Create the specific methodology, including talking points, for cross-selling existing corporate clients to the financial advisory business.
- Write and help implement the strategic marketing plan through pilot offices.

Result: In one year we changed the mind-set of long-established transactional brokers from going for the "quick sell," to taking a longer-term financial advisory perspective. By year three we had two pilot offices in place using the No-Sell Sale™ system, with commissions even higher than projected, and 12 additional offices beginning the migration. Single greatest improvement in a financial advisor? From $275,000 in production to over $800,000 in 18 months!

KATHERINE'S PERSONAL EXPERIENCES MAKING THIS SYSTEM WORK

Some years ago, my husband and business partner, Peter Vessenes, convinced me that I had to dust off my Series 7 and spend some time retesting our systems as a financial advisor. His reasoning was that actual experience using the strategies and methods we had learned and taught over the years would strengthen our ability to help financial services clients in the future.

For several months I worked face-to-face with clients, handling the initial interview, preparing the plan and product recommendations, overseeing the preparation of a plan, and presenting the plan and product solutions to the clients. Taking this experience and adding to it the many different techniques that I had described in my previous two books, *Protecting Your Practice* and the *Compliance and Liability Handbook,* helped us design and refine the systems in this book.

Do the systems work? Beyond my wildest expectations! I was astonished to see how easy it was to become a superstar financial advisor. It was so easy, I frequently felt guilty, thinking this work should be much harder. My closing ratio was over 90 percent. Yes, that number is correct.

As you might expect, some people are skeptical about this statistic. Let me give you a little background on my personal sales ability. First, if we consider salespeople on a continuum of 1 to 10 with Zig Ziglar, Tom Hopkins, Tom Gau, Bill Bacharach, Bill Good, and John Bowen as 10s, on a good day I am at best a 5, a rather average sales performer.

What I did have going for me was an amazing system, where all the dominos were in alignment. When all of these dominos were lined up correctly, I could not help but make a lot of sales. In fact, selling was so easy we called this system the "No-Sell Sale™."

When I worked the system correctly, I could easily succeed and turn prospects into clients. It was easy to close, because it was the natural part of the sales process.

THE PROSPERITY FACTORS™

The longer Peter and I worked with top advisors, the more we realized the key to being wildly successful, and to have the "No-Sell Sale™," was to have the eight key Prosperity Factors™ in alignment. As we worked with numerous clients, we discovered that when these factors were in correct alignment, they produced extraordinary results. Surprisingly, some of the top producers who generated in excess of $2 million or more per year typically had only five of these eight in alignment before we ever started helping them. Our job was to help them get those five in better alignment and add the other three crucial ones to their system.

These eight vital Prosperity Factors™ are:

1. *A star-based business that has transitioned into a team-based business.* Every financial advisory practice that we worked with had one person who was the star. Not just any star, a megastar. They were well known and a natural marketing machine. The operations and structures around the business had grown up to support them and their individual likes, peculiarities, strengths, and weaknesses. They

operated on a simple principle that the star financial advisor should do only those things that the financial advisor does well. Absolutely everything else is delegated. Chapter 1 explains how the star-based business works and how to get to a team-based business.

2. *Strategic planning.* We found a carefully written strategic plan, including tactics for reaching a company's goals, was essential because, as Proverbs says, "Without a vision, the people perish." Putting a plan on paper always seems to increase the chance of it coming to pass. In one instance, by putting a firm's plan in writing, Peter was able to triple its valuation within one year and get a buyer excited about cashing out the principals. If he had not had the written plan, no one would have been interested in purchasing that firm at that price. In Chapter 2 you will see how to create your own strategic plan and how the superstars rated on their plans.

3. *Fiscal and asset management.* Sound fiscal and personnel management is imperative for building value and improving profitability. These skills and tools allow the financial advisor to control costs, forecast growth, and motivate employees with an employee incentive program. In Chapter 3 we discuss ways you can improve your fiscal and asset management.

4. *A marketing system.* A marketing system that puts a steady stream of motivated, qualified, and hot prospects into the financial advisor's office is another key component to making this system work. We call this putting "derrieres in chairs." The financial advisor, when things were working well, never had to worry about where the next prospect was coming from because there were always new people who were interested in his services. Although the superstar financial advisor could be counted on for seminars or radio shows, someone else was managing the day-to-day details of the marketing plan. We also found

a commitment to referrals was essential for increasing revenue. Details about the marketing plans are included in Chapter 4.

5. *Operations.* Superstar financial advisors need abundant support in every possible area. This means strong process and procedures and a solid operations department to make sure nothing is falling through the cracks. Everyone in the firm clearly understood that the financial advisor's job was to meet with clients. Efficient systems were put into place to delegate everything else to a salaried individual. Suggestions on how to improve your operations are discussed in Chapter 5.

6. *Highly effective support staff.* Good staff can make or break a superstar's business. A solid delegation system that puts the right person in the right job was also important to create the "No-Sell Sale™." We always recommend the Kolbe Systems™ to increase the chance of success with new hires. Kolbe is a system for assessing how a person approaches work and solves problems. It identifies a person's natural strengths. Our thoughts on how to manage and coach staff and when to delegate are included in Chapter 6.

7. *A defined sales system.* Each superstar financial advisor had a defined sales system. The good news is you do not have to be brilliant or beautiful to make a sales system succeed. You just need to get all the moving parts (we call them dominos) lined up to create an easy, effortless sale. The sale becomes automatic and runs like clockwork. Sticking to the system reaps extraordinary results. We call this the No-Sell Sale™ system because you do not do any hard selling with our system. Instead you solve clients' problems. This is described in Chapter 7, where we walk you through the entire process, focusing on the critical first client meeting, because we believe that is where the sales are made.

8. *Solid compliance systems.* Finally, we think workable compliance systems are also important, because the financial advisors need to be meeting with clients and not spending their time defending lawsuits or answering to regulators. They are particularly important for superstars because they are targeted by regulators and sue-happy investors. Some tips on how you can tighten up your compliance procedures are discussed in Chapter 8.

Over the next few chapters we will go through and review the kind of systems or Prosperity Factors™ that superstar financial advisors had in place. We will review the many things that they were doing well before we ever walked into their offices. We will also discuss some of the weaknesses of their current programs and the changes that we brought to bring all eight factors into alignment.

In the last chapter, Peter and I discuss the steps you can take to bring these elements into alignment in your own office.

Some of these chapters are written from Peter's point of view, and some from Katherine's. At the beginning of each chapter we list the author so you know who is speaking.

1

THE STAR-BASED BUSINESS THAT TRANSITIONS INTO THE TEAM-BASED BUSINESS

Prosperity Factor #1: Team-Based Business
Businesses based on a team approach, rather
than a star approach, are more profitable
and have greater value.

By Katherine

HOW THE SUPERSTARS GOT TO BE SUPERSTARS, AND WHAT THEY WERE DOING RIGHT BEFORE WE GOT THERE

In a star-based company, everything revolves around the star. Every one of our superstar clients, and we have worked with dozens, began the same way. They were a highly motivated financial advisor, who, over time, discovered techniques that allowed them to generate substantial commissions. They also discovered that the most important thing they could do was meet with the client and close the sale. Let

---

M*ulti-Million-Dollar Principle #1*

The superstar's job is to meet with clients and close the sale. Everything else is delegated.

---

us review that simple thought again, because it is the keystone of this system: *The most important thing a financial advisor can do is meet with clients and close the sale.* Absolutely everything else is delegated. Filling out forms? Delegated. Reviewing products? Delegated. Preparing financial plans? Delegated. Making doctor appointments? Delegated.

As much as possible, these financial advisors stuck to their strong suit, closing the business, and hired others to handle absolutely every other item—in short, all the details. As a result, every firm had extensive support systems to make the financial advisor's life easier and to allow them to spend more time with clients.

One of the key elements that we found in high-producing financial advisors is they liked being the star. They were the center of the universe, the ones that generated the clients, and they were the reason the money was being made. With such strong systems in place, the financial advisor is treated like a prince or rock star. The universe revolved around the advisor. This is nice work if you can get it. Who would not want a whole staff at your beck and call?

This is a wonderful, very seductive position for the financial advisor. It's good for the ego and, if the practice is run well, it makes their life very easy.

I did not realize how deep the delegation and star mentality went until my first day in the office as a financial advisor in a superstar firm. Every financial advisor there had their own client service manager, or registered sales assistant. Some had two or three. I was no exception even though I had not been in production for almost 15 years and had absolutely no client base to bring to the table.

Jean was assigned to be my personal registered sales assistant, or as we called them, "client service manager." Having practiced law since the dark ages, I had strong personal opinions about how I liked my filing systems. So one of the first things I did with Jean was to hand her a document and tell her how I would like her to set up the filing system for my clients. Jean grabbed the piece of paper out of my hand and said, "I'll take care of it."

I responded, "No, you don't understand. I have a system in mind that I'd like you to follow for tracking the documents."

Jean responded with, "I will take care of it."

I said, "No, let me make myself clear. I've been around a long time, I know how I want my filing system to go." Jean responded again that she would take care of it.

Finally, in exasperation, I thought I would try to reason with Jean. "You see, Jean, there is going to come a day when you are at the dentist office and I'm going to need this document. I need to know how to retrieve it."

She said, "You're right, there's going to be a day when I am at the dentist office, but you'll never have to retrieve this document. We have other client service managers that work for other financial advisors here. We're all taught to assist each other. One of the other client service managers will get this document for you." And with that, she walked out of the office. She was right. In two months I never had to pull a single document out of a file. I had no idea where files went after they left my office.

In a superstar firm, the entire staff understands the most fundamental concept of the "No-Sell Sale™": Financial advisors cannot make money when they are filing. Furthermore, if filing is left to the financial advisors, it will either never get done, or be done so poorly, it will be impossible to retrieve the documents. Therefore, someone else will always do what the financial advisor should not do, will not do, or does not want to do.

Although we will be discussing this in greater detail in other chapters, the superstar support system tended to fall into two different groups. One group, similar to American Dream Advisors,* assigned every financial advisor between one and three client service managers, depending on their level of production. The client service managers helped fill out all the applications, processed all the paperwork, handled all the service requests, and by and large fielded most of the financial advisor's phone calls.

American Dream also used a system of having a case-writing department or the financial planning department to create the plans; an insurance department to review insurance policies; an investment department to review current and recommended investments; and a tax department to prepare tax returns and make recommendations for tax-reduction strategies or tax-advantage investments.

At American Dream, the marketing and scheduling was all handled within the marketing department. The financial advisors did not have control over their own schedule. Prospects were assigned to them on a rotating basis.

Mitch Mercury had a different system. Mercury used the junior advisor/senior advisor, or apprentice program. The superstar, as the senior financial advisor, had numerous junior financial advisors with varying levels of ability. The junior advisor would sit in on the end of the meeting with the clients and take notes, then move the clients to another room where he would take over, complete the applications, prepare the paperwork, and handle the service requests. Mercury did not have a separate department for investments, planning, and insurance review. These tasks were all handled by a group of junior financial advisors. Mercury's goal was to mentor the junior financial advisors so that one day they could reach the level of a superstar and have their own junior advisors assisting them.

Multi-Million-Dollar Principle #2

If you want to increase your income, see more people.

At American Dream, every financial advisor had the goal of meeting with 15 clients a week. Approximately half of these appointments were prospects or people new to the firm. The other half were clients coming back for the second meeting where their plan and investment options were presented to them.

Each meeting took me almost two hours, even if I kept my preparation down to 15 minutes. If my goal was to meet with 15 clients per week, in a week I was spending close to 30 hours just in front of clients! I could not help but make a great deal of money when over 75 percent of my time every week was spent face-to-face with clients.

American Dream had an advisor who just did not buy into their system. The reason? He liked to do the financial planning and the due diligence all by himself. He considered himself a much superior intellect to the people in the planning department, and preferred to create his own financial plans using Excel.

Unfortunately, this is a time-consuming and tedious task. During the time he spent creating the plan, analyzing the investments, and running through all the possible tax strategies, he did not have time to do the number one thing that makes him money: Meet with the client and close the sale. As a result, this advisor was not able to meet with 15 clients a week; he probably met with 5 or 6 because the rest of his time was spent

Multi-Million-Dollar Principle #3

Stick with the system that works. Don't try to reinvent the wheel.

creating his own financial plans. The result? His production was less than half of the rest of the financial advisors in the group. Although he was still making more money than the average financial advisor in this country, management decided he would be better suited in another firm, and he moved on to practice his own way with his own system in his own business. He was a good financial planner; he just did not fit their system.

Most of the firms we worked with had clearly figured out how important it was to have the superstar financial advisor focus on meeting with clients. In fact, very few of the superstars we dealt with were Certified Financial Planners (CFP®) or had other designations. The reason? They felt that every day out of the office preparing for the exam would cost the firm between $10,000 and $20,000. Despite the value of becoming a CFP®, they concluded they could not afford the time and resulting reduced revenues.

THE DOWNSIDE OF
THE STAR-BASED BUSINESS

Unfortunately, star-based systems have critical limitations and liabilities. These include an inability to

- increase the valuation of the practice,
- create a succession plan when the financial advisor wishes to retire or slow down their pace, and
- grow the business beyond the financial advisor's own capacity.

Star-based businesses are not very sellable. Very few companies are interested in purchasing financial advisory firms that have a star. Why? It is hard to transfer that star loyalty to the next advisor, and they know that they are likely to lose a great deal of the clients. Without the star, there is no business. Cli-

Multi-Million-Dollar Principle #4

If you want to sell your business for the maximum profit, move from being a star-based business to a team approach.

ents develop an attachment to the star. Without the star, client loyalty evaporates and the new business owner finds they have bought a lot of vapor as the clients have moved their accounts. However, when there is no star but a reputable team, the clients have a great deal of confidence in the entire company and are more likely to stick during a transition to another purchaser.

Star-based systems are also difficult to manage. They become harder as the number of support staff increases. Typically, the talents that make the star such a marketing machine are not the same talents needed to run and manage a business. We have found it is rare for a superstar financial advisor to be able to generate big sales and also have the skills to run a business. Frequently the superstar gets sucked into managing staff and other business matters. This time drag keeps them from meeting with clients, the activity that made them so successful.

This process can become a downward spiral. The financial advisor hires more staff to free up his time. The extra staff requires a lot of time to manage, train, and coach. This time drain keeps the financial advisor from meeting with clients and closing sales. Expenses and frustration go up. Revenue and profits go down.

Financial advisors who want to reduce their stress, must create a system where their clients are happy with their team. Too much dependence on the financial advisor may be good for the pocketbook, but can be very stressful and hard on the financial advisor.

Before we started helping them, most firms would get a B– on a team-based busi-

**Team-Based
Business
Report Card**

B–

ness. While the financial advisor understood how important it is to delegate and free up their time for client meetings, they did not grasp how limiting being a star can be to their future prosperity.

GETTING PAST THE STAR-BASED SYSTEM TO A TEAM APPROACH

Moving a business from the star system to the team system is an important part of building valuation. Here are the three key steps we use:

1. First, we help the superstar financial advisor understand why a star-based system is not in his best interest.
2. Second, we develop a marketing plan based on conveying to clients and prospects why a team-based system is better for the client.
3. Finally, we design the tactics and strategies for creating an enterprise-based system rather than a star-based system.

Let's review each of these in more detail.

Before we get to the first step of our process, we should explain why we are called in to assist a firm in the first place. Whether it is financial advisors or other business owners, it is always the same combination of factors that prompts the call: They are in a lot of pain. They are generating more revenues, but not taking home as much money as they think they should. They are investing a lot of time doing tasks that drain their energy, and they can see that they have nothing to show for their efforts. They look into the future a few years and realize they have nothing to support them in a fun-filled retirement. They know they cannot fix these problems by themselves and they need help. That is when they give us a call.

After performing an initial analysis of the firm, we prepare a plan to help reduce their pain, increase their profits, build valuation in the business, and allow them the freedom to do what they do best. Typically a part of this plan is a strategy on how to transition from a star-based business, which is causing most of their problems, to a team-based business.

The first step: We explain to the superstar financial advisor, who is usually the owner of his own firm, all the limitations of the star-based business. Explaining why the star-based system is not effective can be much harder than it looks on paper. Logically we all know that we are each limited by our own capacity, our own strengths and weaknesses. However, superstars have strong egos. They had to have them to get to where they are. Deep down inside, they believe they can do it all. After all, they have been treated as the crown prince by their own staff for years. They believe their own press releases. Furthermore, few people want to give up being a star. This is the reason the "Caesars of old" had a slave riding with them in the chariot. The slave's duty was to constantly whisper into Caesar's ear: *"You are mortal."*

Peter and I frequently feel like we are in the difficult role of being the slave to Caesar. Initially, the financial advisor superstar may not want to hear the truth about moving to a team concept, because they sense power is slipping from their hands. However, some are in such pain, they will do whatever it takes to make their business healthier and stronger. These are the easy cases for us. The harder ones resist because they like being a star and feel the stress of that lifestyle is worth the many rewards.

Sometimes we have to bring in a superstar's spouse to help us convey this difficult message about moving to a team-based business. After all, the spouse is usually very supportive of the change, because they have not seen much of the superstar. Oftentimes the star has been so busy with the business, not much time has been left for the marriage.

Once the financial advisor finally realizes that his valuation will go up and profits will increase with a team-based approach, the advisor nearly always agrees to the change.

One client, Steve MacDougal of MacDougal Financial Advisors,* was a multi-million-dollar producer who had created a strong reputation within the San Jose community. Our efforts included redefining how MacDougal Financial Advisors provided services, creating an extensive marketing campaign built around branding the practice, rather than the star. We also redefined employee job descriptions so their duties were clearly part of the team.

MacDougal recognized that good financial planning involves a broad variety of disciplines that no single individual could possibly master. It made sense to show his clients that his support team demonstrated a diversity of skills and abilities working to the advantage of the client. MacDougal grasped that it created greater trust in MacDougal Financial Advisors when clients recognized a whole team of people were looking after their best interests.

While we were there on a regular basis, we kept MacDougal and the teams accountable to the strategy. This is a big part of our job. We did this through regular meetings, and by working with the general manager of the office to ensure all the players were properly presented to the clients. We also reviewed meetings with the clients to make certain they were meeting with several members of the team (not just the star), and that their advertising and public relations efforts reflected this team strategy.

A few of our stories did not have such a happy ending. Sometimes after the conclusion of our engagement, when we are longer spending time regularly with the principals forcing them to be accountable, guess what happens? Occasionally the star goes back to being the star, and the tactics and strategies to put more focus and attention on the team are no longer implemented. Why? Emotionally it is too hard on some advisors not to be the star. They must be the top guy.

It is easy for the star to justify remaining top dog. They feel, and justifiably so, that there are certain things that they do much better than anyone else in the organization.

Is this true? In some disciplines it is. Is it the right tactic? Absolutely not! These time-consuming tasks keep the stars from their most important task: meeting with clients. Unfortunately, the emotional ego needs of some of the stars worked to the detriment of their long-term financial objectives.

STAR-BASED BUSINESS

Although being a star can be a great deal of fun and wonderful for the ego, ultimately it is very tiring. The star must constantly be on, focused, and moving the entire organization forward. The weight of this responsibility can take a toll, and more than one superstar had his share of stress-related health problems.

It is also very time-consuming to be the star, because typically they like to be involved in every decision. It means long hours and serious burnout, particularly for practices still playing basketball, where everyone is just trying to get in position to score the next sale.

ALTERNATIVE STRATEGY

For those few financial advisors who do not want to stop the fun and the power of being the superstar, or who find it too difficult to transition into a team, an alternative strategy is needed. They will probably be able to sell their business at some point;

Multi-Million-Dollar Principle #5

If you cannot become a team-based business, increase your profitability. Use your increased profits for retirement.

it just will not receive maximum value, and they need to be pre-pared for that outcome. In this alternative scenario, they need to use the other principles we talk about here to improve their profitability. With increased profitability, they can set aside more funds for their own long-term retirement needs.

SWOOP

We always start our engagements with the star or the business owner by asking them about their hopes and dreams for the future. We see our goal as helping make their dreams come true. Once we have a clear picture of their hopes and dreams, we go on to analyze the firm's **S**trengths, **W**eaknesses, **O**pportunities, **O**bstacles, and **P**lans for the future, and then we prepare what we call a "SWOOP report." As we start our engagement, the financial advisor must commit to several key disciplines for their dreams to become a reality:

- *Work from your strengths.* We think businesses become wildly successful with the least amount of effort, when everyone is working from their strengths. This includes not just the superstars, but every other person in the entire organiza-tion. As we will explain later, the advantages are huge. When people become energized and not drained by their jobs, productivity increases and office morale also increases dramatically. Everyone has a much better time working at the office.
- *Strong moral values.* Strong moral values are also necessary to create a sound business foundation. Sometimes finan-cial advisors are just interested in increasing their income. Others live every aspect of their lives by a strong moral code. All of our financial advisory clients are motivated by increasing their profitability. Over time they come to see that honesty and integrity are key factors for improv-

ing their bottom line and giving the firm a better reputation, and they realize they are more likely to attract top-quality staff and retain great clients when they take the high moral road.

- *Client's best interest.* A shift in the advisor's focus is often necessary to get their perspective focused on the client's best interest. Some financial advisors clearly have the client's best interest at heart. Others, regrettably, are still looking at their own pocketbook. We believe part of an integrity-based business is making sure that every decision is made in the client's best interest.

- *Good ethics and compliance.* Because I have written a great deal about the industry's ethics, financial advisors frequently ask me to help them out with legal, ethical, or compliance issues. A few years ago I got a call from a financial advisor who wanted me to tell him exactly where the line in the sand was, and how far you could get over it without getting caught. I explained to him that I certainly could do that because I had a good understanding of where the line in the sand was, but that I did not do business that way. That is not what we stand for. We stand for helping financial service firms of all types determine where the line in the sand is, and to then stay on the right side of the line, because we think that is what a business with integrity should do. Needless to say, we did not enter into business with that advisor.

- *Happy clients.* The final focus is on keeping clients happy. I have said for many years when you keep your clients happy . . . you keep your clients. Although the superstars usually realize it is the investors who are paying the bills, sometimes the support staff did not fully understand this and share the important underlying value.

Recently, I was in the branch office of a large broker/dealer and happened to overhear some client service managers answer-

> ## M*ulti-Million-Dollar Principle #6*
>
> When you keep your clients happy . . . you keep your clients.

ing calls from clients with service issues. You could tell they were highly put out by the phone calls, and they were irritable with the clients. Frankly, they just wanted to get off the phone and onto the next thing. The staff was not focused on the most important thing: Keeping clients, the paycheck, happy.

This is the exact opposite of the philosophy we think makes the superstar. A superstar is more than happy to help. That is why they are in the business—to help make an investor's dream come true and help them achieve financial freedom. Everyone from the superstar on down to the newest employee needs to buy into this philosophy. We call it "can do."

It reminds me of a trip we make most summers with our family to visit relatives in Greece. At a small family-run hotel on the Greek Islands, we are always met by Jorgo and his father, who own the hotel. Jorgo is not only the owner, concierge, bell captain, and head waiter, he is everything else that you would need. No matter what I asked, the answer was always the same, "No problem." "Could he move us to a different room?" "No problem." "Could I have a different breakfast?" "No problem." "Could you find somebody to do our laundry?" "No problem." "Could we rent a boat to go around the island?" "No problem." Jorgo has one answer and that is "No problem." The result is wonderful. We have such a fabulous time there that we return almost every summer, bringing our family and friends. Teaching those two words, *no problem,* to everyone in the office would help keep clients happy.

SUMMARY

Although every one of the financial advisors we worked with is definitely motivated by increasing their income and building their nest egg, sometimes they do not understand their own inner drive. When a financial advisor has a difficult time moving from a star-based system to a team approach, it is usually their own ego issues at work. Emotionally they cannot tolerate not being the center of attention. It is like asking a diva to stop being a diva. They like the attention. It affirms them. It makes them feel important and worthwhile. Unfortunately, it puts a ceiling on what they are able to produce with their efforts. It severely limits what they can get for their business and the amount of money they are going to be able to realize from their firm. Some may understand this, and some are in a state of denial. Nevertheless, those ego needs can sabotage their entire plan to build valuation.

As a result, we have found that some of the most successful firms we dealt with have a person who is the star, but not a diva personality or an egotist. They are pragmatics. They want to become wildly prosperous and very wealthy. They are willing to set aside their own ego to accomplish that goal. That means they need to shine light on other team members and build them up in the process. Not every financial advisor can make this transition. The ones that do, though, end up making far more money and building more wealth in the long run.

KEY POINTS

1. The most important thing the financial advisor can do is meet with clients and close the sale.
2. Delegate everything else. Someone else should always do what the financial advisor should not do, will not do, or does not want to do.

3. If the superstar is doing everything for himself, he has less time to see clients—his main business—and his income will suffer.

4. Some superstars are not willing to transition to a team-based practice.

5. Superstar firms have less value when being sold and are more difficult to manage.

2

STRATEGIC PLANNING
Tactics That Work

Prosperity Factor #2
Strategic planning is having a written plan that
includes the tactics of reaching the company's
mission and vision.

By Peter

Before we started working with them, top-producing advisors would receive an F on strategic planning.

Much to our surprise, not one of our financial advisory clients had a written business plan before we started our engagement. It

> **Strategic Planning Report Card**
> **F**

frequently amazed us that they could have the revenues they did without this most basic of all business documents. Consequently, we will not be covering the existing strategic plans of the multi-million-dollar financial advisors in this chapter because none of the firms that we worked with had done any significant strategic planning.

THE TRUTH OF DOING BUSINESS

Before we go into strategic planning, I think it is important to understand some fundamental principles of running a successful business.

Let's start with capitalism. When I am on the speaking circuit, I frequently will ask the audience to define capitalism. Rarely do I ever get an accurate answer! In fact, even the founders of a regional bank could not accurately define capitalism.

If the trading partners do not believe they are receiving equal or greater value, they would not make the trade. If they do or must make this kind of trade, they feel cheated. Without receiving equal or greater value, trading partners do not continue working together.

Understanding capitalism raises an important question: What is the purpose and objective of a business practicing great capitalism? Most people believe it is to make as much money as possible for the shareholders. This conclusion is both right and wrong.

Making as much money as possible for shareholders is a good purpose if you and the shareholders understand that making this money is a "forever" objective, not just a short-term push for the end of this fiscal year. Repeating the "short-term push" on a repeated basis is the wrong belief and results in very bad strategies. Why?

Short-term profits can be increased in several ways. Common tactics in business include:

- Reducing the number of employees and pushing the survivors harder (lowering fixed costs).

M *ulti-Million-Dollar Principle #7*

Capitalism is an economic system of barter where people trade for goods and services, believing they are receiving equal or greater value in exchange for what they offer.

- Creating sales promotions that bump revenues this quarter by motivating buyers that would have purchased next year to do it now (boosting this year at the expense of next year).
- Decreasing prices to increase sales without examining the expectations of the market when you want or need to increase the prices later (creating a market that "waits" until you bring prices down again).

These types of strategies do increase short-term profits, but do it at the expense of long-term profit and value.

Why do shareholders, leaders in business, and boards of directors of publicly traded companies make these kinds of mistakes? They do not understand capitalism.

The fundamental force of capitalism in a free-market society does not allow a business to engage in "bad" trading practices with its trading partners for long. The partners will either not give as much in return (the value is not there) or will find someone else to trade with. We call the trading partners of a business "stakeholders." Anyone engaged in trading with a business is holding a stake in the business's practice and their own reward in the trade.

Who are the financial advisor's stakeholders (trading partners)? Certainly their clients are trading partners, and they as owners (shareholders) are trading partners, but the list is much larger than that. Any practice (or business) engages in many trades: with the bank, their law firm, their CPA, the broker/ dealer, the vendors that provide products, the marketing and advertising agency they work with, and most important, their employees, the employees' families, and their community.

If you consistently do not create a "fair" trade in value with your stakeholders, problems will surely follow. Large companies have consequences for laying off large numbers of workers only to improve profits—not layoffs resulting from decreased demand, inefficiency, or outsourcing tasks. This will result in

> All a business can do is leverage its assets to create value in its trades with all of its stakeholders. We call this a Prosperity Factor™.

burned-out, unmotivated, and less-productive employees. Ignoring trading practices that actually create greater value for all trading partners may benefit in the short term, but will destroy over time.

Understanding the basics of capitalism raises another interesting question: Exactly what is it that a business does? Believing that a business's purpose is to create profits for its shareholders is a very shallow view, and it avoids the question that was asked: What is it that a business does, and how does it do it?

Great companies engage in trades where all trading partners (stakeholders) are receiving greater value than what they gave up. How well you leverage your assets and trade with them determines how successful your business truly becomes. This is the core foundation of creating a company with increasing value that returns the highest possible profits forever, not just this quarter. Leveraging your assets to create prosperity for all stakeholders is the foundation of capitalism. All the strategies and tactics in this book are based on this truth. Our clients' dreams and aspirations took life once they understood and believed the Prosperity Factors™.

MISSION AND VISION

All financial advisors have dreams. In fact, all businesses are founded on the dreams and "vision" of the entrepreneur. Financial advisors have hopes and aspirations for both their clients and themselves.

As a practice begins to grow in momentum, strength, and number of clients, eventually it hits a point where the financial advisor becomes so busy providing advice to his clients that any planning for his practice's future falls by the wayside. Even among the larger, more successful financial advisory firms, traditional strategic planning takes on an element that is limiting and prone to failure.

THE LIMITS OF TRADITIONAL STRATEGIC PLANNING

A common problem in the way businesses do strategic planning (that is not unique to our financial advisory clients) is that plans for growth are based on establishing yearly targets for increasing revenue or increasing the number of clients. This may be represented as a whole number, say 100 new clients, or it may be represented as a percentage, for example, a 20 percent growth in revenue, or it may be represented on fees and commissions that are averaged per client. All of these are losing strategies.

Why? The reason is simple. By building your future on incremental growth—that is, this many more clients, or this percentage of increase—you fail to address all the factors involved in growing a business. More importantly, you have removed yourself from your dream, your vision, and now just want more. These two ways of doing things, just wanting more and working from a vision of the future, are incongruous. The vision that gave life to the practice suddenly dies, while the financial advisor focuses on getting "more."

A MORE PRODUCTIVE APPROACH TO STRATEGIC PLANNING

We have found the following process much more successful in establishing a vision, and also in preparing a solid road map or strategic plan for the future.

Our first step with any new client involves asking them to define their hopes and dreams. We spend a lot of time focusing on what they want to accomplish with their life, not just the business. We also look at how the business fits into their life goals and supports or detracts from them.

An entrepreneur's dreams can take many shapes and forms. They may include:

- How large they want the practice to become, in terms of number of clients they service and amount of annual revenue.
- The types of clients they want to serve and the kinds of services they want to provide.
- The number of employees they believe they want to have.
- What their offices look like or where in the community they are located.
- How much free time the financial advisor can take off.
- Aspects of employing family members in the business.

Frequently, the hopes and dreams are even more personal. One of our clients had a large dental practice. His goal was to be so wildly successful financially that he could spend his retirement years doing missionary work with his wife. A real estate developer told us he wanted to help other people become financially independent through investing in real estate so his clients could live a life of significance. The goals also almost always involve the business owner's children. As parents, people want to instill good values in their children and help support them emotionally, spiritually, and sometimes even financially.

Some business owners have a hard time defining what they want their future to look like. They may be so caught up in the day-to-day business that they have not even thought about what their best future looks like. If you are in that position, you may benefit from an exercise that we undertake with our clients, which we call future visioning.

Future visioning. Take a minute or two in a quiet place and imagine yourself 20 years (or 10 or 5) into the future. Then ask these questions:

1. What is the 20-years-older you doing? Is it business? Is it pleasure? Is it both?
2. What kind of work are you doing in the future?
3. How are you doing it?
4. What are the rewards?
5. Where are you doing it?
6. What do you look like? Hopefully you are envisioning your future self as thin, healthy, and energetic with a great positive attitude.

The final question is also important:

7. What sort of advice does the 20-years-older you have for you in general, and for reaching your vision of the future?

When I ran through this exercise, I envisioned myself running a company where I could use all my talents, particularly my ability to manage others and inspire them in their careers. Others appreciated those talents and were grateful for the blessings they provided. At the same time, I saw a company that could do most of its work without me, and during those times, Katherine and I were active in the charitable work that has meant so much to us.

Katherine said she had a clear picture of her future self making a presentation to her own board of directors, showing how to bring the Prosperity Factors™ to 10,000 new businesses in North America. She is also healthy, trim (still fitting into her favorite suits), and actively involved in her family and community. She says this vision helps her stay focused on her desires to work with boards of directors and to keep working on her exercise program to fit into those classic clothes.

No matter what our clients hope and dream for the future, it is our job to help them clearly define and then realize them. After these sessions we may get involved in many tactical projects. However, if you always stay focused on the goals nearest and dearest to your heart, once you have defined them, you will succeed.

ELEMENTS OF A STRATEGIC PLAN

Most entrepreneurs do not know that there are seven specific disciplines involved in helping any business reach its vision and dream. Without having a clearly defined vision with specific tactics in each of the seven disciplines, they will never reach their ultimate dream that fulfills their core underlying drive and desires.

The seven elements cover these areas:

1. Revenue
2. Growth
3. Profitability
4. Technology
5. Quality systems
6. Strategic marketing
7. Corporate culture

Let us review these seven areas in more detail.

Revenue

Revenue is easy to define. It is the number that represents the gross revenues of the firm five or ten years into the future. Most financial advisors who have dreams of the future already have the number in their heart that they believe they can reach.

Sometimes we think their vision is too small. We had one client who was having trouble getting to $2 million in production. After reviewing his firm and getting his financials in order, I told him he could be at $20 million in five years. At first he thought I was nuts. After sleeping on it, he came back and told me he thought it could be $25 million! By year three of our engagement he was at $8 million, well on his way to $25 million.

Growth

Once you have identified your revenue dreams, growth defines how is it going to take place. Most companies can grow in a variety of ways. Some are easier and more profitable than others. Next are some of the things to consider when creating growth strategies.

What are the factors that could contribute to the growth of the business? For some companies they could add new locations. Others might need to increase the number or the type of clients that are served. Ask yourself:

- Does the growth come as a result of tactics such as creating a marketing program around a local radio show, or does it involve marketing to a specialized market?
- Does it require new products and services?
- What would be the impact of new hires: to either provide the same service as the entrepreneur or provide more support to free up the entrepreneur?
- Does pricing affect demand?

Defining growth is an important element in any strategic plan because it is the tactics that are necessary to reach the revenue goals.

Profitability

Most businesspeople never take the time to define profitability. Their view is that they want as much profit as possible. Unfortunately, without planning for profitability, profits become a hope, wish, and a dream with a lower payout than the roulette wheel at a Las Vegas casino. How do you plan for profits? It starts by rethinking your understanding of profits in a company.

We take an unorthodox view of profits. We do not think any company can make and retain a profit. Are you shocked? After all, isn't that why businesses were created—to be profitable? Read Chapter 3 to find out why this is true and learn many powerful and new ideas in the fiscal management of a practice.

Technology

Technology is a complex and expensive element that continues to grow in our day-to-day lives. When evaluating technology, we always start with the end in mind: What do we want to accomplish with this tool? Technology can improve your marketing efforts or make it more difficult and expensive to attract new clients. It can help you create investment strategies that are great for your clients and help them understand complex issues. The technologies available in financial services are indeed leading edge. Having a vision of what this means in the practice is an important element in defining the future of the practice.

Quality Systems

In its simplest terms, effective quality systems include a plan for identifying and eliminating the bottlenecks in your organization. As you grow, you will probably have to increase staff. As you are shifting from being a basketball team to being a football team, you will need to identify all the positions and determine which ones are filled first.

Tracking and monitoring the practice's process and procedures becomes an important element in increasing the quality of services provided to our clients and in creating efficiency within the organization. We discuss this process later in Chapter 3 when we discuss the Money Trail™.

Strategic Marketing

Few business owners understand that marketing covers far more disciplines than just advertising and public relations. It includes branding, image, competitive advantage, competitive analysis, direct marketing, and a host of other disciplines. These combine to define how you are perceived and the value that is placed on working with your firm. Without a clear picture of what you believe your brand, your image, and your marketing strategies can become in the future, the company will be limited in its ability to grow. Marketing plans are discussed in greater detail in Chapter 4.

Corporate Culture

Without clearly defining the corporate culture, the organization will evolve into the worst of all elements. As a business owner you get two options: You can define and create the culture you want, or you can get what evolves from your lack of action. The first one is far better. The goal is to create a work environment where everyone shares in the prosperity that was created, all members are highly effective and productive, and everyone delights in coming to work.

The elements in creating a good corporate culture include things such as job descriptions built out of the Money Trail™, using the Kolbe System™ to define positions, and understanding delegation of authority so that the business's day-to-day activities are fulfilled seamlessly without constant supervision. These elements are reviewed in Chapter 6.

The Fallacy of Incremental Growth Planning

How is defining these seven elements different from creating a strategic plan that uses a flawed incremental growth analysis? The answer is quite simple. By taking the time to imagine what your business will look like five years from now in each of those seven disciplines—what your heart and soul believes you can become—you can clearly define your vision for the company.

IMPLEMENTING THE STRATEGIC PLAN

The process for implementing the strategic plan in a small practice is the same as in large corporation. Whether we first work with the leaders in a practice or with the senior management team, the starting point is to establish the vision in these disciplines. The next step is a simple one: If that is where we believe we can be in five years, where will we have to be in four? If that's where we're going to be in four, where will we have to be in three? If we're going to reach that in three, where will we have to be in two years? And in order to reach that in two years, where will we have to be at the end of the next year?

Now we can have clearly defined metrics in seven disciplines for the next year by breaking down these measures of objectives and performance into quarterly objectives—by team, by group, by department, and by discipline. Thus we will have created measurable, attainable objectives that can be reached, monitored, and managed.

At the end of the first year, redefine your vision and your dream for the next five. How effective is creating a strategic plan this way? A strategic plan we created in cooperation with Mercury Advisors was submitted to their broker/dealer in conjunction with their revenue objectives and projections and needs for support. The response from the broker/dealer: It was a better strategic plan than they had ever seen, including their own corporate strategic plan. The broker/dealer was so impressed, they gave Mercury significant concessions.

Other benefits: The combination of the strategic plan, plus our financial modeling tools, allowed Mercury to go to their bank and secure a $1 million dollar line of credit on an unsecured signature loan. It was also under prime rate! Strategic planning is a critical element in the growth of any business, but especially in financial services.

KEY POINTS

1. Most financial practices, unfortunately, do *not* have a written business plan—the most basic business document.
2. Capitalism is an economic system of barter where people trade for goods and services, believing they are receiving equal or greater value in exchange for what they offer.
3. All businesses can do is leverage their assets to create value in their trades with all stakeholders.
4. All a business can do is leverage its assets to create value in its trades with all of its stakeholders. We call this a Prosperity Factor™.
5. To be successful, you have to prepare a solid road map or strategic plan for the future. Often it is very difficult for a financial advisor to decide what they want their future to look like.
6. Elements of strategic planning are:
   • Revenue

- Growth
- Profitability
- Technology
- Quality systems
- Strategic marketing
- Corporate culture

3

WHY SOUND FISCAL AND ASSET MANAGEMENT IS ESSENTIAL TO GROWTH IN ANY PRACTICE

Prosperity Factor #3
Sound fiscal and asset management is essential
for a firm's financial foundation.

By Peter

It was truly shocking to witness how little financial advisors understood about their own practice's fiscal management. The common belief was that if we come to the end of the month and there is money in the checkbook, I guess we are okay. Truly the story of expenses and receipts being kept in a shoebox and delivered to the CPA at the end of the tax year was not just an urban legend. We witnessed it.

Fiscal and Asset Management Report Card

F

Regrettably, most of the high-producing financial advisors we worked with had a limited understanding of fiscal and asset management of their own practice. Some of this is understandable. They are entrepreneurs. They are good salespeople. They do understand financial planning for their clients. Few of them had backgrounds in accounting or as CPAs, and therefore, understood little of accounting practices and even less about fiscal and asset management of a business.

BENEFITS OF SOUND FISCAL AND ASSET MANAGEMENT

What are the things that fiscal and asset management can provide to a financial advisor? First, it helps them control costs, establish budgets, forecast growth, motivate employees through incentive programs, and provide a methodology for documenting the increase in valuation of their practice.

Many things can cause financial practices and small businesses to reach ceilings and limit growth. None is more critical than understanding fiscal and asset management. When financial advisors know they need to do something about their financial management, they usually look to a CPA firm to assist them.

What the financial advisor does not recognize is that most CPA firms are primarily involved in tax preparation and tax strategy. Typically, CPAs focus on how to shelter the taxes from the financial advisor's practice. Now this is a high and noble endeavor, however, it has little to do with understanding fiscal and asset management and maximizing the firm's profits and valuation. CPA firms that have a background in fiscal and asset management are rare and can be very expensive.

In order to master fiscal and asset management, it is important to appreciate that all a business can do is leverage its assets to create a rate of return, much like an investment. What financial advisors do not comprehend is the magnitude of how much must be leveraged to provide that rate of return. It is easy for a financial advisor to look at a client's assets and say: If we can realize an average 10 percent rate of return a year for over 15 years, we will meet our goals; if we can average 8 percent in a tax-sheltered environment over 8 years, you will be able to retire on time.

However, most financial advisors do not realize what is involved in leveraging the assets of their own practice in order to create a satisfactory return. To understand a financial advisor's practice and how it leverages its assets, we must first start by defining the assets.

All businesses have two types of assets:

1. *Hard assets.* Hard assets may include cash on hand, accounts receivable, furniture and fixtures, and other items whose asset value can be clearly defined.
2. *Soft assets.* Soft assets include items such as brand, image, location, time in industry, number of clients, goodwill, and past performance.

What kind of assets are employees?

Perhaps the biggest challenge is trying to evaluate whether employees are hard or soft assets. We have all heard the saying, "Our single greatest asset is our employees." I agree with this statement, but not for the reason most people expect. Most financial advisors believe that their employees are soft assets because it is hard to put a quantifiable measure to the value of the asset in their employees. Actually, quite the opposite is the truth.

All employees negotiate with their employers for their services based on wages and benefits. We believe unequivocally that the value you pay for the services of your employees is their true asset value. In other words, if you paid an employee $50,000 and they earned an additional $8,000 in benefits, the asset value of that employee is $58,000 each year. This value is what that asset is worth to you in order to create the return you need to maximize your business.

Why is this important to understand? Let us evaluate a hypothetical million-dollar producer. This producer has the following assets:

```
$  25,000 in furniture and fixtures
    10,000 in depreciated value of computer technology
   350,000 in wages (seven employees who average
               $50,000 in wages and benefits)
   135,000 accounts receivable*
  $520,000 total hard assets
```

*Because financial advisors do not receive payment immediately at the time at which they generate fees and commissions, this financial advisor also had $135,000 in accounts receivable.

We now have a total of $520,000 in hard assets. What kind of rate of return must we get out of these assets in order to hit breakeven? Let's examine the cost of operating this practice:

Client generation	$ 65,000
Office lease costs	35,000
Telephone expense, postage	8,000
Computer, office equipment expense	12,000
Marketing costs	100,000
Professional services (CPA, legal)	15,000
Continuing education	10,000
Employee wages and benefits	350,000
Personal salary	300,000
Depreciation	20,000
Taxes	85,000
Total All Expenses	**$1,000,000**

The revenue required to pay all the bills for this financial advisor was $1 million. Remember, the value of these assets is not the same as the cost of running the business. This practice would have to generate more than a 192 percent rate of return on its hard assets in order to pay its bills. In other words, the $520,000 in measurable hard assets would have to nearly double their asset value for the practice to pay its overhead.

Why is this important to understand? For two reasons:

1. Leveraging an asset to its greatest value requires a greater knowledge and discipline on the part of owners than simply trying to increase revenue or profits.
2. All companies will lapse into trying to create profits only for their shareholders if they do not understand that the only sustainable purpose of a business is to create continuing prosperity with all of its trading partners.

All assets must operate efficiently and effectively to maximize their rate of return. For example, any machine at an auto manufacturing plant that was not functioning well would be a cost and production burden on the company. Naturally, all machines in this plant are serviced and maintained, given preventive maintenance, and are run by skilled operators to optimize the efficiency of that machine. By doing this, it creates the greatest rate of return on appreciated asset value of that machine.

Assets in a service-based company are no different. Because the largest hard asset is your employee, they too must be managed efficiently to create the greatest possible rate of return.

Vestment Advisors does this through a number of tactics and strategies.

The first is by creating a *Money Trail*™. What is a Money Trail™? It is nothing more than documenting or mapping every step that occurs during the servicing of clients in a financial advisor's practice. We have asked many financial advisors of all sizes to tell us how many steps they believed are involved in servicing their clients. We have received guesses from 12 to 75 steps. In actuality, the number of steps involved in providing services to clients of financial services easily number 700 to 1,000.

Why is this number so high? Let us examine an advisor's initial step, prospecting for clients. Assume this practice uses seminars to generate new lead opportunities.

What are the steps involved in establishing clients for a seminar? The first step is gathering a list of those who fit your client profile to invite to the seminars. That may include three steps like selecting a vendor, procuring the list, and getting the names on a mailer. Then there's another step of creating the invitation. The next step involves sending the invitation. Another step involves scouting the location for the seminar. There are many more steps involved with the seminar, which include procuring the audiovisual equipment, transporting it, establishing who will be present from the financial practice's side to manage the guests, and so on.

The servicing of a financial services client requires the fulfillment of every step in many operations. These include:

- Prospecting
- Education
- Initial visit
- Building the plan
- Presenting the plan
- Closing the client
- Filing the paperwork
- Collecting the fees
- Documenting things relevant to compliance and regulatory issues
- Setting up follow-up appointments
- Managing employees
- Training
- Bookkeeping

- Business planning
- Answering service requests
- And so on

As you can see, the steps in helping clients through a financial advisor's practice add up quickly!

WHAT IS THE MONEY TRAIL™?

We call the documented list of all the steps involved in running a company's business practices the Money Trail™. The reason for the name is very simple. Irrespective of which step is occurring, the individual fulfilling any given step is holding all the practice's money. If a person does not fulfill their responsibilities, then the firm's money falls through the cracks and is lost. The Money Trail™ follows the practice's (not the client's) money through the chain of events to service the client. The

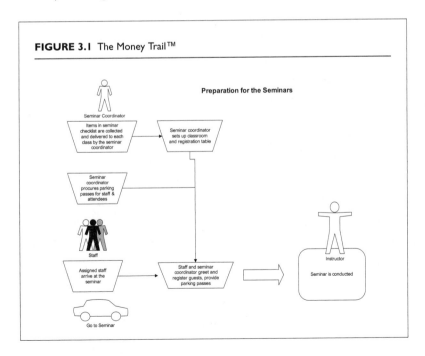

FIGURE 3.1 The Money Trail™

flow chart in Figure 3.1, or trail, represents a small part of the actual workflow process in client generation of a practice.

The Money Trail™ is best expressed as both a graphical flow chart and as a step-by-step process document.

An important outcome of the Money Trail™ is to identify needs, bottlenecks, and limitations of your practice. It also creates a foundation for efficiency in the company. It lets you know not only the tasks and duties of every job that must be fulfilled in the company, but it shows the responsibilities that are affiliated with each of those positions. It clearly defines what level of authority is necessary within each position to fulfill these tasks and duties. Many of our clients have found that they make far higher profits by investing in the additional expense of a new employee to remove a bottleneck than trying to run "lean and mean."

We will be dealing with authority in the Employee/Delegation section of Chapter 6.

Losing Sleep When the Money Falls through the Cracks

In most financial advisory practices, many of the steps are never assigned to an employee. They are just kind of "out there," in the entrepreneur's subconscious. When it becomes obvious the steps or duties have not been done, someone, frequently the financial advisors themselves, step up to try to fulfill them. This is not only an extremely inefficient system, it can keep the business owner awake at night as he remembers dozens of little tasks that have probably not been completed.

A properly designed Money Trail™ will look for tasks that have not been assigned, or bottlenecks—places in the business flow where there are too many needs divided among too few workers. With bottlenecks, processes may get done, it just takes too long. Worse, they may not get done (falling through the cracks) as more pressing tasks take higher priority.

THE CHINESE LANTERN

One of our clients located in Albuquerque had a nine-person financial planning department. Every person in the department was responsible for creating the plans used by the partners. Unfortunately, the partners did not trust the members of the planning department to do the quality of work they felt was necessary. To solve this problem, they hired a well-known CFP® to oversee the department and personally review every single financial plan before it was sent to the financial advisor. The CFP® also screened and reviewed every client's initial information sheet and then assigned it to a person on the planning team.

You can imagine what the desk of the CFP®/manager looked like. With nine people creating plans, he may have had 40 to 50 completed plans per week to review, in addition to scanning the new incoming plans that needed to be assigned. Being a diligent guy, on top of the initial review before assigning them to a planner, he went over every plan with a fine-tooth comb, doing what the partners had hired him to do. Unfortunately, it took him on average an hour per plan—complicated ones took much longer. Anyone can see there is not enough time in the day to complete all of these duties, even if he lived at the office.

We called this bottleneck the "Chinese lantern" because one person controlled all the output—both going in and then coming out of the department. Unfortunately, this particular bottleneck was devastating to the revenues of the firm. It took so long to get a plan back to the advisor that clients had to wait many weeks to get the answers to their financial questions. This

---

Multi-Million-Dollar Principle #9

To get a handle on your fiscal and asset management, create your own Money Trail™.

wait had a negative effect on the clients—their high drive to solve their financial problems waned, and it became harder to close sales.

In short, without prompt and accurate financial plans, this financial practice could not do business. We estimated this bottleneck cost them 40 percent to 60 percent of their potential revenue.

MANAGING CASH FLOW

Another weakness was that many financial advisors did not manage their own monthly cash flow. They had little grasp about where their money was going on a monthly basis. The problem begins with how most firms identify different items in their expense ledger. Most financial practices have their CPAs establish a chart of accounts in order to assign a category based on tax-deductible expenditures. Unfortunately, for the financial advisor, most CPAs create this chart of account for the efficiency and benefit of the CPA in completing their tax returns.

What is missing is an important tool for monitoring and maximizing a firm's growth and profits. In fact, each of these categories should represent a way of tracking and budgeting what is taking place in the practice. An effective chart of accounts has a number of different categories, including assets, liabilities (long- and short-term debt), revenues, variable expenses and fixed expenses, depreciation, and taxes. Each of the items that generate revenue (whether they are fees, commissions, or other sources of revenue) must be detailed in your chart of accounts. Likewise, all expenses, whether they are variable expenses such as marketing costs, prospecting, advertising, public relations, or fixed expenses such as payroll, telephone, lease, computer technology, and so on, must all be itemized in a chart of accounts.

We have taken a structured chart of accounts format for our clients and created the FlexBudget™, a tool that allows the financial advisor to monitor and evaluate their expenditures and revenues, and by that, their asset management, in under 45 minutes a month. Yes, that is not a typo. With the right tools, it is possible to monitor your firm's fiscal health in less than 45 minutes. The good news: You do not have to be a financial wizard or accounting expert to utilize and understand the FlexBudget™.

The FlexBudget™ creates several key benefits:

- It provides the ability to track expenditures on a month-to-month basis in every category in the chart of accounts. This allows you to determine where there are extremely high costs, or anomalies (that is, unexpectedly high costs that were not anticipated), and it allows you to create a snapshot of the company simply by examining month by month each of the revenue and cost items in the chart of accounts.
- It allows you to do a drill down if there is an anomaly in a given category. Let's say there is an unusually high long-distance telephone bill for one month. The drill down allows you to identify an expense that is out of the norm and follow up to find out why. In our example, it would highlight who had long-distance access, and what caused that anomaly within the budget.
- It allows you to get a historical record of where you have allocated money in the company. For example, how much are you truly spending on seminars and workshops? What is the radio show costing? And what kind of return occurs as a result of it? It will allow you to track how effective certain advertising is because you can link it to the number of new clients generated. The history allows you to establish budgets for the following year or period of time, enabling you to determine what is necessary for the continued growth of your practice.
- It helps you determine where the breakeven is in the practice.

- It establishes a clear foundation for creating budgets.
- It becomes the fiscal foundation for fulfilling your strategic and functional business plans.
- It opens the secret to doubling or tripling your profits.

BREAKEVEN

An important element of the FlexBudget™ is showing you what is your true breakeven. What is breakeven?

Most people believe that breakeven is when your revenues equal your expenses plus your depreciation plus your taxes. As in most cases of conventional wisdom, it sounds good but is dead wrong. In reality, breakeven for a business must account for more expenses than these. To understand breakeven, you must first understand that it is impossible for any business to make and retain a profit. I know this sounds like an outrageous statement, but it is true. The hidden word is "retain." Why is it impossible for a business to make and retain a profit?

It is imperative that all businesses make a profit. Without a profit a business cannot survive. But it is impossible for a business to retain a profit, and without this understanding, it is difficult to impossible to effectively leverage assets in the company.

Let me explain: There are only five ways that profits can be used by any company. They are:

1. Cash reserves
2. Money for growth
3. Money for risk—those things that are outside the normal operation of the business
4. Money for employee incentives
5. Dividends to the shareholders

Let us examine whether a company can retain any of these profits.

Item One: Cash Reserves

The company does not retain cash reserves. Why does a company need cash reserves? Not every month is profitable and not every revenue account receivable is paid on time. Every month does not generate the same income, though expenses, at least the fixed ones, are still there. Cash reserves are a normal part of any business's life. Extremely healthy companies can sustain ten months of positive cash flow with only two months of negative cash flow in any given year. Healthy companies may have nine months of positive cash flow and three months of negative cash flow. More months of negative cash flow indicate there are probably problems within the organization. To understand how you can manage yourself through months of negative cash flow, particularly if they are successive, you must have capital (cash) reserve. Naturally this excludes seasonal businesses.

Many practices believe that you can account for your cash reserve needs through getting a line of credit from your bank, to help cash flow. However, banks do not award lines of credit to be floated indefinitely. Bankers call these "evergreen loans," and they do not like them.

Most lines of credit represent a percentage of accounts receivable plus assets with personal responsibility and signed liability on the financial advisor's part. Even with these conditions, most banks insist that all practices are out of the line of credit for 1 month during a 12-month period. Few banks will provide a line of credit that will maintain all cash flow needs in the course of a year, particularly if there are successive negative cash flow months.

As a result of this, all practices must establish a line of credit and a cash reserve. Are cash reserves a profit that is retained by the company? No, they are spent on a monthly basis and function like an insurance policy for the business's bills.

Item Two: Money for Growth

Corporate profits must also be designated for growth. Businesses do not thrive if they remain stagnant. Frankly, businesses do not survive if they do not grow. Growth requires a reinvestment of capital. Growth can come from any number of things, including marketing campaigns, advertising, public relations efforts, increased education, or expanding into new markets. The common denominator is that all of these activities require a front-end investment before there is a return on those expenses. As a result, some of the company's profits must be set aside for growth. The best companies plan their growth and plan their strategies and tactics they will use for growth. As a result, monies for growth may be retained today, but they are spent tomorrow.

Item Three: Money for Risk

Risk involves venturing into something new or different for the company. For example, in a financial planning practice, risk may include opening a second office in another part of the city. Risk capital is the money that would be necessary in opening another location. Many factors come into play in this, including bookkeeping, administrative services, advertising and marketing, lease space, technology, telephone, and so on. Money for risk has to be available to move on the risk strategy. Therefore, risk capital may be a profit today but it is an expense tomorrow.

Item Four: Employee Incentives

We believe employees should be rewarded for work well done, but particularly when they contribute to the company making profits above breakeven. There are only three ways for any business to increase its profits:

1. Increase revenue faster than expenses
2. Decrease costs
3. Increase efficiency

What is the common denominator? All three of these efforts come as a result of your employees efforts. If employees are not motivated to increase profits, profits will only occur as a result of your own efforts, a very strenuous task even with everyone's help. When you make a profit, employees should share in those profits. Significantly raising profits, and understanding how and why it happens, can only happen through your employees when they clearly see how the benefit also reaches them. Employee incentives are also an expense, not a retained profit by the company, but probably the best use of company profits available!

Item Five: Dividends to Shareholders

Finally, shareholders who have invested in the firm and shoulder the risk of its debts and liabilities should reap the benefits of their investments by receiving after-tax dividends of the company's profitability.

What was the common truth in how profits are used? The company ultimately cannot keep any of them! Why is this important to know? Without this knowledge, business owners never get a clear understanding of how a company operates fiscally, or how to create long-term value, stability, and profitability. What is it that a business ultimately does financially? The only thing a business can do is leverage its profits to create prosperous trades with all of its stakeholders. Understanding this is the fundamental foundation of learning how to leverage the assets of any business.

Trading with stakeholders is the very cornerstone of any business and its participation in capitalism. Unfortunately, defining profitability as "getting as much as you can out of the business" prevents the advisor from ever managing his company to a target level of profitability and allowing him to succeed at growing beyond that target in an effective manner.

CAPITALISM DEFINED

Remember, capitalism is an economic system of barter where all parties in a trade believe they received equal or greater value in exchange for what they receive in the trade. Any financial services practice has many trading partners. They include their clients, employees, employees' families, their bank, their CPA firm, their law firm, the community they live in, their product suppliers and vendors, their broker/dealer, and many others.

A good trading partner creates many happy relationships. This is a way businesses leverage their assets: They trade cash, goods, or services with their trading partners and stakeholders. Doing this effectively leverages the assets of the business.

TRUE BREAKEVEN

How does our FlexBudget™ help you understand breakeven? Our contention is that breakeven in a business is when the revenues are equal to the fixed expenses plus the variable expenses plus taxes plus depreciation plus cash reserves plus money budgeted for growth and for risk. We combine money for growth, money for risk, and cash reserves into a category, which we label Targeted Profits. The reason we call them targeted profits is that they are profits targeted as an expense, an expense that is necessary for the business's prosperous growth and survival.

Definition of Breakeven

$$\text{Revenue} = \text{Fixed} + \text{Variable} + \text{Depreciation} + \text{Taxes} + \text{Targeted Profits}$$

Why is this breakeven? It is breakeven because the owners of a financial services practice know that if they generate enough revenue to pay their fixed expenses, their variable expenses, depreciation, taxes, cash reserve growth, and risk budgets, they will sleep well at night. Fiscal concerns for financial advisors are among the most compelling reasons why financial services practices bring us in for advice. It is more than not realizing their dreams; it is the fact that the money management has become so painful that the financial advisor suffers from excessively long hours of work, deteriorating health, less time off, and all the consequences of very high levels of stress.

In addition to establishing breakeven, the FlexBudget™ provides another fascinating insight. You can determine how a modest increase in revenue will result in a large return in profitability. Let me explain.

Let's look at our million-dollar producer.

Multi-Million-Dollar Principle #11

Breakeven in a business is when the revenues are equal to the fixed expenses plus the variable expenses plus taxes plus depreciation plus cash reserves plus money budgeted for growth and for risk.

Total All Revenue:	**$1,000,000**
Client generation	65,000
Office lease costs	35,000
Telephone expense, postage	8,000
Computer, office equipment expense	12,000
Marketing growth and risk	100,000
Professional services (CPA, legal)	15,000
Continuing education	10,000
Employee wages and benefits	350,000
Personal salary	300,000
Depreciation	20,000
Taxes	85,000
Total All Expenses	**$1,000,000**

Now let us split the expenses into two categories, Fixed and Variable. Fixed expenses remain the same each month; variable expenses tend to move up or down based on revenue moving up or down.

Variable Expenses

Client generation	$ 65,000
Marketing growth and risk	100,000
Taxes	85,000
Total, Variable Expenses	**$ 250,000**

Fixed Expenses

Office lease costs	$ 35,000
Telephone expense, postage	8,000
Computer, office equipment expense	12,000
Professional services (CPA, legal)	15,000
Continuing education	10,000
Employee wages and benefits	350,000
Personal salary	300,000
Depreciation	20,000
Total, Fixed Expenses	**$ 750,000**

Total All Expenses	**$1,000,000**

In this example, 75 percent of all expenses are fixed. What does this mean, and why is it important to understand it?

Important thought #1: Fixed expenses are paid once irrespective of revenue.

Important thought #2: Variable expenses go up and down with revenue.

Important thought #3: The percentage of fixed expenses at breakeven becomes a profit contribution on all revenue above breakeven.

What does this mean to our million-dollar advisor? If they generated another $100,000 in revenue, $75,000 of it is profit! Looked at another way, if it costs $25,000 in marketing/growth/risk expenses to generate an additional $100,000 in revenue, is it worth it? Of course it is!

The FlexBudget™ allows you to see how modest increases in revenue generate large increases in profitability. Why is this important? In a very simple way, you can allocate budget costs for growth and risk, with an anticipation of return of increased revenue, and then calculate them in the FlexBudget™. The FlexBudget™ allows you to run these calculations based on the previous year's history, the average of the current year's production, and the current year's budget. These three factors allow a financial advisor to gain control of his assets within the practice. Sound fiscal management through tools like the FlexBudget™ is a powerful way to build your practice!

We have seen fixed expenses in financial services companies range from 35 percent to 75 percent of breakeven costs. The difference in the fixed expenses has much to do with whether financial planners pay themselves a commission, a percentage of commission, or a fixed salary. Reality remains the same: You only pay fixed expenses once.

What have we found in our clients? Prior to us teaching them fiscal and asset management, defining their Money Trail™, and creating a FlexBudget™, very few financial advisors knew how to manage their own money.

It was shocking to see how few of the top salespeople saved enough money to invest in their own financial future. Some were not saving any money. One had been bankrupt twice and was moving close to it a third time. Most of them paid themselves with whatever was left over at the end of the month, and when the negative-cash-flow months occurred, would have to draw money out of their own pocket, usually with loud complaints from their spouses.

How can you change this? First, establish a salary for the principal/owner of the financial services practice. This is important because it allows you to establish true breakeven and a budget for the practice. Does that mean you will not pay yourself additional money? Of course not! But the monies (paid as dividends on a regular basis) were based on the performance of the company and not on needing extra income for a new car. We recommend dividend payments and profit sharing to occur quarterly through the fiscal year.

Second, establish a profit-sharing plan based on incentives that occur on performance above breakeven. Profit sharing is an important part of a successful financial practice. We detail our recommendations on profit sharing in Chapter 8.

Some top-producing financial advisors live a very lavish lifestyle. We know of a very large broker/dealer that terminated the second largest financial advisor in the firm. Fortunately for us, he was *not* one of our clients! It was an interesting case, because the advisor in question had not been a significant compliance risk up to the point of termination. However, his lifestyle was so lavish, and he was carrying so much debt, that the broker/dealer anticipated he would become a problem child, forced to stretch for commissions to keep up his high-flying spending habits. They knew he would eventually be tempted to make recommendations that were not in the client's best interest, or worse, possibly steal from client accounts. The broker/dealer figured it was better to terminate him immediately, before he caused problems, rather than fend off regulators and unhappy investors later.

Lavish lifestyles do not add value to the firm. Establish a salary, make it reasonable, then reward yourself by paying yourself dividends from the firm's profitability.

MANAGING EMPLOYEES AS AN ASSET

Now that we have determined the largest asset in a practice is its employees, how do you manage them as an asset? Very few financial advisors, who have been our clients or come to our seminars and workshops, have a clear system for hiring and managing employees. They provide little to no employee training. They rarely have a solid and fair plan to motivate them with incentives, and they haven't thought about using the employees' best talents to make the firm grow. This would be like a manufacturing company allowing its key equipment to get rusty.

Second, clear job descriptions are not written. How could they be? Without defining the Money Trail™, it is difficult to really understand the tasks, duties, and responsibilities of a position—particularly when you are playing basketball. New hires may have varying levels of competence. Frequently, we have found that there were no employee contracts or poorly written ones. You can rescue your practice from employee lawsuits through the use of carefully written job descriptions and employment contracts.

Job descriptions are important because they clearly define the responsibilities, tasks, and duties of a position. They also clearly define the level of authority that the position entails. One consistent flaw we found among financial advisors was a pattern of delegating responsibility for fulfilling tasks but not delegating authority to complete them. Delegating responsibility, without the authority necessary to fulfill tasks, is a fairly common practice and a very short route to disaster.

Why? Most financial advisors who are principals in successful organizations believe they know how to do it better than anyone else. It can be anything from meeting with clients, to preparing plans, to due diligence on investments, to writing marketing pieces. Frankly, in most cases, they are correct. The business owner can do all those duties and many more, far better than their staff.

Unfortunately, failing to provide adequate training and coaching will ensure that their employees will never get to the level of competence the firm requires. When the work product is not up to the standards set by the financial advisor, they become hesitant to delegate any more duties and responsibilities. The ripple effect of this is devastating.

An extremely stressful work environment is then created. Financial advisors find themselves doing tasks that keep them away from the one thing that builds the business—meeting with clients. The staff is upset because they sense their boss is not pleased with their work, and they do not know how to change to provide a work product that will be appealing to the financial advisor. When employees become concerned about their job security, productivity degenerates.

Some of the Root Issues of Poorly Managed Staff

Many factors contribute to a work environment where the most important asset, employees, is not effectively managed:

- Having no clear definition of responsibilities, tasks, or duties.
- A lack of employee authority from the financial advisor to implement tasks, duties, responsibilities, and projects.

- The no-win situation, part A: Employees believe they have the authority to fulfill their task and duties, but their performance does not meet their boss's expectations. Result: A negative experience with their boss.
- The no-win situation, part B: Employees do not believe they have the authority they need to fulfill their duties, while their boss assumes they should have known that they did have all the authority they needed. Result: A negative experience with their boss.

The end result of this kind of dysfunctional corporate behavior is a system we all know well—bureaucracy. Employees quickly learn how to manage their time in a "CYA" world.

The Solution

Clearly defined job descriptions that include how the position contributes to the mission and objective of the practice should include each of the following elements:

- A job title
- How the position contributes to the practice's mission/vision/value statement
- The job's responsibilities
- The tasks and duties affiliated with the position
- The authority that the position has for fulfilling their tasks and duties
- The reporting relationships, by job title, not name, both up and down
- Affiliated relationships, including those departments or positions with which this position works

These are all critical elements in a good job description. Because of the litigious world we live in, it is also important that job descriptions include OSHA disclaimers. Examples of OSHA items include:

- Requires an individual be able to sit five hours a day or more at a desk and work with a computer.
- May require the employee to lift boxes weighing no more than 25 pounds as a consequence of the filing responsibilities of the position.

Clearly written job descriptions go a long way to improving communication with employees and establishing a healthy and affirmative working environment. The end result is that all the tasks from the Money Trail™ are assigned to employees, and all employees understand what is expected of them.

Sample job descriptions are found in the Appendix.

CONSISTENT PAY STRATEGIES

Another painful flaw we saw among many financial advisors was inconsistent pay strategies. This was particularly true among registered sales assistants, the licensed individuals who help financial advisors with their clients. One West Coast firm had four different registered sales assistants who worked for four different financial advisors. Each financial advisor was free to create their own bonus structure. Some assistants received wages and salaries in the $30,000 to $40,000 range while others received salaries as high as $60,000. Some received bonuses that increased their personal income to as much as $90,000 or $100,000. Others, doing the same work but for a different financial advisor, were only getting their base salary. Unfortunately, there was nothing consistent about the policy and how it was practiced in this firm of four multi-million-dollar producers.

These inequities create very bad environments in terms of morale. The assistants all talked to each other, and it did not take them long to determine some were getting paid two and three times as much for the same level of work. It is imperative when managing your employee assets that there is a consistent system of reward and reinforcement for all employees.

This basic truth was lost on some of our financial advisor clients. They wanted to maintain a disparate system because they were under the false illusion that it would be private between them and the employee. Unfortunately, that is never the case. Rumor and gossip still run rampant in any organization. The best way to quell it is to have consistent policies that apply to all.

SUMMARY

In summary, sound fiscal and asset management necessitates that you have a chart of accounts for tracking and monitoring fixed expenses, variable expenses, and revenue sources. You will also need to use a tool like the FlexBudget™ that allows you to determine breakeven, cash flow, budgets, and the ability to expand profitability.

Great fiscal management demands leveraging of your hard assets, the largest being your employees. Finally, a careful monitoring of resources and rewarding those who help you increase profitability are key factors to financial security.

KEY POINTS

1. Without understanding the fundamentals of fiscal and asset management, your practice is limited in growth and will probably cause you many sleepless nights.
2. To maximize the value of the firm, and create a sound fiscal foundation, financial advisors should put them-

selves on a monthly salary. They should also set aside money into their own savings programs.

3. Most CPA firms do *not* have a background in fiscal and asset management. They focus on how to shelter taxes for your practice.

4. All businesses have two types of assets:
   1. *Hard assets.* These include cash on hand, accounts receivable, furniture and fixtures—and other items whose asset value can be clearly defined.
   2. *Soft assets.* These include brand, image, location, time in industry, number of clients, goodwill, past performance—and employees.

5. The true value you put on your employee is their salary and benefits earned.

6. The Money Trail™ documents every step that occurs during the servicing of clients in a financial advisor's practice. A carefully constructed Money Trail™:
   - Identifies the needs, bottlenecks, Chinese lanterns, and limitations of your practice.
   - Finds tasks that have not been assigned.
   - Creates a foundation for efficiency in the company.
   - Defines the tasks and duties of every job that must be fulfilled.
   - Defines level of authority.
   - Increases profits.

7. The servicing of a financial services client requires the fulfillment of every step in many operations, and for some firms may involve 700 to 1,000 steps. These operations include:
   - Prospecting
   - Education
   - Initial visit
   - Building the plan
   - Presenting the plan
   - Closing the client

- Filing the paperwork
- Collecting the fees
- Documenting items relevant to compliance and regulatory issues
- Setting up of follow-up appointments
- Managing employees
- Training
- Bookkeeping
- Business planning
- Answering service requests
- And so on

8. The FlexBudget™ is a tool that allows financial advisors to monitor and evaluate their expenditures and revenue—their asset management—in under 45 minutes a month. The FlexBudget™:
   - Helps you determine breakeven.
   - Establishes a fiscal foundation for creating a budget.
   - Allows you to track expenditures and find problem areas.
   - Provides a record of past spending.

9. A company can use profits in only five ways. They are:
   1. Cash reserves
   2. Money for growth
   3. Money for risk (those things that are outside the normal operation of the business)
   4. Money for employee incentives
   5. Dividends to the shareholders

10. Breakeven is when the revenues are equal to the fixed expenses plus the variable expenses plus taxes plus depreciation plus cash reserves plus money budgeted for growth and for risk.

4

MARKETING IS EVERYTHING, OR PUTTING DERRIERES IN CHAIRS

Prosperity Factor #4
A marketing system that puts a constant stream of
motivated and qualified hot prospects in front of the
financial advisor is imperative.

By Katherine

Although all eight Prosperity Factors™ are important to having a mult-imillion-dollar practice, a successful marketing system, in my opinion, is the most important factor. The reason superstar financial advisors were able to generate millions of dollars in commissions was they each had a steady of stream of qualified prospects sitting across the table from the advisor. I call this "derrieres in chairs." The best scenario was when these prospects were not just cold or warm, they were hot. They were already motivated to do business with the advisor before they ever walked into the office.

The day-to-day grind of filling the client pipeline was generally left to someone other than the superstar. Other than occasional seminar or radio program duty, most financial advisors never worried about where the prospect was coming from because someone else was taking care of that crucial part of the business.

Over time we were able to convince our financial advisors that everything they did had a marketing component. This included many aspects of the business that most had not considered to be marketing related, such as the first impression of the company, the parking lot, or even employee recognition programs. As Brad Lantz, Vestment's Chief Marketing Officer is fond of saying, *"Marketing is everything."*

**Marketing
Report Card

A**

All of our superstar clients were marketing machines. They worked hard to market their businesses and paid a lot for their prospects. Here are some of the things the superstars were doing right, before we ever started to assist them.

Target Market Segment

Contrary to common understanding, most of our superstar clients focused on the middle-America market, not the wealthy or even very affluent prospects. Although universal wisdom in our industry is to focus on only the top-tier investor, these superstars found that mainstream Americans were being overlooked, and that they had a surprising amount of assets available for investment. They may not be the "millionaire next door," but they had sizable 401(k) rollovers or large insurance needs.

M *ulti-Million-Dollar Principle #12*

Marketing is everything!

Focus on Their Demographic Niche

A well-known Minneapolis-based marketing company that helps large financial services firm tells about the marketing department of one of their large broker/dealer clients. Apparently the home office marketing guys, most of whom had never sold an investment in their life, spent a year getting bogged down in researching the demographics of their investors, nit-picking over age, salary, gender, geographical location, and even their favorite television shows. At the end of the year, they had a lot of great information about their investors but no strategies on how to turn this information into new, paying clients. In other words, they had great information but no practical way to use it to increase revenue.

This kind of detailed evaluation of the market never happened at the superstar firm. Why? They knew this painstaking process took too long to turn leads into clients. It was not helping the bottom line. The superstars stayed focused on their ideal demographic niche and kept it very simple: What is the most immediate thing we have to do to get clients in the door?

As an example, Mercury Financial Advisors* and Mile High Investments* both understood that the key factor was a simple one: How much money did the client have to invest? We call this *investable assets*. Investable assets include 401(k) proceeds that could be rolled over, accounts in other firms that could be brought to the financial advisor's firm, IRAs, emergency funds, and other personal liquid assets. They did not include real estate, corporate pension plans that must be left where they were, or 401(k)s at existing employers, because none of these funds could be transferred to the financial advisor's supervision.

Mercury originally placed the minimum bar at $50,000 of investable assets. When they focused on having clients who had at least that much to invest, they found that eventually they could get their average commission to $8,000, and on their high-end marketing niche, estate planning attorneys, they averaged $24,000 in fees and commissions per case.

Mile High investors set the bar at $75,000 of investable assets. Clients who came in with at least $75,000 were referred to a top-tiered financial advisor. Those who had less than $75,000 of investable assets were referred to a less experienced advisor. This was called an "A" or "B" lead, with "B" leads going to newer advisors. They found that $75,000 in assets would generally lead them to an average commission of $4,500. We helped them get it to $6,700.

Mile High had a number of new financial advisors who were quite happy to get the second-level client leads, the "Bs", or those with less than $75,000 to invest. One rookie managed to generate over $1 million dollars of commissions by his third year just working with "B" leads.

Chicago Capital Investments* (CCI) fell into their demographic niche quite by accident. The company became affiliated with a radio program that provided most of their leads had a deep penetration with 45-year-olds on up. In fact, the station had a higher concentration in that age group than any other radio station in the entire area. Focusing on this group, CCI, by their fourth year in business, was averaging $450,000 worth of investable assets per client.

THE MARKETING SYSTEMS USED BY THE MARKETING MACHINES

Our experience shows that financial advisors use less than ten different systems to generate large numbers of qualified

---

M *ulti-Million-Dollar Principle #13*

Don't ignore the "B" clients. Handled correctly, they can be a major part of your clientele.

hot prospects. These include: radio shows with additional advertising, seminars, referral programs, educational workshops and seminars, centers of influence, events, drip-marketing letters, and niche marketing. The most obvious system, client referrals, was not used successfully by a single firm until we brought them a workable program.

Here is a closer look at what the superstars did to get derrières in chairs:

Local Radio Shows

Chicago Capital Investments had a weekly radio show that became second only to Rush Limbaugh in popularity in their market. Surprisingly, CCI fell into this amazing marketing tool by happenstance. One evening Charlie Chicago was giving a seminar attended by an executive of this radio station. The executive approached Charlie and asked whether he would be interested in doing a regular radio show. Charlie happily accepted.

Charlie's one-hour-a-weekend, call-in show is so successful it is rare to run into anybody in the Chicago area who has not heard of him. It provided instant credibility. Listeners assumed that any reputable radio station would have carefully checked out a financial advisor, reviewing his credentials and history, before asking him to host their own radio show. Nothing could be farther from the truth. The radio station did no due diligence on their new financial expert. It is true they needed someone who was good on the radio, but they also needed someone who was going to pay the monthly $26,000 cost of the weekly show.

This radio station, known for its "voice of the community" format, had over the years held a dominant presence with the "45 and over" crowd who were either retired or approaching retirement. This one happy coincidence, being on a radio station that perfectly matched their demographics, had a huge impact on CCI's prospects. They did not know it at the time, or plan it—CCI just lucked out.

The personality was a big part of this equation. Charlie Chicago was a small-town boy who sounded very credible on air. The listeners liked and trusted him. Charlie continually stated that he was not smart enough to answer all the audience's questions, but the experts in his company were, and therefore he was just one phone call away from the answer to any financial question. This not only made him more believable, it constantly reinforced his "brain trust" branding.

Focusing on this group (over 50 years old, with assets of $75,000 or more), by their fourth year in business, CCI was averaging $350,000 worth of investable assets per client.

Few of the listeners had any idea that this radio show was really a one-hour commercial paid for by CCI. The firm's cost did not stop with paying for the weekly show. Their contract with this established station also required them to purchase ads promoting the radio program that would air during other shows. The station itself would then promote the program, as well. To make sure that the radio show also had good listenership, CCI invested in billboard ads throughout the city, magazine ads, newspaper ads, and seminars, and even had their name on charity events. The total annual cost of the radio show was substantial. This advertising combination increased awareness of the program.

Annual Radio Expenses for CCI

The weekly radio shows annual price tag	$275,000
Radio ads annually to drive more listeners to the show	70,000
Billboards advertising the show each year	110,000
Total	**$455,000**

This does not include the ads in newspapers, magazines, and other activities they did to promote the show.

On the surface, the CCI radio show may have appeared to be a "go-with-the-flow" media event. In reality, it did involve some planning. A different topic was discussed each week. Sometimes Charlie would bring on experts and interview them before he took calls from the listening audience. Once again these shows were carefully crafted to fit in with the advisor's image and differentiation statements. Most of the topics were hot issues with their demographic group.

Was it worth it? Every penny. Once potential prospects had listened to the program, they felt they had a friend and would call to set up a free, no-obligation review. Closure rates were over 90 percent. The cost per lead was $175–$350, depending on whether it was seminar season or not. But remember, clients want to be educated and seminars were an excellent way to educate prospects and eventually obtain more of their assets to invest. With commissions averaging well over $6,000 per case, the initial investment, even at $350 per prospect, really paid off.

We have worked with other financial advisor firms that had radio shows in different parts of the country who have not had nearly the same level of success. Why was CCI so incredibly successful?

- First, they had the right radio station that perfectly matched their demographics.
- The show was on at a key time, Saturday mornings.
- Although Charlie Chicago,* who hosted the show, was certainly good on the radio, he also had a sidekick, a well-known radio personality who became Ed McMahon to his Johnny Carson. "Ed" was brilliant at making our superstar look dazzling. This experienced radio showman was invaluable in fielding the questions called in by listeners, controlling the time, and focusing the star's efforts. When things got slow, or things got hot, the radio professional would put out the fires and save the day.
- CCI realized this type of marketing was patient work. It was not unusual to hear prospects say that they had been listening to this show for two or three years before they

finally decided to call in and make an appointment. It was not a quick fix. It can take a year or longer for this kind of marketing tool to produce the desired results.

- The ancillary marketing, the radio ads, billboards, and the like, were also a key component of making this work. They added additional credibility and exposure and helped establish the brand recognition.

- Finally, let's not forget our superstar, Charlie Chicago. He was terrific with this kind of audience, low-key, unassuming, funny, and self-deprecating. He quickly admitted that he was not the smartest advisor around, but he knew where to go to get help. Whenever he got stumped with a question, he would just refer to his "brain trust" back at his home office. It made him appear very credible, extremely trustworthy, approachable, and believable.

Radio shows run amuck. We have heard horror stories from advisors around the country who went into radio shows without clearly thinking through the process. One firm apparently burned through about $25,000 in four months with nothing to show for it. It turns out that the radio station was a thousand-watt station—so small it was probably operating out of someone's basement. The station had done absolutely no advertising to promote the show. In addition, the time of day, Monday afternoons, was deadly. In fact, in 16 weeks, they had only two legitimate call-ins requesting information. It was a most painful lesson for this small firm that should have looked before they leaped.

The bottom line: Just because radio shows work for some advisors in certain parts of the country does not mean they are a good idea for you. Make sure you do the due diligence to make sure it is going to work in another location. A radio program might have been appropriate, if it had been on a station that fit the demographics of their clientele, advertised the program, had a winning format with an engaging co-host, and was broadcast during a time of day that was appropriate for the audience.

A Series of Seminars

Seminars are certainly not a new marketing tool used by financial advisors. In fact, I used seminars to build my business when I started in 1985. Every single superstar advisor that we assisted was using seminars. Mercury's use of seminars was particularly effective. Although it was not unusual for the superstar to use a canned or purchased seminar that hundreds of other financial advisors were using around the country, they still managed to get a good-size attendance that fit their demographics. Mercury did this by offering a free dinner at the local country club. Forget the boring meals you see at most meetings like this—they splurged on steak, salmon, and other delicacies. The dinners were quite delicious and a good draw.

Mercury Investments* of Greeley, Colorado, also focused on middle America. They may not be the "millionaires next door" but they were certainly the supersavers living next door. Their market was people who were steady savers in their 401(k), savings accounts, and other investments. However, they typically were not very savvy about their investments and had a great deal of fear surrounding new investments and investment professionals. To help them overcome their fear, they liked to attend continuing education classes on investing. Mercury saw this as an opportunity. They called themselves "The Edification People." Working through the local community education system, they provided continuing education on investing to this particular group. About five times per year they would create a three-part workshop held weekly for three weeks. Each seminar cost them about $6,000 to $8,000 including marketing, food, room rental, and giveaways.

Mercury had tapped into a market that was afraid because they were not competent about their own investments. They were also afraid that they were not asking the right questions and did not have anyone to trust. This group generally had investments between $150,000 and $750,000, with the average being

$250,000. Education was particularly effective because it helped them overcome their fears.

Part of the seminar included a free consultation at Mercury's office and an individual financial plan.

To further capitalize on this market, Mercury purchased a list with the identical demographics. These prospects were sent a tried-and-tested marketing letter created by a national marketing firm, inviting them to attend a dinner seminar at a nice country club. The food was delicious and the purpose of the dinner seminar was to encourage them to attend the three-part workshops being held through the local community education system.

The series of three seminars were so important to Mercury's marketing program that they flatly refused to take any clients who had not been to all three seminars. They used this time to explain to the prospect their philosophy of investing and how it was different from other firms'. Mercury showcased their market differentiation during these programs and put it to a great advantage. They also gave the attendees excellent information about their finances and a new look at an old topic. The net result was building a high level of trust with the prospects and preclosing them on retaining Mercury.

What is a successful seminar? We have watched numerous financial advisors give seminars. Some of these presenters were good speakers, but none would win any Toastmaster awards as great orators. However, that is not why the advisors gave presentations. This is also good news for all of us. You do not have to be a great speaker to be wildly successful at seminars. The financial advisor focused on one thing when giving a seminar: Doing a good job at motivating prospects to come into the office. The superstar financial advisor was excellent at this mission. Using seminars they could literally bring hundreds, or thousands, of prospects to their firm over a year.

Part of the reason the financial advisors were so successful with seminar marketing was that they all appeared extremely trustworthy. I have heard dozens of seminars from financial advisors across the country and one phrase seems to leap out over and over no matter where they are located. The speaker will get up and say something along the lines of "I'm just a farm boy from Iowa." This "Aw shucks, I'm just a down-home guy like you," seems to build trust and credibility with the audience. The audience wants to work with someone just like them. They trust the advisor because the advisor seems humble and approachable.

Some of these firms, like Mercury, were especially adept at getting to the close—an appointment for an initial consultation. In Mercury's case, they had set up three different workshops with the first leading to the second, leading to the third, leading to an appointment in their offices. By the time the prospect showed up in their offices, their closing ratio was between 80 percent and 90 percent. Why? The attendee knew Mercury's philosophy, and had decided they were ready to purchase Mercury's services, otherwise they would not have bothered to show up.

Guru Investments,* on the other hand, would use seminars on a hot topic that appealed to their audience, such as "Maximizing Retirement Income." They specifically advertised to the gray-haired set by using the words "seasoned seniors" or something similar in the title. Seminars focused on getting more money in their retirement years, and then the presenter used a soft sell to get prospects to come in for an appointment.

Chicago Capital Investments held 16 two-hour seminars per year. It cost them approximately $24,000 to put the ads on radio shows and in newspapers, and to send direct mail to get the attendance that they wanted. The average seminar attendance was between 75 and 150 people, with about 30 percent to 40 percent being existing clients. Approximately 70 percent of the new people would come in for a free review. The rest of the audience was probably professional do-it-yourselfers there for free food and information.

The best way to drive people to the seminars turned out to be the casual mention on CCI's radio program. It got to be a humorous part of CCI's marketing's department weekly list of duties. People in the marketing department were assigned to listen to the program. If Charlie, the superstar, had not mentioned the seminar within the first 15 minutes of the show, one of his own employees was assigned to call, pretending to be a listener, and request information about the seminar. Two or three of these calls and attendance at the seminars went up dramatically.

Important Lessons about Seminars

- *Prospects want to learn.* The programs need good, solid information and cannot be a sales presentation for your firm.
- *Focus on a topic that appeals to your audience.* Shelly Simon,* who has made a business of tax-reduction strategies for the very wealthy, only gives presentations that appeal to this group—how to get more money into your pocket and out of Uncle Sam's.
- *Good food does help bring out a crowd.* We recommended to one of our clients that she actually print the menu on her invitations. Americans have become more discriminating about food. They are more likely to come for gourmet meals than ordinary chicken.
- *Be prepared to spend some money.* After helping numerous advisors across the country, we have found the average cost for a decent seminar that brings out qualified leads is between $6,000 and $8,000. Shelly Simon, who focuses on the ultrawealthy, would spend between $10,000 and $15,000 per seminar.
- *Radio ads helped generate a greater attendance.*
- *Locations are also important.* Make certain you pick a restaurant with a good reputation in the community as well as one that provides an effective meeting space for your presentation. Against our advice, one of our clients did a

seminar for high-end clients in a local restaurant. The food was great, but the layout of the room was so bad, and the room was so dimly lit, it was hard for her to make eye contact with the audience. Also, surprisingly, during her dinner event, we had two people tell us there had recently been a well-published murder in the parking lot of this very restaurant! No wonder she did not get the response she had hoped for. Many advisors have found success in having programs at their local country club. A surprising number of people would never pay to join a club, but they want to attend just to see what it looks like. Do a little due diligence on your chosen location to make sure it has the kind of reputation you are looking for.

- *Lighting is important.* After having done almost 100 seminars myself in the late 1980s to attract investors to the financial planning practice I had, I learned lighting is one of the most important factors in keeping the audience awake and engaged. Brightly lit rooms are very important. In a dimly lit room, the attendees may actually get drowsy or go to sleep. You need them awake to hear your message!

- *Giveaways can add excitement and help close the sale.* I did a Webinar for *On Wall Street* magazine and Wachovia in 2003. They had an unprecedented 450 people sign up. I was astonished with the turnout. Before I started thinking too highly of myself that I was the draw, I discovered they were giving away a $400 BlackBerry. Okay, it hurt my ego, but it did get sign-ups. Mercury, who did the series of three workshops, gave clients a book by a bestselling author on the highlighted financial topic if they signed up for the personal meeting—again, following the educational format.

- *Use evaluation response cards.* Having tested a number of response cards in my own programs, I discovered a few techniques that increase the chance of getting them back. The most important was to print them up on card stock, or the kind of paper used to mail postcards. I also reduced the size to 3″×5″ or 8.5″×5.5″ (half a sheet of paper). For some reason, the smaller size and the heavier paper drove more evaluation forms and checks in the box of those who wanted to come in for appointments. We would also have a drawing of the response cards that gave the lucky winner a prize.

Drip-Marketing Letters

Drip marketing is a system that works like a gardener who puts a little bit of water—drip, drip, drip—on a plant and by the end of the growing season, you have a full-grown garden of prospects. Common drip-marketing systems used by many superstars were Bill Good's "Gorilla Marketing" program, Jim Cecil's "Nurture Marketing," and Ed Morrow's "Practice Builder." Bill Good's program integrates a comprehensive series of tested letters with a software tracking system designed to attract prospects. Jim Cecil's program uses cleverly written letters combined with attention-grabbing toys. His system can be combined with standard contact management software. Ed Morrow's "Practice Builder" includes a vast library of marketing letters and other documents that financial advisors can use to solidify their relationships with prospects and clients. All of these programs include well-written letters sent to prospects on a regular basis. They vary in terms of their marketing philosophy, approach, and style.

Important lessons about drip-marketing letters:

- Make sure the letters are geared to your market. I can think of one superstar who purchased a system but had to rewrite most of the letters because the letters did not reflect his consultative selling approach. This took him a lot of time and kept him away from seeing clients.

- One of the first campaigns that Bill Good uses is one to "uncover the money." We know most consumers have funds with other advisors and they may not have been honest about the amount of their assets. His letters are good at getting at all of the prospect's money. This is important because it is a lot cheaper and easier to get more of your existing client's wallet than it is to get a new client to do business with you.

- Jim Cecil learned that business executives could not resist opening a letter that had dimension to it. He calls this a "lumpy," something that makes the letter an odd shape. Most of his letters feature a little toy or gadget that makes it more likely the reader will open the letter and read it. The results are great because a large number of prospects will actually call the advisor, based on the letters, for an initial appointment.

- Once again, this is a tool that takes time. Give it at least a year to warm up your market.

- Make sure the letters are professionally drafted. The quality of the professional ones and their ability to draw prospects is far superior to the average letter created by most advisors.

- These letters are considered advertising or sales literature by the NASD and need to be approved by a broker/dealer before they are mailed.

Some sample drip-marketing letters that I created for a broker/dealer can be found in the Appendix.

Niche Marketing

Whenever possible the savvy marketing machine prefers to focus on a niche. It makes referrals much smoother and it is much easier to get depth and experience in the issues that are facing this particular market. It also helps reduce their costs. For example, one superstar worked with the health care niche; others focused on small businesses or estate planning attorneys. Sometimes working the niche market is as easy as asking for referrals from colleagues in the same niche. Other superstars have taken it to the next level and have actually been on national platforms at conventions speaking to their particular niche. They then become one of the most famous financial advisors nationally who address the issues of (fill in the blank)— it could be podiatrists, chiropractors, trial attorneys, or high school principals.

Some successful niches we have seen (and there are no surprises here):

- *Teachers.* Teachers are great savers and good referral sources. If they like you, they talk you up in the lunchroom, so they make great referral sources.
- *CPAs.* One advisor at Mile High had such a good relationship with a CPA firm that their referrals kept him completely busy.
- *Business consultants.* Boston Advisors* works primarily with high-end business consultants from all over the country. Eight to ten consultants and their spouses will fly to Boston for the weekend for a series of presentations and then one-on-one counseling with the principal.
- *Sports figures.* These arrangements usually work best when the advisor has a close relationship with the sports agent.
- *Business owners.* Once again, nothing new, except Shelly Simon* focused on homebuilders and construction companies. Granted they looked pretty rough and tumble in their plaid flannel shirts, but many were making $1 million a year. Shelly provided programs focusing on the issues builders face. She even had articles on how to save taxes published in builders' trade magazines. No one had

gone after this market exclusively and she picked up a great deal of clients in a short time.

Important lessons about niche marketing:

- *Find an underserved niche.* Everyone wants to go after doctors, but the market is crowded and it would be hard for you to distinguish yourself. Consider, for instance, women business owners, chiropractors, or builders.
- *Become an expert on their issues.* Shelly Simon found builders had not been given good advice about sheltering their money from taxes. Their CPA would just advise them to buy more equipment. She discovered some strategies that the builders had not considered and closed many deals because she understood their issues.
- *Be patient.* Like all these strategies, it can take years to be recognized as an expert and penetrate your niche.

Referral Systems with a Center of Influence

Consider using a center of influence to refer up to your niche market. This is both a niche system and a referral process. One of the most successful arrangements we have seen is Bill Brockway's* relationship with National Lawyers Client Development.* National Lawyers is a firm that gives seminars and workshops for lawyers, teaching them how to bring in more business from wealthy individuals who are charitably inclined to make large donations. They have a huge base of lawyers who have attended their programs over the years and use their techniques. This became a gold mine for Brockway because National Lawyers actively promoted him to every lawyer who went through their programs. Brockway's business doubled when he set up this arrangement.

Important lessons about centers of influence:

- *Do not put all your eggs in one basket.* Do not limit yourself to one referral source, no matter how lucrative it is. Sometimes these referrals sources get tired of the relationship or find someone else they would rather send the business to. We watched one financial advisor's business almost tank when their main referral source got angry at the advisor and refused to send over any more prospects. He had a hard time paying his bills when his steady source of leads dried up.
- *Be careful with sharing commissions.* Many referrers will want to share in your commissions. That is illegal unless they are licensed with your broker/dealer.

Client Appreciation Events

Events are get-togethers for the clients, their friends, and prospects that usually involve something other than an investment-related topic. They are meant to build goodwill and exposure for the financial advisor.

Some successful events we have seen:

- One superstar holds a monthly event on topics of interest to his clients. For example, in May he might invite a gardener to talk about different gardening techniques, followed by a luscious lunch. In February, he may invite his A clients to a basketball game. You can imagine his surprise when one of his top clients, an elderly lady he never had met, actually showed up at the basketball game. Our financial advisor had been working with her son to manage her portfolio because she was not very interested in her investments. She was, however, very interested in basketball. The basketball party was such a huge success that she sent a number of her widowed friends to him, and now he has a niche market working with wealthy divorced and widowed women.

- Another firm in the hill country of Missouri does an annual picnic in the country. They only have two rules: have fun and do not talk about investments. The picnic is such a huge success that they have had to do it over two or three weekends instead of the original one-time event to accommodate all the clients and prospects. Clients will call them months in advance to ask for the date because they want to plan their summer vacations around the picnic.
- Big Time Advisors in Austin, Texas made arrangements with the local art museum for a special night for clients and friends. They arranged for docents to give tours and asked product sponsors to pay for hors d'oeuvres. It generated so much goodwill they are looking for another site for a follow-up event.

USING A MARKETING DEPARTMENT

The requirement of having a steady stream of clients is so all-consuming, most of the superstars had their own marketing department. Some hired an outside firm to do most of the heavy lifting. The financial advisor knew they needed to be meeting with clients and closing sales. Therefore, the drudgery of providing leads was primarily delegated to another person or, in larger firms, an entire group.

When prospects called in for an appointment, they usually wanted to meet with the superstar. They were familiar with the superstar through radio ads, seminars, or other marketing tactics. Everyone in the entire office, even the newest receptionist, was taught how to answer the phone and try to schedule an appointment.

Generally they tried to pass the call off to a skilled marketing person who was given additional training on how to handle their call. This was important because most callers wanted to speak directly with the superstar—and rarely was the superstar available. It took careful scripting to convince the caller that it would be more appropriate for them to meet with a "ministar" than to wait a number of months to meet with the superstar.

Their technique was simple. They told the prospect they could meet with the radio star in five months, or they could meet with one of many other qualified financial advisors, who used the superstar's techniques, within the next two weeks. They also focused on the team concept to get the attention away from the superstar. The prospects were primed for listening to this "team approach" because they had heard about it from the radio program or other collateral including printed brochures and bios. The prospects then knew that they were meeting with an expert member of the team.

In addition, each marketing person was taught how to build up and promote the financial advisor. For instance, when I worked as a financial advisor, the marketing person wanted to schedule clients to fit into my schedule. In an extremely cheerful, upbeat manner, the marketing person would say, "You are going to love working with Katherine Vessenes. You may not know this, but she is a national expert in the area of legal and ethical issues of financial advisors. We were so lucky to get her. Everyone enjoys working with her, and I know you are going to like her." It may have only been a sentence or two but it set up the meeting. By the time they met with me, they were not cold leads, but very warm. They had only heard nice, positive things about me, and were looking forward to the experience. The net result: The prospect is excited about meeting with the financial advisor and already moving along the lines of being "presold."

Other tasks of the marketing department:

- Creating all the ads, including billboards, radio, and newspapers.
- Creating and managing the seminars.
- Coming up with new marketing tactics.

- Managing events.
- Creating the employee satisfaction program.
- Managing the newsletter.
- Tracking programs to see what is working and what is not.
- Assigning leads on a fair and impartial basis.
- And anything else that pertains to getting prospects into the door.

Information Packet

Once the marketing person had scheduled the appointment, they sent the new prospect a package of information. It included a short questionnaire about their assets, their goals, etc., which is fairly common in the industry. They learned the hard way that if the questionnaire was too long, some prospects would be intimidated and never get around to completing it. They did not want anything to be a barrier to the prospect coming into the office.

The packet also included a lot of information about the firm: its background, philosophy, etc. The key to this information packet was a one-page biography, or bio, on the financial advisor. Every financial advisor had their own one-page bio. A copy of mine is included in the Appendix. As you can see, these bios were well done—professionally written with professional photos. They were short, to the point, and included some personal information. For example, mine mentioned that I liked to cross country ski and shop for antiques.

I did not realize how effective the bios were until I was actually meeting face-to-face with the client. It is my philosophy that we should never start a meeting off with a new client by telling them who we are and how smart we are. I much preferred the doctor's approach. When you go to the doctor's office, the first thing they ask you is, "What can I do to help?" They never start the conversation by telling you about all the medical sem-

---

M*ulti-Million-Dollar Principle #14*

Build trust in advance of your first meeting with a well-written bio.

---

inars they have been to or where they graduated in the class at
Johns Hopkins. Consequently, all my client meetings started off
by asking the client about them—their goals and concerns, their
hopes and dreams.

However, by the time I got to the end of the meeting (and
we had thoroughly discussed the client's background and goals
and objectives), I frequently asked them if they needed to know
any more information about me. Surprisingly, nine out of ten
had said no. The reason? "We read your bio and we know everything we think we need to know." The bio, accompanied by a
short cheerleading script from the marketing department, had
accomplished what we wanted: It built trust and warmed up the
prospect. In short, bios are a very effective way of building trust
in advance of the first meeting.

Building Trust in Advance

Another key aspect of a solid marketing program is that,
when done well, it builds trust with the prospect in advance.
When the trust level is high, prospects are in an favorable frame
of mind before even the first meeting.

We noticed that the superstars focus on two primary factors
to build trust. They are: 1) building a high-touch relationship
with a client, and 2) educating the client.

Building a high-touch relationship with a client. The superstars understood the importance of focusing on their clients'
needs and staying very high touch, by that we mean building

deep and lasting relationships with their clients. Here are some of the ways they do this that goes beyond the norm:

- Periodic phone calls from their client service manager or registered sales assistant just to check in with the client to see how they are doing.
- "Guarantee" on the financial plan. Although it is illegal to guarantee any investment return, it is appropriate to guarantee satisfaction with the written financial plan. One firm gave each client a certificate that was a guarantee of satisfaction with their financial plan. However, if the client was not completely satisfied with their financial plan, the advisor would refund the fees the client paid for the plan.
- Having someone on their staff drive the clients to the airport so they did not have to hire a cab.
- Engaging a local college student to pick up the client's dog when the client was going out of town and taking it to the kennel. He would also pick up the dog when they returned so the dog was already home when the travelers came back.
- Chelsea Investments* had a special program for keeping the sales on the book. They realized that with large insurance purchases, clients are likely to get buyer's remorse between the time the client signs the application and the policy is finally delivered. They noticed that if they sent weekly follow-up notes, personally written on good-quality note paper, or made a phone call where someone on the staff got in touch with the client, they were far more likely to keep the business on the books.

Educating clients. Numerous studies have found that one of the top desires on a client's wish list is a financial advisor who educates them. Here are some of the ways that the superstar financial advisors work on educating their clients and prospects.

You will notice that many of these techniques overlap with other activities we discuss elsewhere in the book.

- *Ongoing dinner seminars.* As mentioned earlier, the Mercury group was particularly effective at using dinner seminars to prospect, as well to provide ongoing education to their current clients. This was especially true when they had a new investment insight or particular new changes in tax laws that would impact their clientele. Their clients were encouraged not only to attend, they were also invited to bring along a guest or two. I happened to attend one of these educational seminars during our monthly consulting visits with the Mercury group. Across the table from me was an established client of Mercury who had brought along some of their friends because they were very interested in hearing what Mercury had to say about investing. The new prospect was particularly interested in whether they would be able to attend Mercury's annual client appreciation event if they became a client. Apparently, this picnic had been quite a topic of conversation, and it was a big motivator for them in doing business with the Mercury group. I assured them they would be invited!
- *One-on-one sessions, meeting directly with the client.* A good portion of each face-to-face time with clients included reviewing the information from the seminars, radio shows, or other media—and explaining it once again. By the time the client had heard this information two or three times, they very clearly understood how their money was going to be invested and why. I was able to sit in on these personal sessions in dozens of financial advisors offices. It was very interesting to see how few questions each of these clients had. I think they had so few questions because the clients had already heard this information on a number of occasions and had mastered it.

- *Newsletters.* Most of the superstars make good use of news-letters. Although there are numerous "canned" newsletters in the industry, a good number of superstars create their own newsletters. The reason is simple: They want to make sure the newsletters espouse their particular investment philosophy and highlight their market differentiation in every issue. They use them to highlight employees and other activities of the superstar, including their work with different charities. Yet, the newsletters can be a great deal of work for people who are not naturally gifted writers. As a result, some of the firms could not get them in the hands of their clients as often as they would like. Some firms figured out they were much better at answering questions than they were writing an article from scratch. They would typically hire a talented writer to interview them and create their own newsletter. We usually recommended Connie Anderson of Words & Deeds, Inc. (for more information, see WordsandDeedsInc.com.). She would interview each of the financial advisors on the topic in question, write an article for them and take care of all the logistics of sending out a customized newsletter. It was probably less expensive than using the canned versions, and it got their message across extremely well, and, most importantly, it got finished and out!

STUPID MARKETING TRICKS OF THE MULTI-MILLION-DOLLAR FINANCIAL ADVISOR

Although each financial advisor superstar was a marketing genius, even geniuses have their weak spots. Here are a few of the mistakes they made and some thoughts on how you can avoid them.

Tacky Collateral

Collateral is a phrase in the marketing industry that covers the written presentation of your firm. It can include business cards, newsletters, brochures, or even the folders that you would use to present your financial plans. The same financial advisors who would spare no expense on their personal offices, suddenly become "cheapskates" about their collateral. This is incredibly shortsighted because the collateral was frequently the very first impression the prospect had of the financial advisor. It was an invitation to a seminar or newsletter or some other written document about the firm arriving in the mail. It was not unusual for these forms to look like they had been printed in the back office on a computer by their 13-year-old son. And that was not far from the truth. What they did not realize was this created a great chasm between two different messages.

On the one hand their offices could be very plush, including hardwood floors, fireplaces, and leather sofas. It was not unusual to see lavish Oriental rugs and fresh flowers adorning their office palaces. Unfortunately, the tacky collateral printed off their office printers created a subconscious disconnect in the mind of the prospects. The collateral looked cheap, frighteningly cheap. This disconnect can lead a prospect to mistrust the overall message because it is confusing. Does this firm pamper its clients, or treat them like the red-headed stepchild?

The solution: Spend the money necessary to have your collateral professionally produced. This includes retaining a quality design team that can professionally lay out your materials and make it consistent with your compelling story. If you cannot afford to use professionally designed materials, sometimes it is better to have nothing at all. This way the only message the client receives about your firm is directly from your lips. In one case, when our client had a small two-color brochure that was very tacky, we created their compelling story and presented it in a six-page, four-color brochure for less than the cost of the original. How is this possible? Frequently experienced marketing people know where to go for the best deals. The right marketing firm can actually save you money.

The Ego Trip

Gary Smart,* a superstar financial advisor in Boston, terrified his partners one day when he announced that he had just dropped $100,000 of the firm's money on his latest marketing scheme. What was his brilliant idea? He had contracted to have the firm's logo placed on a car in the NASCAR races. He was absolutely convinced this was the most brilliant marketing idea he ever had and could not understand why his partners were furious. Gary loved NASCAR, and he was sure they were going to be able to pick up the accounts of the drivers and people watching the races.

In truth, this is near the top of my list of all-time worst marketing ideas. Gary's logo was not even recognized in his hometown, much less across the country. If he had been American Express or ING, this might have been a fine plan. Those firms have spent millions and millions of dollars to make their logos recognized. The average sports fan watching a NASCAR car with an American Express or ING logo might actually recognize the logo. We could almost guarantee that 100 percent of the viewing audience, not to mention the racers involved with NASCAR, had never seen the logo—and thus it meant absolutely nothing to them.

What did the financial advisor get out of this arrangement? A great boost to his ego! Because he loved NASCAR racing, this gave him an excuse—or the ticket to hobnob with the leaders in this field.

Bottom line: If you want to go on a vanity trip, buy a billboard. This larger than life photo can please the biggest egos but they are also often incredibly effective, creating market awareness for the superstar. Consider your marketing programs and be honest with yourself—if they are just ego trips, you are not going to get the clients you desire.

Using Celebrities as a Draw

George Dean,* from San Francisco, wanted to use a celebrity draw for his next event, a lavish dinner party. They rented a well-known restaurant in downtown San Francisco, hired a band, and invited everyone they could think of, including every client, every prospect, their mortgage banker, their attorney. Even I was invited. The draw was "Mr. Famous." The party cost about $110,000, plus Mr. Famous charged them $25,000 to use his name on the invitation and for showing up at the party to "press the flesh."

Everyone seemed to have a good time at the party, with one exception: Mr. Famous was too famous to show up. A refund to the firm was not possible due to the clever terms of the contract Mr. Famous had prepared. I do not think they got a single piece of new business out of this entire event.

While sometimes using a celebrity can be an effective draw, make sure there is a plan in place to work the room and engage potential clients at the event. Also, make sure that the fee makes sense for the scope and potential return of your event, and that you have a solid contract that guarantees the celebrity's attendance, or else a refund.

Make sure your marketing plans are business-driven and not ego-driven. Sometimes it pays to work with a reputable marketing firm to help give you an insight into what will work and what will not. Remember, to make the business work, we need derrieres in chairs. Hanging out with the rich and famous may be a lot of fun, but it may not bring in new clients.

WHAT WE DID FOR THE FIRMS

Because every firm was already a marketing machine, our recommendations just modified what they were already doing. Unfortunately, this is much harder than it looks. Golfers with handicaps of 15 have a relatively easy time getting their handicaps down to 11. Good lessons and practice can have a big impact. It is much harder to take a golfer with a 4 handicap to a 2. However, that reduction in handicap can have a significant impact in their game, and if they are a professional, in their earning capacity. Take the number one player on the PGA tour and the number 50 player. Number 1 makes $6,000,000 more per year than number 50, and yet there frequently is only a 1.5 of a difference in the average score per round. The same is true of financial advisors. What we did was get that 1.5 per round difference, to improve their income dramatically.

CASE STUDY: GURU

With most of our clients, we bring in Brad Lantz, Vestment's chief marketing officer, to prepare a written marketing plan and develop specific tactics.

"One of the things we did for Guru Investment," said Lantz, "was expand their exposure and improve the demographic level of their client. We wanted to attract clients who had more investable assets."

Following are some of the things Vestment did at Guru.

Marketing Department

Guru already had a marketing department, but we reorganized it so it ran like a real business unit. A few of the things we did in the marketing department:

Marketing plan. We always start with a marketing diagnostic that assesses what is working and what is not, and clearly identifies what their clients think about the financial advisory firm. We also had to tell them the bad news that no one wanted to hear: Some of their current marketing tactics were the worst of all outcomes: ineffective, overly expensive, and frequently conveyed a bad impression about the firm. Some of their marketing strategies were great and others were terrible. No one wants to know that they have burned a lot of money on things that did not work—our job was to gently explain how important it was to avoid ego trips and fund only campaigns that work, meaning they produced new clients for a reasonable amount of money and conveyed a good impression of the firm.

Out of that initial research flows a written marketing plan that is modified as we proceed.

Process and procedures. "The next thing we did," said Lantz, "was set up a system of process and procedures. We particularly wanted to track to see what marketing methods were working and what were not. We were looking at a number of things. One included the cost per prospect. The recommendations we made to improve their marketing programs reduced the average cost of prospecting to about $95 per prospect from about $325." A prospect was considered a person sitting in front of a financial advisor. "The industry average," according to Lantz, "was between $125 and $350 to get a person in the door talking to a financial advisor."

With our new tracking procedures in place we were able to track the cost of every single marketing campaign, even comparing the different printers. This was one of the many ways we were able to get the cost per prospect reduced so dramatically.

Metrics and reports. Vestment Advisors created a number of marketing reports for Guru that summarized the different marketing tactics on a monthly basis. We found it invaluable to report monthly every possible aspect of the marketing process. This included the following:

- Total incoming calls
- Setting of appointments
- Changing of appointments
- Average commission per case
- "No shows"

Each event and seminar was measured carefully to determine effectiveness and yield of a particular program. These numbers were beneficial, because it helped senior management keep focused on which marketing efforts were working, and which were not. It also helped tighten up operations and procedures so that we could find gaps in the process and plug the holes to increase revenues.

Another area that received a lot of Lantz's attention was maintaining key relationships with centers of influence (COI). Most of the superstars wanted to work with influentials who would refer them business on a regular basis. Unfortunately the superstars did not have the time or profile for following through. When these key relationships were not nurtured along, the referrals dried up. It became the marketing department's duty to maintain those relationships and keep the COIs happy. This kept the steady stream of referrals coming in the door.

Scripts and training programs. We then set up numerous training programs for the marketing staff. A key one involved training everyone who answered the phone how to give a good, positive impression of the firm and a specific financial advisor. "We found an early enthusiastic plug for each of the financial advisors to help increase closing ratios," Lantz explained. "Unfortunately, before we took over their marketing efforts, there was no consistency. If another person happened to be answering the phone, they may not be as skilled at promoting the financial advisor. The more enthusiastic the promotion by the marketing department, the more likely the financial advisor was to close the sale," added Lantz. This simple, no-cost marketing technique added thousands of dollars to the firm's revenues.

To solve this problem, we created a script. The script covered all the common questions or concerns that prospects had when they were calling in for an appointment. For instance, one of the common questions was, "Are there any CFP®s at the firm?" Using the script's bullet points, the person on the phone would discuss our team and the members working in the firm that had CFP® designations who were not financial advisors but were creating the actual plans.

Another common question was, "What do you charge?" Our answer was, "We are paid in three ways: fees for the plans, commissions that are built into the cost of the products by the companies we place business with, and by referrals to other like-minded clients." This helped set up the prospect to understand that the business was built on referrals. This thought, impressed early in the relationship, made it easier to get referrals later. The prospect was also advised that there was no charge or obligation for the initial financial review and that they should feel free to come in and make a decision at the end of the meeting whether they would like to proceed.

Another thing we did in training was to make sure every financial advisor's bio was available for anyone who answered the marketing line. It was easy to pick up key points on their bio and use it when the prospects called in.

"Something we found," Lantz said, "is that the younger the person, the more valuable the scripts were. Let's face it, at my age, I've seen just about everything. It was very easy for me to take a fielded call and turn it into a prospect sitting before a financial advisor. That's my business. I've been doing it a long time," Lantz added. "However, young and inexperienced receptionists would not have my level of confidence. So they were particularly helped by having talking points, scripts, and training on how to handle the telephone."

At American Dream we did a number of things to boost their marketing activities. We worked with their receptionists. American Dream Investments had a half a dozen different receptionists in different offices. We actually trained them how to interact with clients. They were taught to smile, be cheerful, offer them refreshments, and even how to chitchat.

The receptionists were taught that there was a proper way to answer the phone: "This is American Dream Investments, Monica speaking. How may I help you?" This last piece is particularly important because we wanted to place in the clients' minds that they were going to be helped at our firm. Their questions were going to be answered and that everyone was there to serve them.

Each of the receptionists at American Dream also had a copy of all the financial advisors' bios. Although they normally would not handle the marketing calls, this additional information was helpful in case they were asked a particular question about the process. However, they were taught to transfer the call to marketing as quickly as possible. Some receptionists found this work very interesting and applied for marketing positions.

SPECIFIC NEW CAMPAIGNS AND TACTICS

All of our marketing plans for financial advisory firms, no matter what their size, have numerous strategies and tactics. Here are some typical ones:

Events

Once again, Guru is a good example here. We reviewed their current events and kept those that were working, eliminated those that were not effective, and then added new ones. One program we implemented targeted clients who had over a million dollars to invest. We set up a golf event at an exclusive and prestigious golf course. The financial advisors were encouraged to invite only a few of their top prospects and clients. By top, we mean very wealthy prospects who were outside Guru's typical middle-income client. The invited prospects and clients were allowed to bring friends. We also targeted some wealthy individuals who our financial advisors knew but had been apprehensive about approaching directly for their business.

This event included free golf lessons given by a nationally known golf pro, plus the golf course's own pro. It also included a free round of golf and dinner with cocktails. The cost of the tournament was $11,000 plus $25,000 for having the nationally known talent attend. All of the clients and prospects were to focus on just having fun, with no discussion of business the entire time. Of course, the financial advisors were strongly encouraged to follow up after the event to invite the new prospects in for an initial meeting. The firm invited over 50 clients and prospects.

Result: One financial advisor made a million-dollar premium sale that more than paid for the entire event. In fact, seven new clients with over $1 million each came from this one high-touch event.

Part of what made the event so successful was retaining the services of a nationally known golf pro. The pro agreed to attend two events each year, and the golf event counted as one of his events. He also agreed to endorse the firm, as a part of his fee.

Birthday Club

One of our favorite recommendations was not our idea originally—but it is a great one. It is called the birthday club.

Here is how it works: The financial advisor calls his "A list" clients about a month before their birthday. The financial advisor asks if they may throw a birthday party luncheon in honor of their "A client." Who would refuse? The client then sends the financial advisor 10 to 15 names, along with addresses, phone numbers, and e-mails, which the financial advisor now has in his prospecting base. The financial advisor sends out invitations to the luncheon, which is usually held in a nice, but not expensive, restaurant. For instance, Chili's, TGI Fridays, or Don Pablo's might be good choices. To save costs, there is never any liquor served. Also one of the reasons we suggest luncheons is that they are much less expensive than dinners and the guests do not stay long!

There is absolutely no selling at all during the luncheon. There are no financial speakers. It is all about the birthday person. In fact, the financial advisor does not even reveal what he does, unless someone asks.

The luncheon usually costs between $100 and $250, depending on how many show up and where it is held. We have found it almost always produces clients. After all, none of the attendees have a financial advisor who is throwing them a party! We have found this to be one of the most inexpensive and effective marketing tactics a financial advisor can do.

Seminars

Guru was already giving seminars, but getting only mixed results. "One of the ways we enhanced Guru Investment's seminar efforts," said Brad Lantz, "was to have special seminars during particularly troubling times. During one bad market downturn, management had our own Peter Vessenes come in and speak on why the market had tanked."

Lantz continued, "The topic was so hot that they obtained a 20 percent to 30 percent increase in the number of attendees. The clients found it helpful to address current events that were causing prospects fear and concern. By helping them deal with the fears and concerns, they became more interested in becoming clients of the firm."

Lantz added, "Sometimes obvious changes can make a huge difference. When it came to helping Guru Investments manage their seminars, we encouraged them to improve the demographics of their direct mail. We focused on higher income and higher investable assets by purchasing lists that fit the higher demographics. With higher-caliber clients coming to the seminars Guru was able to get clients with more investable assets.

"This is one of the many things that Vestment Advisors did that increased their average investable asset by 35 percent in just one year. Although focusing on a niche market seems obvious," says Lantz, "sometimes superstars are so busy selling they miss the obvious—like preparing a marketing plan for the firm."

Centers of Influence

One of the areas we recommended for their niche marketing was to focus on CPA firms that were not currently doing financial advisory business. To make this effort work, we first identified key CPA firms where Guru's financial advisors had strong relationships. We then asked the accounting firms to schedule a meeting for their key members and a few of their financial advisors. This meeting was to explain how Guru did business. We also explained the advantages of working with just one firm, Guru, as opposed to referring their business out to numerous other firms. Our goal was to raise their confidence with Guru and increase the number of referrals. We also encouraged the CPAs to get licensed, so that we could share commissions with them.

To kick off the program, Guru prepared a free financial plan, normally valued at about $2,000, for each of the CPAs. We wanted them to see how Guru worked and to give them confidence in the products and services. They were also invited to participate with their clients in the planning process. They were welcome to attend any meetings with their clients so they could be fully advised of all the recommendations. Although very few of the CPAs actually attended client meetings, the CPAs seemed to appreciate Guru's candidness, openness, and ability to continue communicating back and forth about their client.

We helped Guru focus hard on maintaining close communications with the CPAs. If the client was willing, and signed the proper disclosure form, a duplicate copy of the plan was sent to the CPA. The advisors were also available to discuss the plan privately with the CPA.

This program was so successful that within a year, one financial planner, Brian Fieldman,* had expanded his CPA referral system from one CPA to six. Those six were seasoned, experienced CPAs with large clienteles of wealthy investors. Their comment: "Brian, just the referrals from our firm will keep you busy full-time."

THE MODEL CLIENT EXPERIENCE

In the back of our minds, when we develop a marketing program for any financial advisor, it is based on their "model client experience." This means thinking about all of our marketing from the client's perspective, not the financial advisor's.

No matter where we live, we are all from Lake Wobegone— where all the men are good looking, all the women are strong, and the children are all above average. However, the stark truth is that we generally think we are doing a whole lot better than we are. I call this the Lake Wobegone effect.

Frankly, we have all been spoiled. Who spoiled us? Starbucks for one. We all know we could make coffee at home for about $.50 a cup. We could also get it in a restaurant for about a dollar. Why do we spend three or four dollars at Starbucks? Because of the experience.

How would you describe the Starbucks experience? Here are the words that come to mind: consistent, predictable, comfortable, warm, friendly, secure, safe, and a way to pamper myself.

I think Starbucks has done something few companies have done—they have thought about the experience their clients would want to have—and then they delivered it. They have taken a commodity, something that costs about $.50, sold it for $3.50, and made us crave it, almost becoming an addiction. We can't wait to get back.

This is exactly the same experience every financial advisor should be creating for their clients. Why? For a number of reasons. First, clients who are wildly happy with your experience will not only stick with you, they will send you many wonderful referrals. Also, it makes the selling process so much easier. If your prospects are having their expectations met at every step of their relationship, your closing ratios will increase dramatically and the sales process becomes so painless. I call it the No-Sell Sale™. There is no selling—you just systematically deliver exactly what the client wants at every stage. Net result? A lifetime relationship with a happy, satisfied client.

Broker/Dealer Application

We were hired in 2002 to create the model client experience for North Star Tax and Financial Advisors.* When the president, Guy Nelson,* called us, he stated his problem: North Star Tax had bought a discount brokerage firm a few years before, and they had been having a difficult time making the transition into a financial services firm that meshed with North Star's tax base. They wanted to move from doing transactions over the phone to face-to-face consultations.

I'll never forget what Nelson said to me: "I am concerned about the client experience. What does the client expect from us?" The question was simple but profound. What he was really asking is, "How do we want our clients to feel, think, and act because they are doing business with us?" One thing Nelson knew for sure, it had to be consistent across the country. They have thousands of tax pros and hundreds of financial advisors—they all have to be on the same page, delivering the same message—no matter where they are located.

Part of our engagement was to create the Client Experience Model for North Star, which they started to roll out in 2004. Regrettably, creating the Starbucks experience is not always fast, but it is a sure way to improve sales and create clients who become raving fans.

This process has many moving parts and can take a long time to execute. However, in its most basic premise it is incredibly simple. What do you want your clients to experience by being in a relationship with you? If your clients are having Starbucks-like experiences that rates an eight, nine, or ten at every stage, it is highly likely that you will not only make the initial sale, you will create a raving fan that refers many more clients.

If the experience is only a mediocre Lake Wobegone five, six, or seven, it will be much harder to close the sale and even more difficult to generate referrals. If your clients are experiencing a two, three, or four, you could be looking at investors who are so unhappy that, in the best case, they will leave you, and in the worst, they will be looking for an attorney.

Here are the steps that we take to help our advisory clients or broker/dealers create the ideal client experience for their investor clients. In taking a moment to answer the following questions and reexamine your firm, you can look at all of your client touch points and determine if you are creating the experience you want your clients to have.

Meet with your staff and coworkers and brainstorm on these questions:

- *What do your clients want in their relationship with you?* It is likely to be a lot like being in Starbucks: a consistent, predictable, comfortable, warm, friendly, secure, and safe relationship that helps bring them a sense of peace about their financial future. Make a list of the most common attributes your clients desire and use this to evaluate your entire service continuum.

- *Compare client touch points with the ideal client experience.* Next make a list of the major touch points your clients have with your firm in chronological order and evaluate them from the clients' perspectives. It may look something like this:
  - A marketing presentation in a seminar or brochure
  - An initial meeting in your office
  - Follow-up meetings
  - Client appreciation events
  - Quarterly reviews
  - Service requests

At each point, think about what the client would want at that stage in the relationship with you. It may be helpful to physically walk everyone in your firm, even the file clerks, through the office, covering each step in your process while thinking like a client.

For example, take the first initial meeting in your office. In working with one of our financial advisory firms, I was having some trouble getting the concept of the Model Client Experience across to the financial advisors and field managers. They kept thinking of the experience from the broker's perspective. Everyone said the same thing to me: "But Katherine, this office is so much nicer than it used to be!" My response? "That may be true, but does a new prospect know what it used to look like or even care?" They had not yet gotten used to looking at everything through the client's perspective. These financial advisors were still thinking about the office from the viewpoint of what suited the advisor.

Finally, I took the managers out into the parking lot and said, "Let's pretend you are a brand-new prospect to the firm and this is your first visit here. You are standing in the parking lot. How are you feeling about the firm so far? On a scale of 1 to 10, how would you rate your experience?"

Their answers were very insightful. The signage was poor so it made it difficult to find the firm. They recognized this would make a prospect uncomfortable because they may not be sure they are at the right location. A little stress makes the sales process more difficult. On the other hand, the parking was easy and close to the office. The outside of the building was neat and clean. The parking lot score was an 8—so far so good.

What happened after we walked into the reception area was more disturbing. The receptionist was AWOL. The space was dark, dingy, and messy. There were no artwork or plants. The chairs were uncomfortable and there were no reading materials. They offered their prospects water served in a disposable cup.

The advisors and managers scored this part of the experience a 4. I thought they were being too generous. In my mind, it was a 2. They had just taken their score from an 8 to a 2 in less than 50 feet! This made their entire sales process much more difficult. All the other prospect contact points would need to be 8s or above to have a good chance at solidifying a relationship with a new prospect, and to make up for the poor initial impression.

We then continued a few more steps, reenacting the prospect's visit as they walked back to the financial advisor's office, meeting staff along the way.

Once we went through this simple exercise, their eyes seemed to open and they could finally start thinking about what a client would want to experience when working with them.

Once they started thinking like a client, we could get to some strategies on how to improve things for the clients. My recommendations on the reception area were to clean the place up! Change the paint color from insane asylum white, to something rich and warm, like deep green, camel, or even navy. Order some better furniture. Make sure the lighting is bright and cheery.

Provide decent reading material. All of this would get the score to a solid mediocre, Lake Wobegone 5. Let's face it. Almost every financial advisor in the country meets this minimum standard.

If you want to get up to a Starbucks 9 or 10, then you should add these extra touches that we have recommended to a number of firms:

- Go to Tuesday Morning or Home Depot and get an Oriental carpet for the floor (approximate cost, $250).
- Buy a small toaster oven and keep refrigerator cookies on hand. Make sure every client and prospect gets a freshly baked cookie when they arrive (toaster oven costs about $60).
- Offer cheese and fruit for those prospects on a low-carb diet.
- Serve juice, bottled water, and coffee in sparkling clean crystal glasses or china cups. These are available at Mikasa for about $3 per glass. Also, make sure you use a tray and quality napkins.
- Play soft music like jazz or classical, not elevator music.
- Teach the receptionist to say, "You must be Miss Jones. We have been expecting you."

Note the expensive part of this process was just getting to Lake Wobegone. It was the paint and furniture that cost the most money. Creating a Starbucks experience is not expensive; it just takes some thoughtful planning, and making sure everyone in the office understands they are in Starbucks, not Lake Wobegone.

I happened to be in a field office of one of our broker/dealer clients last year during a firm-wide conference call. To free up the advisors, one of the registered sales assistants was answering the phone. It was painful to watch him deal with clients who called in with service issues. He was short-tempered, rude, and far from helpful. You could tell he did not think responding to service requests was part of his job. Clearly this did not even come up to the Lake Wobegone level. Forget about getting referrals from this client. They had gotten a level 2 experience and after enough of them, they will be looking for another advisor.

Unfortunately, this situation could have been easily resolved with little to no cash outlay. By bringing the assistant into the model client experience discussions, he would have known his job was to treat clients well and go beyond the service provided by other firms. Like everyone in the firm, he was responsible for making every contact a client has with the firm a Starbucks experience.

Once you have reexamined all the client touch points in your office, start to think about your ads, marketing materials, seminars, and telephone staff. These, too, will probably need to be reworked to match your model client experience.

Over time you should notice happier clients, easier sales, and many more referrals.

THE MARKETING PLAN

Once you have clearly defined what you want your client experience to be, you can start by creating a written marketing plan. If none of our superstar clients had a written strategic business plan, it follows that none of them had a written marketing plan. They were all good at marketing; they just did it on the fly by inspiration.

Here are some thoughts on building your own marketing plan.

Branding and Image

Perhaps the most important element in marketing for a financial services company is *branding and image.* It's important to establish who you are and what your point of differentiation is to be effective in getting prospects/potential clients to work with you.

One of the most fun parts of our work is helping our clients decide on their brand and their image. We start the process by helping them identify something few of them have consciously considered—their mission, their vision, and their values. We do this by helping the financial advisor ask the most important question of all: Why would a client want to work with me? What do I provide that is so compelling and unique that clients would choose me over my competitors? Once we establish this, we can help them synthesize it into their brand and their image.

We went through the process with North Star Advisors, working in conjunction with their marketing firm. After brainstorming different reasons clients would want to work with them, we came up with this tagline to describe their brand: *America's trusted tax and financial team for life.*

Each word became crucial in explaining their position in the market.

- *America's.* They did not want to focus just on the upper end of the market. No one liked the terms "everyday" Americans, "mainstream," or "Main Street" Americans. We finally decided they wanted to work with all Americans—so we left it simple.
- *Trusted.* It showed the public that they know trust is crucial when choosing an advisor. They want to be worthy of that trust. It is also a huge advantage for CPAs because the public trusts them more than most other advisors. They wanted to capitalize on the existing trust they already had with their clients.
- *Tax.* Reminds them of the importance of considering tax consequences to investing.
- *Financial team.* This message conveyed that financial planning is so complicated it takes many experts to create workable strategies. We have an entire team to help you, the client, with your financial future.

- *For life.* North Star is in this for the long haul. We value long-term relationships, and we want to work with you for the rest of your life. Our company has longevity, and you can count on us being here for that period of time.

Public Relations

The second most important element is *public relations.* It is critical because it establishes trusted third parties to validate your practice as being worthwhile. It outweighs the impact of advertising ten to one. Public relations includes getting quoted in your local newspapers or on local radio and TV. Few of our superstars had a knack for PR. If you are in that boat, it probably pays to hire an expert.

Advertising

Generally the third element of a good marketing plan becomes *advertising.* What is it that you are promoting? How do you do it in a way that complies with regulations? What is the advantage to your clients? Frankly, most of the superstars either did not use advertising or used it sparingly, say to promote a seminar. Although ads could be an effective way to build attendance at a seminar, I cannot think of a single financial advisory client we have ever served that could claim to have gotten a client from an ad in the newspaper or telephone book. Traditional advertising is more effective in other industries.

Sales and Customer Service

Sales and customer service, though separate elements, are considered here together within the context of marketing, as they both establish the strength of the relationships. The focus here is keeping the clients happy and creating a client-retention plan. Because it costs at least six times as much to get a new client as it does to keep an existing client happy, this was an important part of the marketing plan.

Creating WOMP clients: Tom Peters has urged companies to create products and services that would delight consumers with the "WOW!" factor. However, there is a higher standard than "WOW!" It's what Dale Dauten, nationally syndicated columnist, referred to as " WOMP," for Word of Mouth Potential. We do not just want people to walk in and say, "Wow, this is cool." We want them to walk out saying, "I have got to tell my friends about this place!" That is WOMP. Its goal? To take clients from satisfied customers to WOMP clients!

A satisfied customer:

- Will leave you for a 10 percent price differential.
- Will leave you for perceived value-added.
- Is satisfied until you fail.
- Will leave you for the "last man presenting."

A WOMP client:

- Has a vision of the end.
- Considers the financial advisor as their source.
- Values the financial advisor.
- Can't wait to tell friends about this place.

Any successful marketing plan needs a WOMP campaign that is focused on delivering the WOW! factor to new prospects and existing clients.

Demographics

List your ideal client, including everything you know about their demographics. This includes age, income, marital status, job type, hobbies, investment experience, and their deepest concerns.

Services and Products

Describe what it is that you provide to your clients, and why they would want to buy it from you. This includes not only the features (we provide retirement planning), but also the benefits (so you can retire with confidence).

Specific Tactics and Campaigns

This describes the specific tactics you plan to use to generate new leads. Although we included some specific tactics and campaigns throughout this chapter, one thing that needs to be considered with every tactic is how it contributes to top-of-mind awareness (TOMA). Top-of-mind awareness means that you and your firm occupy that valuable piece of real estate that belongs to your client's brain. When your client thinks, "I have a financial problem. Who should I call to help me solve it?" You want them thinking of your name first. That is top-of-mind awareness.

Our research has shown that the A-level client in a firm that is going after the middle market expects 12–18 touches per year in order to reach top-of-mind awareness. However, recent research has shown that wealthy clients may expect twice as many touches in order to stay in the top-of-mind category. A touch is a client meeting, a birthday card, an event, a golf date, or a thank-you note, but it is *not* a confirmation statement.

Once the financial advisor understands the importance of creating a campaign based on the number of touches per year, the marketer's job is to create a series of inexpensive, easy to execute interactions with your clients and prospects to keep your name at the top of the prospect's brain to build the awareness and interest necessary to get them to move to the stage of action. Ultimately every message the client or prospect gets should present an offer from the financial advisor that is hard to refuse.

Costs

Like any good business, it is important to budget your marketing efforts.

Build Your Database

Regrettably few of our clients had thought about the importance of a good database when it came to streamlining marketing efforts. For instance, one advisor wanted to do a specific campaign to attract teachers in his area. He told us he already had a lot of teachers as clients and that he wanted to focus on this group because he understood them and had great results. We asked him to go through his database and see how many teacher clients he had so we could do an event aimed at them and their teacher friends. This would have been an inexpensive way to penetrate this market niche.

Much to his chagrin, he found out his staff could only locate one teacher out of hundreds of clients. The reason? Their database called for the husband's occupation and left the wife's blank. Because most of his teacher clients were wives of other clients, he had no way to identify them to maximize his marketing to this group.

This turned out to be a very expensive oversight. To go after teachers, he had to purchase lists and do mailings. This cost a lot more than our original plan: have an event for your teacher clients and get referrals.

Profile your current clients and customers. Match that against who you want to be your clients. Define each client into a group: A (top 20 percent, clients you enjoy working with), B (middle 60 percent), C (lower 20 percent). The more information (including interests, birthdays, special times, and, of course, dreams) you have on your clients and prospects, the higher your retention rate.

Your database should be able to quickly identify many different factors about your clients including their holdings, their age, the ages of their children, their profession, their annual income, the amount of investments they have to invest, and even their hobbies. Any of these topics can be used to customize a marketing campaign that focuses on your existing clients and their like-minded friends.

Performance Objectives

Set realistic goals and measurable, time-phased objectives, strategies, and tactics that produce the desired results. Establishing performance objectives, and monitoring them, is a crucial element in a marketing campaign. Understanding expectations, performance, and results establishes the value and performance of a company's investment in marketing.

Monitor Results

The marketing plan is a dynamic, not static document. Marketing goes through organic change, just like the people it has identified as prospects. Marketing strategies must change as your market conditions, products, services, and personnel change. Marketing requires updating and monitoring. You must expect the unexpected, which will mean constantly refining the process. The only way to receive results in marketing is to constantly monitor and refine.

THE COMPELLING STORY, ELEVATOR STATEMENT, AND SHORT COMMERCIAL

We believe every financial advisor needs to be able to communicate what they do succinctly, passionately, and in a manner that encourages the listener to want to learn more about the advisor's services. Three key components to this are the elevator speech, the short commercial, and the compelling story.

Before you can successfully build your marketing plan, it is important to create what we call the compelling story, a two- to three-paragraph description of the benefits that your firm provides clients that describes the firm's differentiation in a story format.

The compelling story is then distilled down to a one- to three-minute commercial.

The commercial is further refined to an elevator statement. If you are in an elevator and someone asks you what you do— what do you say in the 30 seconds it takes to get to the next floor?

Finally, you can take the elevator statement and reduce it into a tag line.

Crafting a good compelling story, short commercial, and elevator statement can take days. Paraphrasing one sage, "I would have written you a much shorter letter, but I did not have the time." It is more difficult to be succinct than wordy.

Here are some things to think about when writing compelling stories, elevator speeches, and short commercials:

- What is in it for the client/listener? It is human nature to be selfish. Consider that as you craft your statement. What do you do that excites and motivates the average listener? What would flip their hot buttons and move them to want to meet with you? What problems do they have that you can fix? It gets them to listen rather than tune out.
- What is your market differentiation put in terms that benefit the client? Although we have seen many differentiations, two common ones we have seen with superstars are using a team approach and planning from a net-tax perspective.
- KISS: Keep it short and simple. The whole reason for using this approach is that it does not get into the detail of what we do—this can turn them off immediately because they

may have a preconceived notion of a financial planner. It focuses on what we do for our clients. It builds a vision of an experience that 95 percent of the American public is not currently getting from their brokers and financial advisors.

- Finally, it is usually best not to volunteer this information about who you are and what you do. Wait until someone asks you.

Take the elevator statement of All Star Team Advisors.* They wanted to get across four different concepts that could be big advantages for their clients:

1. All Star uses a *team* approach because a client's finances are too important to be left to a single individual.
2. They place a high value on *educating* their clients.
3. Planning investments from a *net-tax perspective* will leave more money in the client's pocket.
4. High-touch *service* keeps clients happy.

One good template that we use when creating these statements for clients is like this: We provide A, B, and C, so our clients can D. Another way to think about this is we provide benefit, benefit, benefit so that our clients can solve a major problem. See how this plays out below.

Elevator Statement

We use a team of financial experts, education programs, and personal service managers so that our clients can accumulate and preserve wealth in a way that puts more money in their retirement and brings them peace of mind. Therefore our name, All Star Team Advisors.

Let's look at how this fits the template. We provide: a team of financial experts (A), education programs (B), and personal service managers (C) so that our clients can accumulate and preserve wealth in a way that puts more money in their retirement and brings them peace of mind (D). Each of the top areas is covered—the team, education, net tax, and service.

Here is the elevator speech that we created for Shelly Simon,* who was focusing on wealthy individuals who wanted innovative tax strategies:

> I own a business that works with successful professionals and business owners who are feeling the pain of paying too much in taxes. We are a team of tax-advantaged wealth builders, focused on putting more money in your pocket.

She clearly identified that her target clients are successful professionals and business owners. Furthermore, they must be seriously motivated to doing something about reducing their taxes. She, too, wanted to focus on the team approach, and to what is in it for the listener—more money in your pocket.

Bad Elevator Speech

If you come out and tell people that working together as a team, you provide clients the five disciplines of finances with nonproprietary products and a high degree of service, their eyes immediately glaze over because they cannot visualize what you are talking about. They do not know what you are saying and how it relates to them.

Another poor choice is stating the obvious: "We are a financial planning firm." They already believe that they have one because their insurance salesman told them he did that. This is boring and not focused on what is in it for the client.

Research shows that people are not excited about meeting someone in financial services. If you can paint an engaging picture that your prospect would like to experience, then the prospect will go to the next step—a meeting with you. If you repeat the same tired, vague descriptions that everyone else does, they will flee or shut you out.

Short Commercial

Here is the expanded version we created for All Star Team Advisors:

Because our firm offers full capabilities using a team approach, your question is probably best answered by some examples about how we work with and have helped clients. First and foremost, All Star is a financial education company. Our clients receive sound financial education and research through our radio show, one-on-one meetings, and in-depth seminars. We want our clients to understand their financial alternatives so that they can make the best decision for their unique situation.

Secondly, our clients learn how to protect their assets from tax inefficiencies, which can be devastating to them at retirement and to their estates. In some cases we've seen people who could have lost over 70 percent of their retirement or pension plan due to poor planning and taxes.

Thirdly, and perhaps most importantly, looking at the marketplace, the industry is spending 90 percent of its time on sales and 10 percent on service—and we are trying to reverse that with over 24 professionals (8 service personnel to 1 sales) who just specialize in taking care of our clients and treating them in the way that they deserve to be treated.

So you ask what do we do? All Star Team Advisors is a financial advisory firm that provides customized financial alternatives that fit the needs and desires of our clients to enhance their wealth and enrich their lives.

Here is Shelly Simon's* short commercial:

> Our clients have worked hard for their money, and we believe they should be able to keep as much of it as they legally can. Don't you agree?
>
> We provide clients with innovative strategies to help them conserve, optimize, and receive distributions of wealth in a tax-efficient manner. Our goal is to help people, like you, keep more of their own money. Generally, that comes in the form of using the latest tactics to reposition your wealth in a way that is tax-advantaged, or finding "lazy" money and developing a plan to make it work harder. (Here Shelly told a story about one of her clients.)
>
> Let me ask you this: When was the last time you had your portfolio reviewed for the devastating effect of taxes?
>
> That's what we do. We are very bottom line. We help our clients conserve their assets from tax inefficiencies, because the amount of money you can withdraw from your assets can have a dramatic impact on your lifestyle and retirement.
>
> We have seen cases where some people, who did not do any planning, have lost over 75 percent of their retirement funds to unnecessary taxes. (Shelly told another story here.) Our goal is to conserve these assets so they can contribute to your lifestyle and not make Uncle Sam the senior partner in your retirement.

The short commercial allows you to go into even more detail, eliciting more emotion. The statement talks about results that everyone wants and gets them to question in their minds whether they receive those results. Because it does not fully answer their question, they, if they liked the results expressed, will need to go to the next question, which is, "Tell me about that?"

Multi-Million-Dollar Principle #15

Every person in your practice should be able to deliver an elevator speech
that motivates people to work with you.

That is when you have them hooked and they will allow you to
get into what you do.

These statements are so important, we advise our firms to
make sure everyone in the company, from the newest employee
to the most senior advisor, can say this statement backwards and
forward. When that happens, you have the entire company focused on the things you need to get your business to the next
level.

ABSOLUTE ADVOCATES™/ CLIENT RETENTION PROGRAM

We have coined the term Absolute Advocate™ to define
the kind of relationship we would all like to have with our best
clients. We do not want just clients, we want clients who are so
wildly happy with our services that they cannot stop talking
about us to others. They become the captain of our marketing
team and send us a steady stream of new prequalified clients.
They go beyond the regular clients and become an outspoken
advocate or cheerleader for our firm.

No marketing program would be complete without client-satisfaction and client-retention programs. A key component to
keeping your clients happy is discovering how they feel about
the service you are providing them. You can do this two ways:
you can ask them in writing or you can ask them personally.

In the Appendix we have included a written client-satisfaction survey that we created for one of our clients. This should be mailed at least once a year. If you get some negative feedback, it is important to act on it right away and get back to your client with a good solution.

Other firms have made good use of telephone surveys done by outside firms or even their own marketing departments. It never ceases to amaze me what clients will tell a disembodied voice over the telephone.

Sometimes the client-satisfaction surveys are not as positive as we would like. One firm learned this lesson the hard way when they discovered a significant number of their clients were angry. Why? The financial advisors did not get back in touch with them after the sale was made. This was particularly a problem with financial advisors who were low Follow Thrus on the Kolbe scale, which is discussed in Chapter 6.

To overcome these issues, Brad Lantz created a client-retention program that is reproduced in Figure 4.1.

FIGURE 4.1 Client-Retention Program for Anderson Wealth Advisors

Memo to: Anderson Wealth Advisors*
From: Brad Lantz
Re: Improving our client-satisfaction scores and retaining clients

As we all know, our success and rapid growth has created a lot of challenges. As a company, we continue to be exceptional in many areas. However, we have also been aware of mounting challenges in client service and retention. As suspected, the results of the recently completed client-satisfaction survey clearly show a need for improvement in this area.

Therefore, we created a Client-Retention Committee.*
The committee's purpose is to identify business practices that create satisfied clients and to develop the processes and systems to achieve standardized levels of service for clients. Our long-term goal is not merely to create satisfied clients, but Absolute Advocates™ who will refer friends and family to us without hesitation. To accomplish this, we must create a standardized process (with some flexibility for financial advisors) of client service.

FIGURE 4.1 Client-Retention Program for Anderson Wealth Advisors, continued

---

The following are some of the ideas generated

Communication: setting expectations. During the introduction and presentation meetings, we should clearly establish the following:

1 What the client should expect of us, and
2. What we expect of our clients.

As a company, we want to avoid a situation where we promise services that we cannot reasonably deliver. Likewise, we want to avoid any misunderstandings that the client may have about us and our services.

- Provide each prospective client a written document that clearly illustrates all of the expectations.
- Remove statements from the plans that imply services we do not provide.
- Present different levels of annual services where the client can choose the services they wish and pay an appropriate advisory fee to receive.
- Identify the client service level (A1, B1, C1) in the financial advisor's meeting notes and any plan developed would have that designation on the information given to planning. Different level clients will pay for and receive different levels of service.

Here are some brief examples of how this might be handled in the introduction and presentation meetings:

- Listen to the client's expectations of us.

  "There are two things that I believe are imperative going forth in our relationship. The first is your expectations of what you want from us as your financial advocate. The second is our expectations of our clients."
    - Let them tell you their expectations, listen well, and repeat back to them so they know you are listening.
    - Let the client know what to expect going forward in the way of additional meetings and reviews. "You may not hear from us until next year, but rest assured, our team is working constantly behind the scenes."

- Communicate our expectations of the client.

  "We've talked about all of the things we will do for you (money management, taxes, estate planning, etc.). Here's what we expect from you. If there is any change in your financial situation—job, family status, address, inheritance, stock options, bonus, whatever—I need a call from you! If you have a major concern or question, please call."

(continued)

FIGURE 4.1 Client-Retention Program for Anderson Wealth Advisors, continued

- Communicate a strong team concept.

  The financial advisors should personally introduce the client service managers to the client, as well as describe some of the key professionals who work on their behalf in all five disciplines.

- Additional communication and client contact.

  We are all busy. However, are we busy with the "important" or the "urgent?" We need to prioritize each day with our team and reorder and schedule those things that are important both long term and short term. If indeed our clients are our top priority, are we fully using each team member's skills in the best way? We need to be focused and intentional about our communications to our clients. Our communications need to be in-person, on the phone, and in writing to our clients, depending on their specific needs.

The client service managers should have already completed their task of identifying the A, B, and C clients. The A clients generate ten times more income than C clients, so the financial advisors need to concentrate on them. This should not mean that we ignore our C clients, however. We have proposed some client communication guidelines:

A Clients
- Contact a minimum of 6 times per year: one review and three phone calls/personal contacts, send personalized birthday card and Thanksgiving card.
- Marketing touches (mailers and ads, etc.) should be over and above the 6 minimum contacts.

B Clients
- Contact a minimum of four times per year. One review (in person or by mail) and one phone call/personal contact, plus birthday card and Thanksgiving card.
- Marketing touches should be over and above the four contacts.

C Clients
- Contact a minimum of three times per year. One phone call/personal contact. Operations sends a birthday and Thanksgiving card signed by the company president.

These guidelines appear very time demanding, but we estimate that the phone calls would take about five minutes. Are any of our clients not worth five minutes of our time? Jane Wellspring* has the most C clients at 154, and it would take her less than 13 hours to call all of them, or about 20 minutes a week over 40 weeks. Nevertheless, making these contacts will mean blocking calendars and reprioritizing roles for your client service managers and financial advisors.

FIGURE 4.1 Client-Retention Program for Anderson Wealth Advisors, continued

---

Other additional important client contacts our committee proposes.

- Send out a thank-you note after each meeting.
- The following should be done within 90 days of plan presentation:
  - Send out a client survey.
  - Call all A clients to confirm completion of account transfers and transactions.
  - Set up a Phase II meeting.
- Set up pending file for all recommendations that were not implemented at the presentation. Follow up on these pending issues in six months.

Reviews

- **One month before the annual review, send one of two review letters to the client.**
  1) Review appointments.
     - Include checklist of what they will need to bring with them to the review.
     - Send out goals and objectives.
  2) Mail out reviews.
     - Send out goals and objectives.

- **Two weeks prior to review meeting.**
  - Advisor team will review checklist, gather and review materials.

- **One week prior to review meeting.**
  - Check review.
  - Determine what has or has not been implemented.
  - Update financial inventory.
  - Review confirmation and send the client a checklist of what to bring.

Client Retention Specialist

We are going to hire a junior financial advisor reporting to the senior vice president, marketing. The position would extend for a period of six months to one year and will be responsible for the following:

- Identify client's needs and create market specialty product events.
- Work with review team to identify product and planning opportunities.
- Ensure that all C clients have a phone call or meeting once per year.
- Ensure that all B clients have a phone call or meeting twice per year.
- Ensure that all A clients have three phone calls and one meeting per year.
- Send out client-satisfaction surveys and tabulate the results.
- Send out review questionnaires and call to verify and gather data. Prepare the client for the review.
- Work with financial advisor teams to contact clients for events and seminars.

MARKETING TO YOUR EMPLOYEES

If marketing is everything, any marketing plan would be remiss if it did not include strategies aimed at your own employees. Employees are key stakeholders and crucial at making your business succeed. Keeping them happy reduces turnover, increases your profits, and reduces your stress.

Figure 4.2 shows an employee-satisfaction and retention program that Brad Lantz created for one of our clients.

FIGURE 4.2 Gold Star Club Employee-Recognition Program

Executive Summary
The "Gold Star Club" is the name of the North Star Financial* new employee-recognition program. The Gold Star Club will initially consist of these components:

- *Gold Star Thank-You.* Instant recognition program. Thank-you card program designed to instantly thank one of our employees for going out of their way to help you.
- *Gold Star Service Award.* Ongoing quarterly/annual program. Employee nomination program that recognizes employees for constantly performing at a higher level of service than what is expected of them.
- *Gold Star Ideas.* Ongoing idea-generation program. Tapping into employees will help uncover ways to make North Star Financial a more profitable and a better place to work
- *Future components* might include sales contests, client-referral program (by employees), or new North Star Financial employee-referral program.

The following three sections state the goals and attributes that were built into the entire Gold Star Club program. Each of the three components has its own section.

Goals

1. To recognize and reward employees for their efforts that go above and beyond normal expectations.
2. Increase employee morale, create an ownership attitude, and challenge people to be their best.
3. Turn our employees into Absolute Advocates™ of North Star Financial. Have one monthly award celebration with cake, cookies, ice cream, or other treat to publicly recognize the winners.

<u>Attributes of recognition</u>

- Must be public or visible.
- Should be personalized.

FIGURE 4.2 Gold Star Club Employee-Recognition Program, continued

- Should be given on various levels (i.e., instant, quarterly, annually).
- Should promote teamwork and strengthen morale.
- Should be attainable by all employees.
- Should be fun.

<u>**Attributes of the reward**</u>

- Must carry perceived value of either emotional or monetary value (depending on level).
- Reward should be visible, something they can display in work space.
- Reward should be something employees would like to receive that they may not purchase themselves.
- Lowest level of reward should be attainable by all.
- Highest level of reward should be attained by 10 percent of employees.

"Gold Star Thank-You" **Program**
Instant recognition of peers is a great way to promote a team atmosphere and increase employee morale on a daily basis. Employees need a way to thank other employees for going out of their way to help someone else.

1. Employees have a postcard-sized preprinted thank-you note that they fill out when someone provides them with service that goes above and beyond the call of duty.
   - The sending employee will notify HR on our internal Web site of the person they want to send a "thank you."
   - The recognized employee will post the original in their office.
   - Copies will act as an entry into monthly contest for employee (or Gold Star) of the month.
   - As employees receive thank-you cards, they will be given a small something (to be determined) every time they receive a total of 20 cards.
2. Provides an immediate recognition, an emotional boost.
3. Must be available to everyone, at all times.
4. Provides a visible token that will be displayed in work area.
5. Provides an opportunity for greater prize by receiving employee of the month honors or by receiving 25 cards.
6. Employee of the month:
   - Person receiving the most thank-you notes per month.
   - Reward: special parking spot, lunch with a board member of choice, day off, etc.
   - Employee can only win once a year.

"Gold Star Service Award" **Program**
Some employees demonstrate a higher level of performance/service every day. These people need to be recognized for their ongoing efforts. At the end of the quarter, employees nominate someone who they feel has demonstrated a level of performance that is far greater than what is expected of them.

- Nominations go to a committee and five are chosen as winners.
- Employees become quarterly winners and receive a gift certificate for $100.

(continued)

FIGURE 4.2 Gold Star Club Employee-Recognition Program, continued

- Winners from each quarter are then eligible to be the annual winner.
- Annual winners—2 out of 20 will receive a significant prize such as a weekend at a lake resort or at a bed and breakfast.

Important information about the service award:

1. Nominations can come from peers and from management.
2. Open to all levels of employees.
3. Nominations and awards given on a quarterly basis.
4. Annual award based on quarterly winners.
5. Recognize all nominations in internal newsletter.
6. Rewards for nominated winners should be both visible and have monetary value.

"Gold Star Idea" **Program**

Employees need to be encouraged to provide input to help North Star Financial continue to perform and be successful. Ideas should fall within the following areas:

- Cost savings
- Revenue generating
- Process improvements that save time
- Customer service improvements

1. Employee should be thanked and recognized for their idea (no matter how big or little their suggestion).
2. Committee awards monthly/quarterly recognition for the best ideas.
3. All ideas will be sent to team leaders for review and possible implementation.
4. Track and report results to show employees the difference they are making.

Reproduced in Figure 4.3 is a short summary of a much longer marketing summary of the plan Brad Lantz created for All Star Financial. This plan was written to attract a buyer to the firm.

M *ulti-Million-Dollar Principle #16*

Retaining good employees is crucial to your success.

FIGURE 4.3 Sample Marketing Plan

Public Relations/Media Relations: The Story

All Star Financial* is unique in the marketplace. At All Star Financial our financial advisor is the person who guides the financial planning process: goal identification, data organization, analysis, problem identification, recommendations, and most important, plan implementation and the ability to monitor results. Financial planning is not simply a numbers game. People make the plans, and make the plans work.

Experienced and expert. Personable and helpful. These are the qualities of our team. We approach financial planning as a team. The financial advisor is the coach of the team. They then relay this information (depending on the client's needs) to five different teams that provide in-depth strategies and resources all under one roof. They are experts in their field who together build strategies to shape your financial future.

Because All Star Financial is an independent firm, we are limited to offering specific lines of products; we offer the products and services that are in the best interest of our clients.

Few, if any, firms in the marketplace offer all of these disciplines and services.

Corporate Marketing Goals

1. To grow All Star Financial to over $50,000,000 in revenue per year in five years.
2. To define All Star Financial as a full-capabilities financial advisory firm in each of the following disciplines: Financial Planning, Estate Planning, Insurance, Tax Strategies, and Investment Management.
3. To build a significant number of new clients through an Absolute Advocate™ program.
4. To continue to educate our clients and stakeholders in the various disciplines in wealth management.

Client Profile

Currently, All Star Financial has over 3,000 clients. They are typically 37 to 70 years old, white collar, and worked for their money. Profiling the audience is an important element of the marketing plan. This profiling allows us to be effective in several key elements of marketing, including market research and competitive analysis, products and services, pricing, public relations, merchandising, and branding.

The opportunity

The operations and direction of the marketing for All Star Financial is changing from:

1. A one-city operation to regional.
2. An opportunistic tactical direction to a strategic direction.

(continued)

FIGURE 4.3 Sample Marketing Plan, continued

3. A primarily outward-focused company to one that must build campaigns internally so it will be able to sustain and support the incredible growth expectations outwardly.
4. A client organization to an Absolute Advocate™ organization.

Our goal is to differentiate All Star Financial in the minds of investors by providing:

- *Teamwork.* The services we provide are reviewed by an internal team of experts in five fields: Financial Planning, Investment Management, Tax Strategies, Insurance, and Estate Planning. Your financial future is too important to leave in any one person's hands.
- *In-depth expertise.* Team members are highly regarded specialists in their fields who have earned the highest professional credentials.
- *Independence.* We are beholden to no one but you. All Star Financial is an independent firm that is not committed to selling anyone's products. Instead, together we pick and choose strategies and products designed to meet your needs.
- *Financial life planning.* We address all three phases of an investor's financial life: accumulation, distribution, and legacy.

The marketing energy of All Star Financial is focused on five different fronts to realize these changes:

1. Keeping the pipeline full.
   - All Star Financial is in its third year broadcasting the radio show "Talking Financial Futures," heard each Saturday morning. The show is the most widely listened to radio show each weekend in the market. It also is the top radio show for the over-35 demographic market in the 13-county metropolitan area. The station reaches an audience of more than 80,000 listeners. The closest competitor has less than 29,000 listeners. This program generates most of the leads. Billboards and seminar ads point to the show and build the audience.
   - Increasing educational seminars. The "Righteous Retiree Seminar" and the recent seminar "Why Has the Market Been So Dicey?" are showing good response from the community.
   - We will move to generating a majority of our leads by referrals or "recommendations." Our emphasis is changing to gaining recommendations from our clients.
   - Billboards, radio commercials, and direct marketing are creating awareness and growth.

2. Building the team image of All Star Financial.

   Noted securities writer and author John Bowen states, "The writing is on the wall. If you want to generate 'apostles' rather than clients, you need to provide them with world-class service, not in just one area, but in three or four."

   All Star Financial has five! These include Planning, Tax, Insurance, Managed Funds, and Estate/Trust work.

FIGURE 4.3 Sample Marketing Plan, continued

The *key* is our plans! In reality, each of the five teams stems from our planning. We must become proficient at selling that point of differentiation to our prospects and demonstrating its worth. If the relationship is built solely on the relationship with the financial advisor, a dip in the marketplace creates concern and erodes trust. If it is built on the relationship and solid plans, there is a greater feeling of being able to weather through current market situations.

Each team will have its own strategies to accomplish this. Everyone must present a consistant image in their strategies and presentations to clients, especially the financial advisors. We are dedicated to discovering and considering all aspects of a client's financial needs and selling the team concept. And as Tom Peters, author of *In Search of Excellence*, says, "Build quality into every part of your company experience."

Financial Planning Team: To truly provide the personalized strategies that our clients deserve, we have shifted to selling four distinct levels of financial strategies and custom plans for niche markets. These levels are based on the complexity of the client's needs and the size of the portfolio. Marketing is creating the packaging around each of four new plans.

Tax Strategies Team: Tax issues are the single largest factor in clients keeping more of what they earn. Marketing is creating a campaign that shows that effective tax deferral and legal tax avoidance have a greater impact on a client's financial worth than even a significant increase in annual rate of return on securities.

Insurance Team: Nationally, the top 5 percent of financial planning firms average 30–35 percent of their overall sales in insurance products versus All Star Financial's average of 9 percent. This is an area that we believe has possibilities for growth, and we have brought on one of the top insurance and estate planning people in the area to address this issue. Internal training is needed. Our client reviews will help us discover additional client needs, which will result in more complete financial service for our clients.

Investment Management Team: Registered Investment Adviser (RIA) is an important area of priority because of its significant long-term impact (recurring fees and better client service) to the company. The flexibility it provides is also very good for our clients. An internal and external plan has been developed to launch, build, and maintain All Star Financial's RIA.

Estate Planning: This has been an area of increasing interest and need to our clients. Jonathan Jones* and Gary Ellsworth* will be laying the groundwork and building this element of our teams.

3. Branch launches.

We believe our systems and strategies have great opportunity in other major metropolitan areas. Our experience in launching the Bloomdale*

(continued)

FIGURE 4.3 Sample Marketing Plan, continued

---

branch has led us to the conclusion that the best way to expand into another city is through the association and assimilation of an existing practice in that area. Typically, this would be a practice whose principal is nearing retirement, or a practice generating over $300,000 per year in fees and commissions. In this practice, the principal is interested in our systems and would enjoy the ability to focus their activities on their natural talents more than the executive and support roles of running a practice.

From last year's experience in supporting offices in five bordering states, we have concluded that we are better served by expanding our market in concentric circles. This means staying closer to our core city until we better master the challeges of connecting technology and the cost of travel in managing these sites. Our current strategy is investigating opportunities in cities with a population over 75,000.

4. Verticals/Niches.

The Business Professional Division was launched with an objective of serving professionals like doctors, lawyers, CPAs, etc. We have met our goals for last year in total number of professionals retained. This is slowly proving to be a successful market niche.

Because most of the professionals we are targeting love tennis, we are also sponsoring two professional tennis players: David Long* and Maryanne Green.* We will be building campaigns to maximize those relationships.

- *CPAs.* Strategic alliances with many more well-connected CPA firms can be an excellent relationship where it is a win/win situation for the CPA firm and All Star Financial. We will be identifying those CPA firms with five plus CPAs and those who presently do not have a relationship with a financial advisory firm.
- *Women.* This is an increasing market that must be given strong consideration. Women are seeking to be educated in the financial world and are increasingly controlling much of the disposable income. We are currently designing a campaign to address women through large corporate organizations. The direction will encompass financial, life, legal, and health issues.
- *Small/medium-sized business owners.* We are designing a program for this market for roll-out the fourth quarter of this year. The program is designed to differentiate All Star Financial from other planning organizations. This strategy includes management of 401(k) plans, custom planning for executives, and educational seminars that go beyond financial planning and include workshops on how to more effectively manage the organization.
- *Professional associations.* We currently have some opportunities for sponsorship into these niche markets by national associations. Limited resources are preventing us from pursuing these opportunities this year.

FIGURE 4.3 Sample Marketing Plan, continued

5. Corporate marketing.

Tom Peters states that a company seeking to build brand equity must build quality into every part of their company experience. When people think of your brand, they should conjure up a lifestyle that goes along with it.

Our mission, vision (internal and external), and values statements form the foundation of our brand equity. The process of defining these statements developed synergy and brought concensus and strength to the people at the top.

This mission, vision, and values statements are being carried out. The marketing department's job is to increase the market's recognition and identification of the brand. Think of the brand as an iceberg. Most of it is hidden deep under water. It is the part you can't see that gives an iceberg its solidity. People take an iceberg seriously for good reason. Our equity-creating process is all about giving All Star Financial the solidity and depth of an iceberg.

Building from the bottom up is creating a momentum that will be unstoppable. We have continued to develop and standardize our core compentencies; and we are building from there.

Keeping our brand entails: *creating, positioning, training, building, and maintaining* both internally and externally. It requires consistency in everything that we do. Our corporate marketing strategies and campaigns, ranging from the radio shows to educational seminars, to charity work and to customer satisfaction events, all contain elements that continue to strengthen our brand. Our future challenge is to broaden the market coverage of our brand to new markets in a systematic and effective way. This is being accomplished through a top-down buy-in, and personalized relationship building with current and future associations in our newly targeted markets.

Absolute Advocate™

The All Star Financial's Absolute Advocate™ system is an organized approach to generating new clients through greater client service. It follows a specific process of identifying and defining client expectations, exceeding them, and seeking a "recommendation/referral" from the client to someone they know and believe would benefit from our services.

All Star Financial has made a practice of providing annual reviews for our clients who have adapted plans. This department will review over 1,700 financial plans this year. This is unusual for most financial planning practices. For All Star Financial, it represents a critical element in our Absolute Advocate™ program. Changes are the only constants in the financial services industry. Our

(continued)

FIGURE 4.3 Sample Marketing Plan, continued

review strategies coupled with continuing education and Absolute Advocates™ allow All Star Financial to maintain the level of trust in our relationships that better serves the client and provides us referrals to better serve more in the community.

Another element to Absolute Advocates™ is our internal emphasis, the Star1 Club.

The "Star1Club" is the name of All Star Financial's new employee-recognition program. The Star1 Club will initially consist of three components:

- Star1 *Thank You*, instant recognition program. Thank-you card program designed to instantly thank someone for going out of his or her way to help you.
- Star1 *Service Award*, ongoing quarterly/annual program. Employee nomination program that recognizes employees for constantly performing at a higher level of service than what is expected of them.
- Star1 *Ideas*, ongoing idea generation program. Tapping into employees will help uncover ways to make All Star Financial a more profitable and a better place to work.

Future components might include sales contests, client referral program (by employees), or new All Star Financial employee referral program.

Ensure that our Clients and Stakeholders Are Well Educated

All Star Financial has traditionally placed a strong emphasis on continuing education and training for clients and prospects. Research has shown that clients want to be well educated about their finances. Keeping clients well advised of their financial alternatives allows them to make better financial decisions. We are accomplishing this through the following mediums:

a. Radio Shows
b. Seminars
c. Newsletters
d. All Star Financial Web site

KEY POINTS

1. Marketing is everything!
2. Everything you do in your practice has a marketing component.
3. Differentiate your firm in everything you do, but first you need to determine what your differentiation is!

4. Always do due diligence when entering to a new market/ location. Marketing systems that work in one area may not work in another for different reasons.

5. Stay focused on your ideal demographics for all your marketing.

6. Radio shows, with an easy-to-like, easy-to-trust financial advisor as the spokesperson, can be very successful, driving referrals to your firm.

7. Seminars are about educating prospects and clients— and are highly successful if the presentation is well done, the food is savory, and the facility is right.

8. People want to work with a financial advisor just like them. It is important that your firm's philosophy and branding demonstrate this to the client.

9. Successful firms develop (with expert help) a series of drip-marketing letters mailed on a regular basis. Areas could include a small business, retirement, children, social security, etc.

10. Find a niche and work that most diligently.

11. Attendance and client satisfaction will increase if you have fun, well-planned events for clients and prospects. With increased attendance comes more business.

12. Every client deserves ongoing contact from your client service manager. Your firm will also benefit from frequent marketing touches/contacts to clients and prospects.

13. Newsletters can be a very effective way to tell your firm's story.

14. Use a writer and designer to send out quality collateral to represent your company.

15. Create individual bios for every financial advisor, using professional photos, and anyone else who will be in contact with clients.

16. Tacky brochures and other printed pieces are worse than nothing at all.

17. Financial advisors' ego trips can be very expensive and ineffective if they let personal desires get in the way of spending marketing dollars effectively.

18. Process and procedure are the way to track what is working to get people in the door.

19. Develop scripts for use by those who answer incoming prospect calls. They are the cheerleaders of the firm.

20. Everything is part of your image package, from the parking lot to the offices to printed materials, down to the smallest detail (how you serve the coffee).

21. Every employee, regardless of their level, needs to be able to deliver your elevator speech and short commercial.

22. High-touch service keeps clients happy.

23. No marketing program would be complete without client-satisfaction and client-retention programs to discover how they feel about your service.

24. Employees need marketing programs, too.

5

OPERATIONS THAT PROVIDE A FINANCIAL ADVISOR WITH SUPERIOR SUPPORT

Prosperity Factor #5
Superior support is needed in every area of the
business to free up the financial advisor to do what
they do best: meet with clients and close the sale.

By Peter

WHAT ARE OPERATIONS?

A key strategy for reaching superstar status is to free up the financial advisor's time
so that they are only meeting with the client
to close the sale. Financial services require

> **Operations
> Report Card
> B+**

daily attention to lots of detail. This detail work should be
transferred to support staff whenever possible. These are the
tasks in a practice we call operations.

The operations of a practice revolve around an understanding of the Money Trail™, a method for mapping the organiza-

tion that is discussed in Chapter 4. Operations include elements of the business that are not sales or marketing related. This would include administrative duties, process and procedures, and data management, as well as relationships with vendors, broker/dealer, research, compliance, training, and general management.

Operational issues tend to be ignored by financial advisors during the early stages of their practice. A new financial advisor's primary goal is to establish a base of clients. The "work flow" is very fluid. Remember, we are playing basketball. Operational issues rear their ugly heads as the practice grows and the details of the business start to become overwhelming. The financial advisors start finding themselves bogged down in paperwork, unable to meet with as many new clients. This not only increases their stress level, it also decreases their income. This is why prevention is better than cure. The Money Trail™ helps define operation issues that require management, supervision, and implementation within the organization.

Here is how the different firms used their support staff.

The Mercury* group had a junior/senior focus. Mitch Mercury was the senior member of the team. His junior team members were fully licensed Series 7 Registered Sales Assistants (RSAs). They might sit in on an entire session with a client or they might be brought in toward the end of the meeting. They had the timing down to an exact science. They knew how long Mercury would spend with a client and without even being called, they would show up in the office at the appropriate moment toward the end of the meeting. To us it looked like a well-choreographed ballet.

At that time, Mitch Mercury would introduce his client to the RSA and describe a little bit about what the RSA would do to help them. Mercury would usher the client out the door and the RSA would take them into another office or to a conference room. The assistant would complete paperwork, answer questions, and really perform a variety of mundane tasks that were keeping the financial advisor from closing more business. At the same time, Mercury would quickly clean his desk for his next prospect waiting in the reception area.

These RSAs had a wide variety of duties and responsibilities. They were primarily responsible for:

- Creating the financial plan.
- Completing all the necessary paperwork and illustrations.
- Making insurance selections relative to picking out a particular product, also running the illustrations.
- Handling the transfer of assets from other firms.
- Any other service work.
- Keeping the business on the books—by making sure the weekly contacts took place.

Earlier we mentioned implementing a system of weekly follow-up letters, phone calls, and meetings to make sure the large insurance sale stayed on the books. These sales assistants were responsible for all these aspects of the sale. (See examples of various follow-up letters in Appendix.)

Guru Investments* had a different approach. Every financial advisor, even the new associates, had their own personal client service manager or RSA. New associates may share an RSA with another new financial advisor. Some of the top superstars created so much business that they actually used three or more personal RSAs in addition to a larger staff to do other tasks.

At the end of each meeting with the superstar, the clients were introduced to the RSA. There they would work with the clients to sign all the paperwork. They would have completed each of the applications for the product(s) the financial advisor would be recommending and answer any specific questions about the investments or the process prior to the client visit. They were responsible for making sure all the money was accurately transferred to the right account and handled follow-up service work. The sales assistants did not create the plan, look at the insurance, or analyze the taxes or the investments. Guru had a large staff to do each of these tasks.

Guru had an extensive *planning department* where the actual financial planners were required to have a comprehensive tax background. Although the financial planner attempted to get accurate and complete information on the client intake/data gathering form, in most cases there was crucial missing information. The members of the planning department were charged with tracking down the missing information. The financial advisors used a one-page list of instructions for the planning department to alert the planning department on the type of recommendations they expected to see on the final plan.

The client service managers were responsible for photocopying all the statements, wills, and other important information, and then would send this important stack of information over to the financial planning department.

The *financial planning department* then input the information into financial planning software and worked on creating the plan. This department was responsible for coordinating input with the insurance department, tax department, and investment department. The insurance department reviewed current insurance policies, analyzed them, and made recommendations on whether it was appropriate to hold the policies or do a 1035 exchange into a new policy. If a new policy was being recommended, they created a worksheet explaining why it would be appropriate, and handled the additional marketing materials around the policy.

The *tax department* may be consulted for tax information when it came to handling accounts. This is particularly important because they had used tax-efficient investing as part of their differentiating strategies. The tax department was also used for preparing tax returns and year-end tax planning.

The *investment department* reviewed the current investments. This could be a tedious task if the client has a variety of individual stocks or other issues. Once the investment department had recommended what should be sold and what should be held, they also recommended what should be purchased. They would include the marketing materials and subscription agreements needed for these purchases.

The planning department put together the plan and included all appropriate sales literature for a particular product recommendation. Everything was then placed into a nice color-coded binder. Two copies of the plan, an attractive one for the client and a plain version for the financial advisor, in addition to necessary subscription agreements were then forwarded back to the financial advisor's RSA.

Their job was to complete all of the forms before the client arrived at the office. This made the presentation to the client much easier and actually increased the closing rate.

The financial advisor would focus on the big picture, reviewing the major issues of the plan, and talking conceptually about products. If a variable annuity was being recommended, the advisor would briefly review the advantages and disadvantages of the variable annuity and perhaps provide a few sentences on why they were recommending a particular company.

At the end of the plan presentation meeting, most clients just kept nodding in agreement and would move with the RSA into their own office or conference room. At that time, the RSA would present and briefly explain each application in the stack. As they reviewed them individually, the client would sign on the bottom.

In this streamlined manner, most of the clients could be handled in two meetings. Even the presentation meeting was rarely over two hours in length.

By Katherine

This is a far cry from the way I was taught to do the business. When I started in financial services, we did not even think about filling out the applications until you were sure the client had agreed to make a purchase. As a result, we may have spent 20 minutes or more per application as we were going through and asking these tedious and repetitious questions, including the client's name, age, address, etc.

What Guru learned early on was during the 20 minutes it took to fill out the application, the client's mind is wandering to places it is better not to go, such as, "Why am I making this purchase?" The clients are actually talking themselves out of the sale. This is far less likely to happen, when all the client has to do is sign on the bottom line and move on to the next application. The closing ratios increased dramatically. When the clients completed all the paperwork, the RSA would warmly and kindly escort them out the door, and then proceed to submit all the paperwork, posting it to the ledgers and putting it on the daily blotters.

Once the client left the financial advisor's office, it became the RSA's responsibility to maintain the relationship. Out of sight, out of mind for the financial advisor, but it was one more case for the RSA.

SCHEDULING

Every superstar firm we worked with clearly understood that they had one item in inventory—their time, and that it was extremely valuable. At many top practices, where goals include striving for 12 to 16 meetings per week, face-to-face with clients, managing their time inventory, their scheduling, was absolutely key to good control. The financial advisors had very little say about their schedules. It was possible for them to block out an afternoon for a dental appointment or a haircut or even to list a time they would like to arrive and leave each day. However, once in the office, their time belonged to the firm. Someone in another office was actually managing their schedules for them—

usually the marketing department. When calls would come in from a prospect, the person in the marketing department would assign them to a financial advisor's calendar on a rotating basis.

Katherine's Challenge

Putting this type of system into place was one of the hardest challenges for me during my tenure as a financial advisor. This process demanded that I transfer control over a huge portion of my day. On any given day I would have no idea who was coming in to see me. I would be aware that I had three new prospects, but I would know almost nothing about them. In a typical day I might see three prospects/clients for approximately two hours each visit. Six plus hours is a lot of time to be "on." By the end of the day I was absolutely exhausted. I found I had to take detailed notes about the client's goals, objectives, backgrounds, and desires in order to keep them straight. I also found myself taking notes about their personal appearance or other key factors. It was not unusual for me to get to the end of the day and not be able to even remember what the first client of the day looked like. I would look back at my notes and see something like "wife wore a polka dot blouse, husband carried a cane." This helped me put names with faces.

This was far different from how I managed a financial planning practice 20 years ago. I was quite distressed about it at first, however, when I talked to one of the other financial advisors in the office, I asked how she could possibly keep all these clients straight. Her response, "You need to understand this is an assembly line." She was right about this particular firm. I needed to understand their approach, which worked for them, was to move as many people in and out as quickly possible. An assembly line system may not be right for everyone, but it sure made this company a lot of money. Their process was the direct opposite of my practice 20 years ago where I had the time to work with only three or four clients per week. Here we were expected to see that many clients per day!

CLIENT SERVICE MANAGER AND THE CLIENT EXPERIENCE

By Peter

To show how invaluable the right RSM or client service manager (CSM) is in providing a model client experience, we have outlined in Figure 5.1 the "ideal" CSM involvement. We are using the term CSM here. In some firms they would call this position an RSM.

FIGURE 5.1 The Ideal Client Service Manager Involvement

STEP ONE—INITIAL MEETING

Prior to Initial Meeting with Prospect

- When prospect agrees to consultation meeting, the CSM schedules the meeting on the FA's calendar.
- CSM sends appointment reminder cover letter, financial advisor biography, firm's brochure (6"×9"), and worksheet to prospect.
- CSM calls the potential client (prospect) to confirm the appointment the day before.
- CSM prepares consultation meeting folder for the financial advisor to conduct consultation meeting, including anything the client mailed ahead of time (such as worksheet, financial statements, etc), meeting notes template, and the financial plan disclosure and client to-do list.
- CSM informs the receptionist of duties such as preparing fresh coffee, serving bottled water, cookies, and/or other refreshments. The receptionist will prepare the reception area for guests and should make it respectable (remove waste, straighten furniture, rugs, clean windows on doors if necessary etc.).

Initial Meeting

Purpose: Establish trust, build excitement about the firm, and close for preparing a plan and the solutions meeting. Set groundwork for getting referrals.

FIGURE 5.1 The Ideal Client Service Manager Involvement, continued

Beginning of consultation meeting
- Receptionist greets the potential client (prospect), offers refreshments, and introduces them to the financial advisor.
- Financial advisor conducts consultation meeting.

Conclusion of consultation meeting (if the client/prospect *does* wish to sign up for a plan)
- Financial advisor alerts CSM to sit with the client and review and complete the necessary paperwork to start the financial plan process including:
  - Financial plan disclosure.
  - Client is given a "to-do" list with postage-paid envelope to send any additional information.
- Set a date for the solutions meeting and provide client with an appointment reminder card.
- CSM to give client their business card and let the client know that they are the person to contact if they have any questions (use this opportunity to build client relationship).

Conclusion of initial meeting (if the client/prospect *does not* wish to sign up for a plan)
- Financial advisor sends a thank-you note.
- Financial advisor files the prospect's information for possible follow-up.

After the client leaves the consultation meeting (if the client *does* wish to sign up for a plan)
- CSM sends a thank-you note.
- CSM contacts clients after one week of the consultation meeting if the information on the client "to-do" list has not yet been received.

STEP TWO—ANALYZE DATA

Compile and Enter Data

Plan creation process
- Upon receiving all necessary information from clients, CSM enters all client data into the financial planning software workbook.
- CSM meets with the FA to review the workbook and get financial advisors' recommended product solutions.
- CSM notifies planning department when all client data has been entered.
- CSM creates "plan file" to house all physical copies of client financial statements, worksheets, etc. CSM keeps plan file while in process with the planning department.

Client Contact

Plan creation process
- CSM calls clients to confirm the solutions meeting appointment.
- CSM calls clients as needed, never letting more than two weeks lapse between contacts.

(continued)

FIGURE 5.1 The Ideal Client Service Manager Involvement, continued

Assemble Plan and Complete Implementation Paperwork

Plan creation process
- Planning department notifies CSM/financial advisor when financial plan is complete.
- CSM prints and assembles the financial plan at least one day before the solutions meeting.
- CSM and financial advisor review the plan for accuracy.
- CSM completes documents to implement all product recommendations outlined in the financial plan prior to the meeting (e.g., new account forms, applications, transfer forms, including prospectuses, switch letter, etc.).
- CSM informs the receptionist of duties such as preparing fresh coffee, serving bottled water, cookies, and/or other refreshments. They will prepare the reception area as they do before any prospect or client arrives.

STEP THREE—SOLUTIONS MEETING

Solutions Meeting

Beginning of solutions meeting
- Receptionist greets the potential client (prospect), offers refreshments, and reintroduces them to the financial advisor.
- Financial advisor conducts solutions meeting.

Conclusion of solutions meeting
- Financial advisor alerts CSM to sit with the client and review and complete the necessary paperwork to start the product implementation process including:
  - Account applications
  - Policy forms
  - Transfer forms
  - Switch letters, etc.
- CSM answers client questions and should use this opportunity to establish rapport and to establish CSM as the person to handle all of their service needs.
- CSM gives the client a CSM business card (if they need another one).

Conclusion of solutions meeting (after the client leaves)
- CSM sends another thank-you note.
- CSM creates "master client file" if there isn't already a client file in the branch and places the completed "plan file" in the client file.
- CSM creates "transfer file" and/or "account/policy file" and keeps the material until all transfers or new accounts/policies are complete.
- CSM sends the paperwork to the department that will process it and makes file copies in the "transfer file" and/or "account/policy" file.
- CSM monitors the securities transfer process and/or new account/policy process. Follow up on and take necessary action with transfers and/or new accounts/policies to make sure that the funds/securities are transferred and/or processed.
- Refer to "client records" section for details on filing procedures and best practices.

FIGURE 5.1 The Ideal Client Service Manager Involvement, continued

Maintain Client Contact

As each transfer is complete, the CSM will send a handwritten note card or personally call the client to give an update on the transaction.

Client Service Requests

- The CSM will work with the client to complete all service requests.
- Clients may call with service needs (e.g., address changes, need distribution, etc.). CSM will process all of those requests.
- Complete paperwork necessary to finalize the request and mail forms to client for signature when necessary. If problems occur, the CSM will work with appropriate people to resolve all issues.
- CSM creates "client service request" file to keep record of all pending client service requests and follow up as necessary.
- See "client records" section for details on procedures and best practices.

STEP FOUR—MONITOR AND MODIFY

- Between six months and one year after all transfers are complete, the client should come in for a review.
- CSMs will be responsible for alerting financial advisors when it is time to contact clients and schedule their Monitor & Modify meeting.
- CSMs will contact clients to schedule appointments.
- CSMs will send appointment reminder letter and contact client by telephone to confirm appointment.

Beginning of Monitor and Modify meeting
- Receptionist greets the potential client (prospect), offers refreshments.
- Financial advisor conducts Monitor and Modify meeting.

Conclusion of Monitor and Modify meeting
- Financial advisor alerts CSM to sit with the client and review and complete the necessary paperwork to start the product implementation process including:
  - Account applications
  - Policy forms
  - Transfer forms
  - Switch letters, etc.
- CSM answers client questions and should use this opportunity to establish rapport and to establish CSM as the person to handle all of their service needs.
- CSM gives the client a CSM business card.

Conclusion of Monitor and Modify meeting (after the client leaves)
- CSM sends another thank-you note.
- CSM creates "transfer file" and/or "account/policy file" and keeps until all transfers or new accounts/policies are complete.
- CSM sends the paperwork to the department that will process it and makes file copies for the "transfer file" and/or "account/policy" file.

(continued)

FIGURE 5.1 The Ideal Client Service Manager Involvement, continued

- CSM monitors the securities transfer process and/or new account/policy process. Follow up on and take necessary action with transfers and/or new accounts/policies to make sure that the funds/securities are transferred and/or processed.
- Refer to "client records" section for details on filing procedures and best practices.

Maintain Client Contact

As each transfer is complete, the CSM will send a handwritten note card or personally call the client to give an update on the transaction.

Ongoing Client Touches/Communication

CSM maintains ongoing communication
- Sends birthday, graduation, Thanksgiving, and anniversary cards.
- Sends invitations to client appreciation events (birthday in a box concept, etc.).
- Sends invitations to client seminars.

KEY POINTS

1. The most important commodity a financial advisor has is their TIME. Great operations is all about freeing up the financial advisor's time so they can spend more time with the clients, closing the sale.

2. In a financial planning practice, operations revolve around the Money Trail™—who is doing what in the process.

3. Operational elements are not sales- or marketing-related, but include administrative duties and process and procedures

4. An important aspect is the relationship with vendors, broker/dealer, research, compliance, training, and general management.

5. Some practices use junior financial advisors to work with the senior advisor or superstar.

6. Other practices use a registered sales assistant who is responsible for all the administrative work of a financial advisor.
7. All-important, but time-consuming paperwork should be prepared prior to the meeting. This not only saves time in the meeting, it helps close more sales.

6

EXCELLENT EMPLOYEES

Prosperity Factor #6
Having the right employees on the bus, in the right
seat, and the wrong ones off the bus, is crucial for
becoming a multi-million-dollar financial advisor.

By Katherine

Hands down, the number one
frustration for most small business owners is employees. Financial advisors are no exception. The time they spend hiring, training, and retaining employees is generally frustrating. We found it very rare to find a financial advisor who had complete confidence in their staff.

One of them summed it up quite well when they said, "We have learned to hire in leisure and fire in haste." Nothing can be more draining and demanding on a financial advisor's time than an incompetent or undependable employee.

As we have seen in previous chapters, it is impossible to be a multi-million-dollar producer without help. Every client we worked with understood the importance of finding the right employee and then delegating to them—they just did not do a very good job at it.

It is true that financial advisors like to delegate. Typically, they will pass off whatever it is they do not like to do: completing forms, returning phone calls, or even service work. Unfortunately, they usually give little thought to the type of person they need to delegate to, or how to ensure that person has the tools and skills necessary to make the delegation work.

Typically the financial advisor trusts these people because they have hired someone just like themselves, one who comes close to matching them on the Kolbe index. Unfortunately, the hired position is supposed to fill in the gaps of what the financial advisor cannot cover, and not replicate what the financial advisor can already do well. Now they have two people with the financial advisor's strengths, and no one to fill in the weak spots. This is a natural tendency, because we want to hire people that we like and trust, and they tend to be just like us.

Every firm had some delegation system in place. Like any star-based business, they were all designed to make the star's life easier. They did free up a lot of the financial advisor's time so they could spend it with clients. Although every firm had a few stellar employees who were so crucial to the organization that the financial advisor could not maintain superstar status without them, they also tended to have just as many problem employees. The problem employees tended to be black holes, sucking in everything and everyone around them.

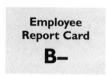

The financial advisors were resourceful in finding the help they needed, however, they had no system for managing or hiring their employees. For many firms, their success with employees was largely accidental.

This chapter will focus on these areas of employees:

- Recognizing common pitfalls.
- How to hire the right fit.
- Using the Kolbe System™ to increase employee success.
- Establishing a delegation protocol to improve employee performance.
- Creating an employee incentive plan to motivate current employees and improve retention.

COMMON PITFALLS

There are many ways that improper management can cause problems with employees and staff. Here are just a few:

All the Employees Have the Same Strengths and Weaknesses

We have seen the entire upper-level management of large broker/dealers have problem-solving skills that almost exactly mirror the president. Yes, it is true, they all get along great, and they are great fun at barbeques, but it is very difficult for them to move the business ahead, because they suffer from what Kathy Kolbe, who we'll discuss in the next section, calls "inertia." Everyone thinks exactly alike. They all have the same strengths and the same weaknesses. This makes it very hard to accomplish important goals and targets.

We saw one firm that was a collection of "Quick Starts." They had plenty of wonderful new creative and innovative ideas. However, they did not have any "Follow Thrus," or people who could take those ideas, turn them into a reality, and keep customer service high. Though a high-energy group, they could rarely accomplish anything of significance. Naturally, reaching quarterly objectives was a challenge. The Quick Starts are far more interested in their latest idea than they were in the Follow-Thru task of following the financials.

Wrong Fit

Another management pitfall is delegating to a person who is not naturally wired for the assigned task. This may take the stress off the delegator in the short run, but in the long run, the delegatee will be frustrated, unhappy, and not able to contribute their energy to what is needed. Sometimes these employees become so unhappy they leave the company, creating high turnover, an unnecessary expense for the entrepreneur.

Ineffective Testing

Some firms used tests that were not very effective at predicting how a person would succeed in their position. A common example is a personality test. I like personality tests, but as a group, they are *affective* tests. They test personality and beliefs. They do not test how a person approaches work or solves problems. It has not been as effective in helping find the right person for the right job as other indicators.

WHAT WE DID

When we work with a company to build valuation or improve profits, one of the biggest impacts comes from using the Kolbe System™. Because it can maximize the productivity of every employee, it literally affects everything in the company.

The Kolbe System™ identifies your natural instincts, strengths, and problem-solving abilities. It has been used by hundreds of thousands of people and countless businesses to help make them more productive with less effort and stress.

I do not exaggerate when I say it has changed our lives and the lives of our clients. First, a little history. Kathy Kolbe created The Kolbe System™. She is the daughter of E.F. Wonderlic, who developed the Wonderlic Personnel Test, an IQ measurement used by employers and the U.S. government for many years. Kathy, who started working for her dad when she was just seven years old, noticed it was impossible to predict who was going to be successful based on IQ tests. She discovered some geniuses did not know enough to come in out of the rain and some people with mediocre scores were wildly successful and became very wealthy. At that time neither Kathy nor her father could identify the key factor for success.

Many years later, a near-fatal auto accident left Kathy with a severe brain injury. As she lay in her hospital bed teaching herself to read again, she made a huge discovery. She was solving problems in exactly the same way she did before the accident, when she could read! She knew then we are born with certain instincts that do not change over time. Kathy concluded that each of us is created with a unique method of operation, our own *modus operandi*, or MO, which is where we get our energy. It is how we solve problems and approach work or other chosen acts.

During her extensive study of the brain, she, like many other researchers, confirmed that the brain has three main parts. The *cognitive* (left hemisphere) controls thought and determines intelligence, skill, knowledge, expertise, and reason. The *affective* (right hemisphere) controls feelings and determines personality, values, beliefs, attitudes, and emotions. Finally, the *conative* (front section) controls action and determines instinct, mental energy, talents, and drive.

Kathy's studies led her to focus on how people succeed, as opposed to how well they follow instructions. "I discovered that achievement multiplied when individuals of any age or status were able to use their knack for getting things done," she said. In other words, Kathy found out that "I will" can be more important than IQ.

Conation, or drive, is about a person's ability and energy to get things done. It is separate from intelligence, emotions, or personality type. Nothing happens until you use your instinct—your Action Mode®.

Moreover, our instincts do not change over time. They will govern how we act, react, and interact. Striving instincts are not affected by genetics, education, social status, or environmental surroundings. There is no bias by gender, age, or ethnicity. Thus, working with, rather than against, your natural Action Mode allows you the freedom to be your authentic, true self. This is true in your professional life as well as your personal life.

Kathy determined there are four Action Modes®: Fact Finder, Follow Thru, Quick Start, and Implementor, and every-

---

FIGURE 6.1 Kolbe Impact Factors™

Positive strengths in each Action Mode®

Operating Zone		Action Mode®				
		Fact Finder	**Follow Thru**	**Quick Start**	**Implementor**	
Prevent	1 2 3	Simplify	Adapt	Stabilize	Imagine	**Rather Not**
Respond	4 5 6	Refine	Rearrange	Revise	Renovate	**Willing**
Initiate	7 8 9 10	Justify	Organize	Improvise	Construct	**Will**

Multi-Million-Dollar Principle #17

Financial advisors who work within their natural instincts can increase their productivity and energy and at the same time reduce their stress.

one has at least some energy in all four modes. In addition, each of these modes is on a continuum that ranges from "won't" to "willing" to "will" (or degrees from preventive/resistant to adaptive to insistent or initiating). Through the use of a test to gauge conative acuity, the Kolbe System™ identifies 12 problem-solving approaches as determined by each person's own method of operation.

Fact Finders

People who are primarily initiating or insistent Fact Finders have a need to research, probe, outline, investigate, set objectives, prove, and evaluate. They also can have a tendency to get bogged down in details, research what already has been done, prove that they are right, and fall into paralysis by analysis. In order for a Fact Finder to work in their groove, they should avoid guesswork. They need a lot of data to feel comfortable. Because their time mode is the past, Fact Finders are especially adept at putting events into historical perspective and using stories as anecdotal evidence.

Three years ago I had a young marketing assistant, Steve Gibson,* who was an insistent Fact Finder. When we first started working together, Steve would come to me for advice. Instead of asking me a question, he would start with a long fact pattern, giving me every detail imaginable in chronological order. This was great if I had a lot of time, but if I was in a hurry it created a lot of tension in me—I wanted him to cut to the chase and be more succinct. I finally explained to him that he was a Fact Finder in a Quick-Start world. There was a better way for him to communicate with me, the Quick Start, when I was pressed for time, which would be a lot more productive for him and more efficient for both of us. I suggested he phrase the issue succinctly and then give me three to five main points in bullets. I know this took him some extra time, but it was good practice for him in communicating with managers, who were mostly Quick Starts.

I also knew he would not be satisfied just giving me the bullets. He wanted me to have the advantage of all of his research. To accommodate his style, we would frequently have walking meetings. We would spend an hour or more walking while he ran through the detailed background that he had researched and what his conclusions were. It was great for me: I got a lot of exercise and it was good for him, as he felt valued, appreciated, and listened to.

At the other end of the spectrum are resistant or preventive Fact Finders. They like to simplify things, and avoid getting bogged down in details and minutiae. Rather than specializing in a particular area, they are more likely to be generalists. These folks never ask for more information and seem to have a knack for taking complicated subjects and getting them down to the most elementary basics. They are also masters of fire, ready, aim. Too many facts seem to bog them down, and they are likely to make a decision without enough due diligence into the alternatives and consequences.

Follow Thrus

People who are primarily initiating or insistent Follow Thrus have a tendency to complete what they start, bring things to closure, work sequentially, avoid interruptions or distractions, and work with graphs and diagrams. They will use their

MO to structure, systematize, plan, coordinate, budget, integrate, chart, prepare, and provide service.

On the other end of the spectrum, those who are primarily resistant Follow Thrus have a tendency to avoid finishing everything they start, go with the flow, avoid following a routine, and resist staying within a structure.

One of our children is a resistant Follow Thru, and he is the greatest person in the world to travel with. "What should we do today?" I'll ask.

"Whatever you want, Mom!"

And he is truly happy doing whatever anyone else wants. However, when it comes to following through with a task, he may not think it is worth his time.

Insistent Follow Thrus are great at creating process and procedures. They make sure nothing falls through the cracks and are very adept at customer service. We have some friends where the husband is an insistent Follow Thru. The first time we were at their lake place, I opened the front door, only to discover that every single light switch had a neat, machine-made label under it. The label identified which light went with which switch. Even the remote controls for the TV were neatly labeled. This was a Follow Thru demonstrating his need for order and structure.

We once did a marketing analysis for a Fortune 200 Company. When it came time to interview the chief marketing officer, he came into our meeting room and dropped a report on our table. It was at least four inches thick and had to be a minimum of 300 pages. The first words out of his mouth were, "I just thought you would be interested in the process and procedures we use to make our marketing decisions." I almost laughed out loud. I have known dozens of top-level marketing people and not one of them has ever expressed any interest in process or procedures. It seemed apparent this fellow was an insistent Follow Thru in a Quick-Start job. I predicted he would not last three months. I was off a bit—it took six months before he was in another position.

We have done hundreds of Kolbe indexes on our clients, and unfortunately we have rarely found any insistent Follow Thrus, even though they represent 20 percent of the general population. This is a great loss for our industry because it is the Follow Thrus who love customer service and get the details done. They can be a huge prize for a financial advisor.

Quick Starts

Initiating Quick Starts thrive on brainstorming, innovation, deadlines, acting spontaneously to future-oriented issues, and bouncing ideas off other people. They will invent new solutions, improvise, and play their hunches.

However, resistant or preventive Quick Starts will resist acting at the last moment, avoid flying by the seat of their pants, seek stability, avoid chaos, and resist constant change.

A huge percentage of successful financial professionals are Quick Starts. One study done by Kolbe Corp. found that 68 percent of the high producers in the insurance industry were insistent Quick Starts. All of the superstars that we studied were initiating Quick Starts. This does not mean you cannot be a superstar if you are another Action Mode®; it just means you will need different support systems.

For the past few years I have been working with a high producer who is an initiating Quick Start. Naturally, because he is so much like me, I find him fascinating! Our respective spouses (both of whom are insistent Fact Finders) give us a hard time, because when the two Quick Starts get together for an hour, we come up with four ideas for new products and two ideas for other business ventures. Unfortunately, few of these brilliant ideas ever see the light of day, because we need the Follow Thrus to bring something to closure and the Fact Finders to research all the competition.

Some time back, Vestment Advisors was asked to create a daylong retreat for a large Eastern seaboard financial planning firm. They had a lead financial planner supervising a staff of ten that created plans for the financial advisors to present to clients. The entire financial planning staff was insistent Fact Finders and insistent Follow Thrus. There were no Quick Starts in the planning department and Jim, the department head, was no exception. Jim was asked to give a 30-minute presentation on the new plan we had created for the firm.

Jim clearly did not want to give this speech. I met with him on three different occasions and laid out the presentation for him, including the key bullet points. He continued to resist but seemed like he would reluctantly do what was required: Give a brief presentation on a topic he knew inside and out.

The day of the presentation, I arrived a few minutes late, only to be met in the parking lot by an agitated meeting planner. She was beside herself. Jim had called in "sick" and was not able to do his presentation. Would I fill in for him?

Now I knew almost nothing about his topic, beyond the few key points I helped him create. My response to her? No problem! I got up and gave a 30-minute presentation on a topic I knew very little about. It even got very high marks on the evaluation form from the audience.

Was this stressful for me? Not at all. In fact, I had a great time. Quick Starts love to fly by the seat of their pants and ad lib—it is what we were created for. I was struck by the fact that a task that was simple and fun for me, giving a presentation, could actually make someone who was wired differently physically sick. What is a treat for one person could be poison to someone else.

A few years ago I had a resistant Quick-Start assistant. I should have known this was not the right job for her after we had the following exchange: I asked her to change the flights on my next trip, an itinerary she had booked a few weeks earlier. I was expecting "Sure thing. No problem." Instead, I was told in a huffy voice, "I can't change your reservations. I've already made them!"

My assistant was primarily a strong "stabilizer" on the Quick-Start scale, a preventive or resistant Quick Start. There is nothing wrong with being in this mode; in fact, such people can provide a very good balance to a Quick Start who is off on a new tangent every day. Resistant Quick Starts hate ad-libbing and going with the flow. Preventive Quick Starts love stability and hate chaos and change. No wonder she did not want to change my schedule—she wanted to carve it in granite, because that made her more comfortable.

Some time ago we had to change the job responsibilities of a resistant Quick Start for one of our client firms. I think she was at 1 on a scale of 10. Two months after the job change, she was still depressed because she hated any change. Every insistent Quick Start in the organization wanted to fire her! They loved change and could not understand why she was having so much trouble. The change was her undoing. She finally could not take it any more and quit.

Implementors

The term *Implementors* refers to working with tools, that is, implements. This includes objects such as hammers, knitting needles, scalpels, earthmovers, and computer CAD/CAM systems. Initiating Implementors have a need to handcraft solid solutions, and to shape, fix, demonstrate, display, and build. Think of the surgeon who likes to work with her hands, or the architect that enjoys building models. Not surprising, these people are few and far between in our industry because we deal with intangibles, and there is little place for concrete models.

We have a friend who is an insistent Implementor. Two years ago he put a new deck on our house. It was beautifully done and a work of art. Every mitered corner fit perfectly. Unfortunately, within a few months the pristine mitered corners fit less perfectly as the fresh wood dried. Every time he comes to our house, he is out on that deck, working to get those corners back to perfection. It is not unusual for him to take out one of the cross bars, if they are warped, and replace it with a new one. As a resistant Implementor myself, I would never have noticed.

In all the tests we have done with financial advisors and their teams, I have only seen one with a score of more than 5. The reason is simple. By and large, insistent Implementors are not in financial services. They are in manufacturing or some other job where they can use their talents. This is an industry of concepts, with rarely an opportunity to use concrete examples or hands-on solutions.

Resistant Implementors avoid concrete examples, hands-on solutions, and operating mechanical equipment. I am a prime example here. Everyone in our company knows I cannot get within two feet of a piece of equipment. It once took me an hour to fax four sheets of paper because the machine kept jamming, and I could not figure out how to fix it.

USING KOLBE TO HIRE THE RIGHT EMPLOYEES

The Kolbe System™ has had a dramatic impact on how we approach our own work and hire employees for Vestment Advisors, our own business, and for our clients. Now when I interview a potential new assistant for me who fits the "stabilizer" area, a resistant Quick Start, I either pass this person up and hire someone else, or make a joke about the situation up front. I tell them that I will probably drive them crazy changing travel plans and coming up with lots of new ideas. I explain that I need them to help me stay on task, sort through all my wonderful ideas, and just stick with a few projects. The balancing effect of someone from the other end of the spectrum is crucial for moving forward. Full disclosure helps me meet their expectations. If I have an assistant who is a go-with-the-flow "adaptive" on the Follow-Thru mode, I make sure they understand my need for uninterrupted time and give them enough time every day to get their questions answered.

As a manager, you can be trained in the Kolbe System™ so that you can recognize the primary Action Mode® of current employees as well as job applicants. You can use your newfound understanding of human motivation to restructure your office for maximum efficiency. Or, you can ask every employee to take the test and share the results with you. Using the Kolbe profiles to hire new employees is one of the crucial factors that must be in line for success. If you can get a good Kolbe match, you have an 80 percent chance of that person succeeding in their job. This is much higher than any other indicator including references or IQ tests.

KOLBE AND TEAMS

The best mix of staff, employees, or any team is a bell curve across the four Action Modes®. The most successful groups will have 25 percent of their members preventing problems, 25 percent initiating solutions to problems, and a broad band in the middle of 50 percent bridging or accommodating the differences. The more out of alignment a group gets, the harder it is for the members to be productive. The right Kolbe mix on your team provides the maximum productivity, profitability, and efficiency. A poor mix means that a team, staff, department, project, or the entire business can become polarized, inefficient, unprofitable, or stymied by inertia.

A few years ago we consulted with a dot-com client. The company had a short window of opportunity to launch a new prod-

If you would like to find out your Kolbe profile, visit:
http://www.kolbe.com/vestment

uct. After the first few hours on site, I knew they were in trouble. The president was equal parts preventive Quick Start and preventive Follow Thru, a deadly combination to lead a company that must move quickly and have a high level of customer service to succeed. As you can see, it is vital that people in leadership not be at odds with the organizational goals in terms of their natural way of problem solving. The chairman was a strong initiating Quick Start. The stress between the initiating Quick Start and the preventive Quick Start was painful to watch. Sometimes they would get so angry with each other they would literally start yelling and screaming. It was impossible to get anything done because they disagreed on everything.

Every month when we returned to visit the company, we could see they had made absolutely no progress. In fact, on month nine they were asking the same questions they had on month three! Not surprisingly, they did not meet their deadlines, but they did manage to alienate almost every client they had. Sadly, this problem was completely fixable! If they had agreed to adopt a Kolbe approach, we could have pinpointed a lot of their problems, restructured their teams, and had a much higher chance of success. All the business strategies we brought to the table were useless because the right people were not in the right job. This company at the very least needed an adaptive Quick Start and an adaptive Follow Thru who were open to others' input. Regrettably, their window of opportunity closed while the principals argued with each other and laid off most of the staff—an unfortunate ending that could have been much different.

Leaders, managers, and supervisors—you can optimize individual and group performance by assigning jobs suited to the instinctive strengths of those reporting to you, or you can watch your company become stagnant. Doing it right results in

- improving morale by allowing everyone the freedom to be themselves;

Multi-Million-Dollar Principle #18

Use Kolbe for all your hires and increase your chances of getting the right person in the right spot.

- building synergistic, profitable, and efficient teams;
- using time more effectively; and
- allowing people to be rewarded for unique energy.

On the other hand, when people work against their Action Modes®, it can be devastating. It can lead to high levels of stress, strain, burnout, and depression, and it can disrupt the flow of energy.

When I have to deal with an extensive amount of organization or details (Follow-Thru energy), such as an entire day cleaning out the filing system and putting new labels on folders, I find my energy being zapped out of me and I will feel positively blue. After three or four days of this continuous activity, a feeling of depression sets in. But when an assistant works on those pesky files, and I am doing what I do best—creating a new marketing program—I am back to my old, cheerful self, excited and full of energy.

It is important to spend most of our time working within our natural Action Mode®. That is, what will bring us extraordinary results with the least amount of effort.

USING KOLBE WITH YOUR STAFF

One of our financial advisor clients was actually considering reducing his production and slowing down business, thus taking a considerable cut in income, all because he was so frustrated managing the staff. Because he found it so agonizing to deal with his employees, he decided to reduce the size of his staff even though he knew it was going to also reduce the size of his income.

Peter worked with him to instigate the Kolbe System™ and coupled it with the Money Trail™, described in Chapter 3. Finally they set up appropriate delegation of authority, and this advisor was set free. Today he is happy, continuing to grow, and no longer facing the employee problems that plagued him a few years ago.

Kolbe can be used a number of ways to improve the output of your teams and your individual hires.

First, when the financial advisor is hiring a personal assistant or registered sales assistant, it is important to find people with MOs who have less than four units of differentiation from the FA's profile, yet still play to the strengths of the hire. Kathy Kolbe has found that where there is a difference of four or more in any mode, between two people there will be conflict. For instance, as a 9 QS, myself, I will need an assistant who is at least a 6 or more, or we will be in conflict. Therefore, finding someone with the proper strengths who is within three of the financial advisor's profile is ideal.

Take a look at the actual Kolbe profile of Jan Jenson* (Figure 6.2). She is a 4383, an insistent Quick Start. She is very typical of the superstar advisors we have worked with. A person with Jan's Kolbe profile is very good at handling chaos, going with the flow, and balancing a lot of balls in the air. She would make a particularly good financial planner, because as a 4 FF, she can handle the research necessary to understand the complex issues of investment recommendations. However, Jan is the last gal we can count on to get her paper work properly filled out on time and sent to the home office with duplicates in her own filing system. It is not that Jan cannot file, it is just that she would really rather not. If her life depended on it, she could get those forms properly filled out. However, if she had to do

FIGURE 6.2 Jan Jenson's Profile

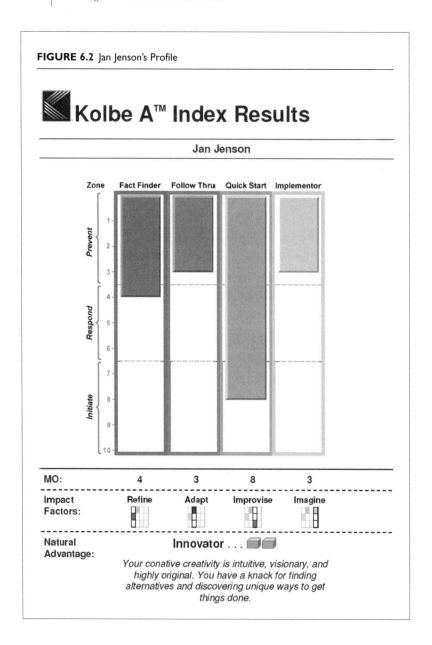

that kind of work day in, day out, over time, it would so sap her of energy, it would be the last thing Jan would want to do.

Jan, to her credit, is great in a sales meeting. Her grasp on the facts and details of the investment business, from her mid-

FIGURE 6.3 Millie Pike's Profile

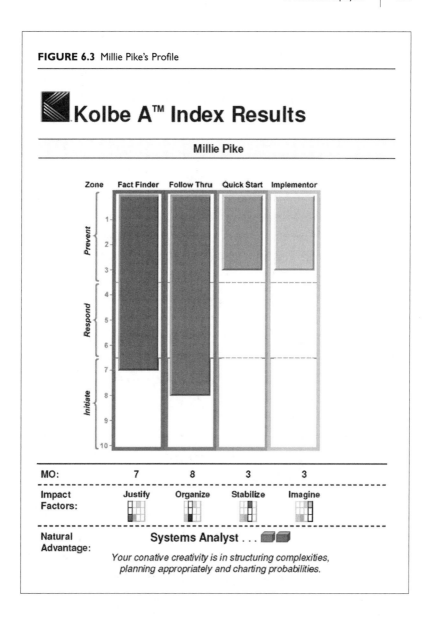

level FF and her ability to be flexible with a resistant FT and initiating QS all contribute to being a stellar financial advisor. However, if Jan is going to see more clients, she needs help. She will get bogged down in the details and service work of the business, leaving her tired and less time to do what she does best: Meet with clients and close the sale.

Four people have applied to be Jan's RSA: Brad Simmons,* Wilma Hunter,* Sally Jones,* and Millie Pike.* Let's assume we have interviewed them and they all pass the cognitive tests for the job. They have the necessary experience and their personality or affective traits would be equally a good fit. We just need to see which Kolbe fit would be better for Jan.

As we can see in Figure 6.3, Millie Pike, a 7833, at first glance appears to be the answer to Jan's needs. As an initiating FT, Millie is organized, on track, and never lets anything fall through the cracks. She meets deadlines and is great with customers. There is only one problem: Millie is in conflict with Jan in two different modes. Millie's 8 FT to Jan's 3 is a difference of 5, enough to be stressful to both parties. Also, Millie's QS, at a 3, clearly puts her in the stabilizer slot—the exact opposite end of the spectrum from Jan, who falls in the innovator category. Millie likes the status quo; Jan likes new and different. Another difference of 5 in this mode would probably be difficult for both of them to overcome. Anticipating a great deal of stress in the relationship, it would be better to pass on Millie now than find that she is not a good fit down the road.

Brad Simmons, a 5393 (see Figure 6.4), would not be a good choice as Jan's assistant. Brad has the exact same strengths and weaknesses that Jan has. If Brad is interested, he would probably be better in front of clients. The very tasks that Jan needs him to do—service requests, filling out paperwork, and keeping the office organized—are the very tasks that are draining for Brad. Let's offer Brad a junior financial advisor position and see if he enjoys sales.

Sally Jones, a 6463 (see Figure 6.5), is considered a Mediator because all of her Impact Factors land in the mid range. She is neither initiating nor resistant in any mode. Sally's profile is rare in Kolbe standards, only 10 percent of the population has three of four impact factors in the four to six range. Sally would

FIGURE 6.4 Brad Simmons's Results

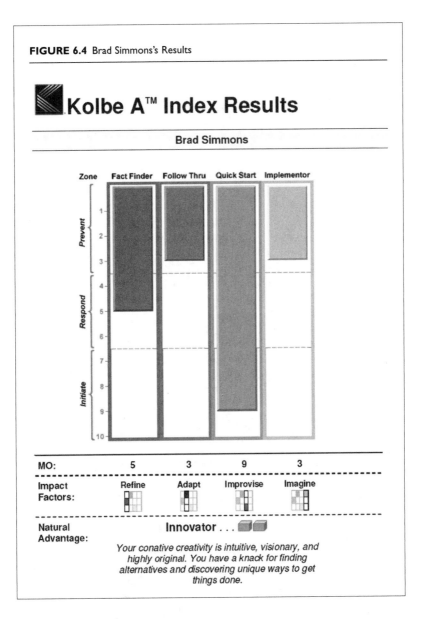

Kolbe A™ Index Results

Brad Simmons

Zone	Fact Finder	Follow Thru	Quick Start	Implementor

MO: 5   3   9   3

Impact Factors: Refine   Adapt   Improvise   Imagine

Natural Advantage: Innovator . . .

Your conative creativity is intuitive, visionary, and highly original. You have a knack for finding alternatives and discovering unique ways to get things done.

be a great person to bridge the gap if there were other people in the organization who differed significantly from Jan. However, Jan needs someone with significant FT skills. As a 4 FT, Sally probably does not have the problem-solving skills Jan needs, but could be a great addition to the team in another job.

FIGURE 6.5 Sally Jones's Profile

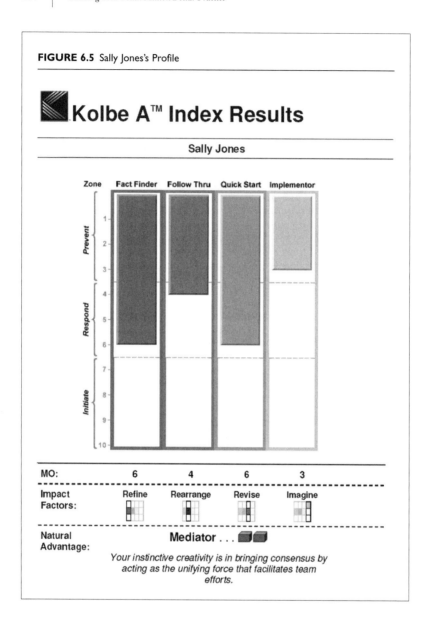

Kolbe A™ Index Results

Sally Jones

Zone	Fact Finder	Follow Thru	Quick Start	Implementor

MO:	6	4	6	3
Impact Factors:	Refine	Rearrange	Revise	Imagine
Natural Advantage:	Mediator . . .			

Your instinctive creativity is in bringing consensus by acting as the unifying force that facilitates team efforts.

Our last candidate is Wilma Hunter, whose profile is shown in Figure 6.6. Wilma is a 7654. Wilma would not be in conflict with Jan in any mode because there are no modes where there is a difference of 4 or more when comparing Wilma's Kolbe A™ to Jan's Kolbe A™. With a 7 in FF, Wilma would be able to

FIGURE 6.6 Wilma Hunters's Profile

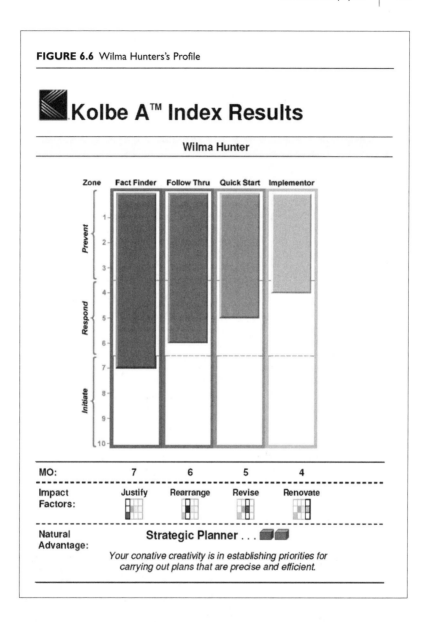

Kolbe A™ Index Results

Wilma Hunter

| Zone | Fact Finder | Follow Thru | Quick Start | Implementor |

MO: 7 6 5 4

Impact Factors: Justify Rearrange Revise Renovate

Natural Advantage: **Strategic Planner . . .**

Your conative creativity is in establishing priorities for carrying out plans that are precise and efficient.

organize priorities and do much of the research that would be needed in this position. Also with a 6 in FT, we would expect her to be able to handle the customer service requests, create process and procedures, and make sure nothing falls through the cracks. Fortunately, she is not an initiating QS, so she would help keep Jan, who never lets a day go by without a new idea, stay focused on the tasks at hand. Although Wilma may not be a perfect candidate because Jan would probably prefer someone with a little less FF, we think Wilma is the best choice of the three and should be offered the position.

Sometimes the job market is such that it is not possible to find a perfect Kolbe fit. This happened to me a few years ago when I, a 9 on the Quick-Start scale, could only find one candidate for my assistant position and she was a 3 on the Quick-Start scale. With a difference of six points between us, I am sure she felt a lot of stress. I handled the situation by acknowledging to her that there would likely be conflict between us. I made a joke about it and said, "These are the ways I am going to drive you crazy. I am going to change my mind at the last minute. I will have a dozen projects going at the same time, and I will never give you enough information when I assign you a project." Fortunately for me, her personality, the affective part of her makeup, was very cooperative. I am sure working with me was stressful, but her naturally cheerful nature came through and she made the best of a trying situation. I came to really appreciate her.

Which shows, although the Kolbe System™ is an important part of any business or personal relationship, it is not the only factor. Personality, or right-brain activities, and cognitive, or left-brain functions, also play an important role in finding the right support team.

As a manager of someone who is four or more levels of difference from you in any mode, try to think of what they need from a conative perspective to be more effective in their jobs. If the job does not require a Quick-Start mind-set, do not expect them to think like you do. Give them the freedom to solve problems in their own way. They will be empowered and present many solutions you had not considered.

Peter worked with a top-producing financial advisor in the Phoenix area who had been the strongest performer in his broker/dealer for many years. Yet the advisor had not captured his dream. There were 13 employees plus the financial advisor. The financial advisor was a 10 on the Quick Start, one of the highest Quick Starts I have ever seen. He was accommodating in fact finding, which meant he was brilliant at creating financial solutions for his clients and good at gathering the information to help avoid risk without getting bogged down in the details.

Unfortunately, the job duties for everyone in the organization ran like this: "Okay, you 13 people, this is what I need to get done—get it done." As you can imagine there was not only a lack of synergy but there was a lack of efficiency, which led to high levels of frustration for the financial advisor as well as the employees.

We came into the organization and did the Money Trail™. From that we defined the job descriptions. We never recommended that he fire anyone, just reposition the existing employees into tasks, duties, and responsibilities that matched their Kolbe profile. Within three months, revenues were up nearly 30 percent and profits had tripled (far exceeding our fees for the year). Needless to say, it was a validation of how applying the Kolbe System™ with the Money Trail™ proved to be the best way to create efficiency, trust, and success in the organization.

DELEGATION

By Peter

We all know we need to delegate. There is too much to do, and a lot of it involves things we do not like to do. Frequently, it results in an inability to do much of anything well. Every top financial advisor we have met has dealt with this in a simple way: Hire someone and assign them the work. What are the most frequent results of this strategy we have seen? High turnover, high stress, and a game of musical chairs between employees and their the tasks and duties.

Why do most people's efforts to delegate break down? Why is it when we are looking for help that the Dilbert Principle joins Murphy's Law? I believe that we all grow "gun-shy" when it comes to delegation.

Delegation is a structured process with five different levels of authority. Following the steps in Vestment's Five Levels of Delegation of Authority™, detailed later in this chapter, will set you and your team free to love coming to work, understand each other's needs, work seamlessly with one another, and build the long-term value of the practice.

Effective delegation must solve many questions. These include who do you delegate to, how do you evaluate their performance, how do you monitor their efforts, and the biggest concern: Can they do it as well as you can? How do you solve the dilemma? The need to delegate is self-evident. Experiences with delegation of authority are frequently not good ones. Many of us would rather "see that it gets done right the first time, even though I hate doing that part of it." This chapter offers a strategy on how to break the cycle.

Everyone in an organization who relies on the efforts of other people needs to learn how to delegate authority. Our own personal efforts are attached to everyone else's efforts in a practice, and the types of tasks we all do require different skills, abilities, and capabilities. Some of us love to do the detail work; others do not. Some are natural communicators and very extroverted; others feel if they are left alone they get more work done. A few of us love mathematics and number crunching, while some capture big-picture visions and inspire those around them. Everyone is unique, with unique gifts, skills, and abilities. Unfortunately, our job responsibilities and duties do not always match our own uniqueness. Delegation of authority, when understood and properly implemented and managed, sets you and your team free to prosper.

Everyone explains what to delegate. No one explains how to delegate.

Many times our view of delegating becomes a thought process that runs along the lines of "I have the authority to assign this to Judy. She may not like it, but I can have her do it anyway." What we don't recognize is the number of underlying assumptions that are contained in this thought. Without recognizing and addressing these assumptions, the effort is more likely to fail than succeed.

Here are some of the common underlying assumptions that we pass over in our desire to be free of our burden in the responsibility:

- The assigned party will have to do it.
- They understand how to do it.
- It is something they can do effectively.
- They understand what they were asked to do.
- They understand the value the task or duty provides in the greater scheme of things.
- They are capable of effectively reporting back on their activities.
- Others attached to or affected by their efforts will follow through on their efforts.
- They are capable of making the moment-to-moment decisions and value calls to succeed in their efforts.

A few years ago, I was vacationing in Colorado and was able to indulge in one of my passions, playing golf. I was teamed with a husband and wife. As our conversation developed over several holes, I asked him about his career. He told me that the sale of his manufacturing company had just moved past the period of time where he was still part of management, and that now he was retired.

I asked him if he minded sharing how much the buy-out was worth to him. He told me that he had received $40 million for two-thirds of the company stock, and did I know of anyone who was interested in the last third. I next asked when he had

Multi-Million-Dollar Principle #19

You can delegate authority, but you can only share responsibility.

started the company. "Sixteen years ago." What was the toughest part of building a business from scratch to a value of $60 million? "Trusting that others could do things as well as I could" was the reply given without a moment's hesitation. He went on to explain that his inability to delegate authority and responsibility in the early years of the business cost him years of growth, and many millions in the current stock value.

Why was it so hard? He was competent; however, he felt his direct reports were not when he provided the opportunity to share authority and responsibility. Lesson: It is the fear and the cost of failure that makes delegating so difficult.

We take many tactics to protect against failures when we delegate. One of the most common is delegating accountability along with delegating authority. This is a strategy usually known as CYA. "You are empowered with this great responsibility, but if it does not work, you and you alone are responsible." This approach is used for many reasons, including the delegator not having a clue as to how to personally make the project or duty successful, but a primary law of delegation is always violated. That primary law: You can delegate authority, but you can only share responsibility.

The Perfect Job

Everyone dreams of having a job where they only do what is fun for them. In the early phases of our professional life, our understanding of what would be "fun" is tempered by being managed. As we matured in our career, we learned the things that school does not teach us, and the good old-fashioned "paying your dues." Hopefully, as we mature in our jobs, whether that means 5 or 25 years, our understanding of what we truly enjoy in our labors begins to merge with these efforts of being prosperous and productive.

For some, our jobs never get to the point where we are primarily doing what is "fun," the things that we are naturally gifted at. For others, our jobs do include what we are naturally brilliant at, but it seems that too many other duties and responsibilities always get in the way.

Most of all, I am a pragmatist. I want people who work in a company to be spending most of their time doing things in their job duties and responsibilities that they are brilliant at. I want this not because it is fun for the employee, though that is certainly an important benefit; I want this because it is the most efficient and effective way for the company to prosper. My pragmatic nature tells me that companies that do not build a way for most of their employees to spend most of their time doing what comes naturally and with excellence is a good way to waste money.

Whether you own the practice or you are a producer in someone else's, it is critical to create a strategy that sets you free to your brilliance. Not doing it is robbing yourself and your company. This process involves five steps:

1. Self-evaluation.
2. What am I currently doing?
3. Who reports to me, and what are they brilliant at?
4. The five levels of delegation.
5. Establishing and assigning authority:

Self-Evaluation

Self-evaluation starts with making a list with four topics:

1. *At what am I brilliant?* Write down the things that you do in your job that are natural, come easily, and energize you. Perhaps you are great at talking to people to accomplish a joint task, or you are particularly good at negotiating terms and responsibilities of joint efforts. These are tasks where very little effort brings extraordinary results. Do not list your job tasks or responsibilities unless they are exactly something you are brilliant at (e.g., I love to meet with clients; I hate filling out the insurance forms).

2. *At what am I excellent?* Make a list of the things that you are very adept at, but that are not a passionate desire of your inner being (e.g., I majored in mathematics at college, and am very good at building financial plans for clients, but I view them as just another tool. I do not dream at night of the wonderful time I am going to have creating a computer model with 7,000 equations).

3. *At what am I only good?* List the things that you do in your job in which your performance is acceptable but not to a level of excellence. This may include items such as filling out a performance report, interviewing job candidates, or attending company meetings.

4. *What are the items that I should never be asked to touch?* Most of us have job duties or responsibilities that we not only do not like to do, we are not good at them. This is not a case of neglect or irresponsibility. It is just an issue of capability.

Conventional wisdom says get training or go to a continuing education class to improve your weak areas. If you are early in your career and see that more training will help your skills, by all means, follow conventional wisdom. Otherwise, I think it is a major mistake. Each of us has natural tendencies and abilities. Most of us acknowledged this among our friends in high school, and it was the reason certain people were athletes, others were musicians, and others competed in the math club. An introverted person can learn good social skills. Just do not expect them to have an easy time succeeding in an extroverted job duty. Stick to the skills and passions you love best. Build a strategy and work to eliminate the ones you do not.

I was privileged to assist a business owner client for over five years. He is brilliant in technology and sales. He is not even modestly good at being the president of the company. The greatest challenge for this owner was to acknowledge this in his skill list. When he allowed his general manager to run the business, the company prospered. When he insisted on taking back "control," it did not. Be honest with yourself, not brutal. What are the areas you should not touch? Ask others about the things you wind up doing that they feel would be better placed with someone else. These people may or may not be at your workplace, but seek input outside of yourself.

Self-Evaluation—What Am I Currently Doing?

In order to be set free to your own brilliance, you must first document what your job calls on you to do. The areas I want you to document are "macro" goals and objectives, responsibilities, and duties.

Goals and Objectives

Goals and objectives are the net sum results of what your position is to accomplish. Every job has broad goals and objectives. These are tied to the overall corporate objective. Write down your goals and objectives.

As an example, let us assume that your position is in the marketing department of a mutual fund company. The company's goals and objectives may be identified as capturing a certain market share for all their products, or as dominating their competition in five key demographic markets. Your broad goal may be "to provide timely and effective competitive analysis that enables your company to evaluate ways to increase its market share and gain dominance in five key markets." Write down your position's macro goal and objective.

Responsibilities

Responsibility is easy to define. It is where the buck stops in the fulfillment of the objectives and goals of your position. What must your position accomplish?

Every position has responsibilities. Responsibilities are different than duties. Duties are tasks, (e.g., you are a computer programmer, your *duties* include writing computer code. You are a computer programmer; your responsibility is to write bug-free efficient code). Write down your *responsibilities.* These responsibilities may include supervising the staff that report to you, creating annual budgets, participating in departmental budgeting, or ensuring that assigned projects are completed on time and at-or-under budget. Write down all the responsibilities of your position.

Duties

Duties are the defined tasks connected to your position. All positions in a company have duties. Examples of duties may include employee reviews, writing project performance reports, managing a development team through its projects, or attending departmental meetings. List all of your duties.

Who Reports to Me; At What Are They Brilliant?

In the simplest terms, delegation of authority is nothing more than sharing your own responsibilities and duties with people who report to you in order to more effectively realize the goals and objectives of your position in the company. In the same way you built your own self-evaluation, build or assign to build a self-examination document of each of the people who report to you.

The strategy for this is a simple one: We want to keep the duties and responsibilities at which we are brilliant and excellent. We want to delegate as many of the duties and responsibilities we are only good at, or should never touch, to others. If we delegate these items, they should be delegated to individuals who are brilliant at them (or at least excellent). Unless you know their core strengths and limitations, delegation is a gamble at best.

The Five Levels of Delegation of Authority

The primary reason delegation of authority fails is that those who delegate do not understand that there are five levels of delegation. To delegate authority to someone at a level that is beyond their capability, regardless of their level of brilliance or excellence, is a fast ride to failure. Not only are there five levels of delegation but there are rules that are attached to making these levels succeed.

1. *Find out and tell me.* The first level of delegation of authority asks a simple question: Is the person you wish to delegate authority to capable of gathering information and reporting on it accurately? This may seem like a very basic request, but have you ever gotten a note from a receptionist asking you to call Mr. Glockenspiel, without a telephone number, and you do not know a Mr. Glockenspiel? Three days later you find out that Mr. Gary Spiegel, a very important client, has been trying to get hold of you and was wondering why you had not called him back.

This is a simple example of "find out and tell me." The ability to gather information and report back accurately is the founding block of any delegation.

2. *Find out, think about it, and tell me.* The second level of delegation of authority is predicated on the first level being proven as valid. Once I know someone can accurately gather information and report on it, I want to know if they can apply that information in a cognitive, problem-solving way. A simple example: My new receptionist takes a call from Gary Spiegel while I am out of the office. The note to me states that Gary Spiegel called, wants a return call, and, if he calls again when I am not in, should she (the receptionist) schedule a time with him for a callback from me? This example shows that the new receptionist has proven that she can accurately gather information, report back on it, and do some simple problem solving. In our example, the receptionist showed that she understood the importance of the phone call, had determined a strategy to possibly implement at the next call from the client, and was informing me of her strategy.

3. *Find out, think about it, tell me, and do it.* The third level of delegation of authority is predicated on the second level being proven as valid. At this level I know that the individual can accurately gather information, report on it, come to conclusions on what should be done, and be assigned to do it. Another simple example: My new receptionist has taken enough calls from important clients and reviewed her strategies with me sufficient times that I authorize her to use her own best judgment on follow-up to these calls. This example displays that level three delegations can be implemented even within administrative positions. Typically, level-three delegation is indicative of an individual with a staff position.

4. *Find out, think about it, do it, and tell me.* The fourth level of delegation of authority is also predicated on the third

level being proven as valid. At this level, the individual has proven to me that the conclusions they draw and the decisions they make are consistently good. I trust their decision-making process and only want a report back on the results of their efforts. This is a line-management level of employee, usually with people reporting to them. Drawing off our last example, my receptionist has proven so effective in managing voice communications that I determined she should be promoted to the position of office manager. Once a week we meet for a report on efforts with the administrative staff.

5. *Do it, and tell me only if.* This is the fifth level of delegation of authority. At this level the individual has proven they have strong abilities in gathering information, drawing conclusions as to what is to be done, implementing solutions or changes, and keeping them consistent with the company's overall business plans, budgetary needs, and general goals and objectives. The only time we want to hear a report is *if* there is an exception to the general direction or strategy of that individual, group, or team. We want a report if there is variance from our expected objectives. This is typically an individual at an executive level of management, though it could be a team leader of a research and development project, or an individual in charge of a mature product or service the company offers.

A third-year MBA student may be able to name the five levels of delegation of authority. They may also be trained in how to evaluate job descriptions and match the levels of authority to the job positions. Perhaps they are analytic enough to even identify different levels of authority based on the position's responsibilities and duties. Does this mean that when the position has a good job description with logical levels of authority attached to it, that delegation of authority will be effective both in the position and under the position? Probably not!

Some years ago, I was introduced to a top-level executive of a Fortune 100 corporation. We became friends and met for lunch on a regular basis. His corporation had nearly perished some years ago. He had been the head of the company's Far East operations and was brought back by the new CEO for an interesting task. His assignment was to eliminate over 150 top executive positions within the corporation, and to replace a majority of the positions with individuals who were more capable of moving the company toward its new vision. He was an important part of the team that restored the global strength of the company.

Our discussion went something like this:

Me: "Can I ask you some questions?"

Him: "Of course."

Me: "These are high-level positions in your company. Did you replace them with individuals from inside the company or also from outside the company?"

Him: "Normally, we like to promote from inside the company, but there were times when we brought in people from other corporations."

Me: "How did you go about confirming that so many executives met the company's expectations in such a short period of time?"

Him: "Well, actually it was fairly easy. We would meet, I would tell them of the situation we felt their division or department was facing, and then I asked them to spend a week investigating it. The following week we would meet again and they would provide me a report. If I was satisfied with what they told me, I would tell them of another situation in the department, and ask them to evaluate it and come back to me with suggestions. If I were satisfied with what I heard, I would tell them of another circumstance within their group, and ask them to report back on both the circumstances and the strategy they would like to implement. We would agree on a course of action, which they would then go back and implement. . . ."

Me: "Wait a minute! Are you telling me that you put them one step at a time through the five levels of delegation of authority?"

Him: "Of course."

Me: "Weren't these individuals who already had level-five track records?"

Him: "Of course."

Me: "Why would you start them out at level one when the company's needs were so critical? Didn't you feel they were qualified for the positions?"

My friend leaned over the table, looked me straight in the eye, and in a very forceful voice said, *"We hire you for what you have done, but keep you for what you are doing, and don't you ever forget it!"* In other words, regardless of what your employees have accomplished in the past, they *must* prove themselves at every level of delegation of authority in each new job position.

Validating ourselves is a regular part of life. It takes place in dating, courtship, sports activities, charity efforts, community involvement, political activity, and, yes, at work. Validation at a simple level is a requirement to moving on to a greater level. We must validate ourselves, and those who report to us, at each level of authority before granting or receiving authority at the next level. This is regardless of what level of authority is assigned or required by the responsibilities and duties of the position.

This is the most common failure in delegation of authority. People who delegate usually do so because of the duties and burdens of their efforts. They want help and they want it now. Who has the time to spend patiently delegating to someone who reports back at each of the levels? They need help right now.

Multi-Million-Dollar Principle #20

The first rule of the five levels of delegation of authority: You *must* prove your staff at every level of delegation of authority in each new job position.

The ripple effect of this mind-set is terrible. The individual to whom a job or task is delegated may not be able to fulfill it to the satisfaction of their supervisor. They may be able to fulfill the task effectively, but not with all the nuances that their supervisor is inherently aware of and they are not. If my friend in the Fortune 100 company did not trust senior executives earning six-figure incomes to effectively hit the ground running during the time of severe crisis, why would anyone believe that merely assigning the task to someone during the time of personal stress would result in relief?

Delegation must occur before there is a need or crisis. The delegation process must be understood and assigned before a need arises, not during a crisis. Anyone who has lived through crisis management knows it is not a fun experience. Companies who have become trapped in perpetual crisis management are always in jeopardy of dying. When an employee does not understand the levels of authority necessary to effectively fulfill a job's duties and responsibilities, it is a ticket to crisis management. When a manager does not understand the levels of authority necessary for his staff to fulfill their job duties and responsibilities, it will radically increase the likelihood of disaster.

Only authority can be delegated—accountability and responsibility must be shared. You must understand what can be delegated and what cannot. Three things must accompany any delegation. They are:

1. Authority
2. Accountability
3. Responsibility

Authority can and must be fully delegated or there is no true power to act. Accountability and responsibility cannot be delegated. They can only be shared. Delegating accountability and responsibility is one of the oldest political games in management, and it has no good effect. Frequently, accountability and responsibility are delegated and authority is not. This is also an old political game, and one destined to fail. If you have authority, success still depends on your efforts and abilities. Accountability and responsibility can be managed, even though your manager should share them with you. Without authority you can only be accountable and responsible for efforts over which you have no control.

This is an easy rule: You must delegate authority; you can only share accountability and responsibility.

Establishing Delegation of Authority with Those Who Report to You

What is the primary objective of delegating authority to those who report to you? It is to set you free to do the things that you are brilliant at and that you do with excellence. By spending most of your time at work doing what is easiest for you, the company benefits, your employees benefit, the shareholders benefit, the stakeholders benefit, and your family benefits. To do otherwise is to cheat everyone, especially yourself.

How do you do it? Pull out the documents you created for your "self-evaluation" and "What am I currently doing?" explained earlier in chapter. Identify the items that you are only good at and that you should never touch.

Next, think about those that report to you and the makeup of their teams. Who is brilliant or has excellence in the areas that you are only good at and should never touch? Meet individually with each of these people or with them and the person they report to. Review what you would like to assign to them. They should like it. After all, you are matching an assignment to an area in which they are brilliant or excellent.

List the task, project, assignment, or authority attached to what you wish to delegate. Follow the example of my Fortune 100 friend. Review with them what the finished work will look like, then validate them one level at a time. The ripple effect of this is far different from crisis management. Everyone will have a higher perspective of the goals and objectives of your team as they relate to the company. They will see you trusting in their abilities and your willingness to delegate authority while sharing accountability and responsibility. The worst situation for any employee is to be delegated accountability and responsibility with no authority. The energy created by breaking this typical pattern creates a very healthy environment.

In Summary

- Delegation is a must!
- Delegation allows us to spend more of our time doing the things we are brilliant at while allowing others to spend more of their time the same way.
- Delegation starts with self-evaluation. Delegation culminates in helping everyone improve his or her job performance.
- Delegation has five highly defined levels.
- Delegation must be proven and validated at each level before advancing to the next.
- You can set yourself free by delegating to those who report to you.
- You can capture authority from your supervisors by understanding the rules of delegation and following a patient process.

JOB DESCRIPTIONS

The first step is building accurate job descriptions that flow out of the Money Trail™, described in Chapter 4. Each job description must contain six different elements:

1. *Mission.* How does this particular position contribute to the purpose and mission of the company?

2. *Responsibilities.* What are the job responsibilities of the position? Responsibilities are defined as what you are responsible for delivering. Note that they differ from tasks and duties.

3. *Tasks and duties.* These are specific activities required by the job.

4. *Authority.* What level of the five levels of authority does the position demand? Levels of authority can be defined either by the position itself or by specific responsibilities or tasks and duties in the position.

5. *Reporting.* To whom does the position report, who reports to the position, and who does the position work with laterally?

6. *OSHA requirements.* Does this position require someone to be able to sit for long hours in front of the computer screen, or lift weight up to certain amounts in order to do filing or office organization, etc.

These six elements, the way the position contributes to the mission and goals of the company, the job responsibilities, the job tasks and duties, the levels of authority, the reporting, and OSHA requirements make up an effective job description. Sample job descriptions can be found in the "Employment" section of the Appendix.

The question becomes, where does the Kolbe System™ fit into an effective job description? Kolbe elements are found within the responsibilities and tasks and duties of the job description. For example, if the responsibilities of a position require filling out paperwork, making sure that content and detail are completed for clients, then chances are you want a Kolbe profile that initiates in Fact Finding and initiates in Follow Thru, or initiates in Follow Thru and is adaptive in Fact Finding. Similarly, if the position requires the ability to create and manage seminars, workshops, or a radio show, the creative element is important here. In this position you may want someone who either initiates in Follow Thru or is adaptive in Quick Start, or that initiates in Quick Start and is adaptive in Follow Thru. These elements allow people to work within their natural energies in the fulfillment of job duties and responsibilities.

Basketball and Football

As the team gets larger, when you move from three to five employees, or five to ten, the job descriptions become more highly defined. This creates an environment where we transition from playing basketball to playing football. Playing basketball involves only five teammates flowing in continuous motion at any and all tasks to score points. On a football team, every position must learn its exact set of plays and execute them perfectly in order to succeed. As an organization grows, so must each job, duty, and responsibility be fulfilled in the correct manner for the company to succeed. Having employees with the most complementary Kolbe profiles allows people to work off their strengths with enthusiasm and get up every morning, thinking, "Boy, do I love my job."

How about hiring based on Kolbe profiles? The Kolbe Corporation works with many large corporate clients who have found that using accurate job descriptions, along with Kolbe profiles, provides an 80 percent probability of success in the position. This is truly an astonishing figure as other testing profiles, and other ways that human resources have used to monitor or manage potential for success, never exceed 50 percent. Some are less than that.

Now that we have people who have job responsibilities and duties that match their conative energy, how do we provide motivation and incentive for them to go above and beyond the call of duty in the practice's growth? Human resources studies that evaluate what employees look for in job satisfaction tend to highly list three elements:

1. *Being appreciated for what they do.* Are you as the supervisor praising them, acknowledging good efforts, and affirming them in their job duties and responsibilities? People want to be recognized for doing a good job.

2. *Working out of their instinctive energies.* People love their jobs, and they like when they get to do what comes naturally to them. It seems simple, and they enjoy the effort. Does the job match their conative profile?

3. *Being rewarded sufficiently for their efforts.* Are they being paid enough, and are they being offered incentives for performance?

Employee Incentive Plans

We have devised an employee incentive program that when combined with the Money Trail™ and Kolbe elements creates an opportunity for profitability that can be shared by all. This actually increases the performance of the organization without costing the owners of the practice any money. In fact, it makes them more money.

The first step is in understanding certain elements of a company's fiscal and asset management. This involves a little bit of accounting work. (See Chapter 3 on Fiscal and Asset Management.)

If you recall, breakeven is when all of the revenue is equal to all of the fixed expenses plus all the variable expenses plus depreciation plus taxes plus targeted profit. Targeted profit is what you need in cash reserves, money for growth next year, and money for risk (diversifying your services).

Our incentive program's core element is that you do not provide profit sharing to employees until the company exceeds breakeven. This means you must exceed the revenues needed to account for your targeted profit. Targeted profits are an expense, not true profitability. Again, following the guidelines, the financial advisor pays themselves a salary. They do not consider their salary "whatever is left over at the end of the month."

Commissioned employees do not participate in employee incentives. Their commission is the incentive. The higher they produce, the more their income goes up.

How do we provide employee incentives for everyone else on the team? The key element is understanding how fixed expenses do not change month to month.

Let me explain. Assume that a million-dollar financial advisor has a break-even monthly revenue of $100,000. Also assume that the practice's monthly fixed expenses are $50,000. The other expenses are made up by variable expenses, depreciation, taxes, and target profit. That means 50 percent of breakeven is in fixed expenses.

How does this relate to an employee incentive program? Quite simply, every dollar of revenue that is generated above breakeven will have $.50 of bottom-line profit. Why? Because once you have paid fixed expenses, you don't have to pay them again. In this example, 50 percent of break-even revenue is fixed, therefore, all revenue above breakeven will have approximately 50 percent profit going straight to the pretax bottom line.

A company can only increase profitability in three ways:

1. Increase revenue faster than expenses increase.
2. Decrease costs of operations.
3. Improve efficiency.

The consistent key element in all three is your employees. Only employees, including the principal, can increase revenue faster than expenses. Only employees can help you curtail the cost of operation. And only employees can improve efficiency.

Why is this important to know in an employee incentive program? If the employees believe that they will receive a percentage of profits above breakeven as an incentive, they will work to increase revenues faster than expenses, to minimize or reduce costs, and to increase efficiency. Why wouldn't they? Some of that money is going into their own pockets.

The question becomes: How much of the profits do they share?

This varies with the number of employees and size of the organization. Generally, we recommend that it should be somewhere between 20 percent and 33 percent of all profits above breakeven. Many of you may be thinking, "What! 20 percent to 33 percent of my profits going to the employees?"

I will explain. Assume we have an organization that determined 25 percent of profits above breakeven would go toward an employee incentive program. This means if I were your employee, I'd be telling you, "Give me a quarter and I'll give you a dollar back. How many quarters will you give me if I give you a dollar back?"

How can this be? It is quite simple. By offering 25 percent of profits above breakeven, I will generate that dollar for you by increasing revenue faster than expenses, by containing and reducing costs, and by improving the efficiency of our operation.

How effective is this? I'll never forget an experience we had with Alexandria Financial Advisors.* We initiated the employee incentive program that called for 20 percent of profits above breakeven to be distributed quarterly. I happened to be in the office the day the first employee incentive checks were distributed. The receptionist was a single mom with two teenage children. She was the lowest paid employee at the practice, and it was the best job she had ever had. When the president handed out her employee incentive check, she immediately said, "I think you gave me the wrong check."

The president took the envelope back and said, "I'm sorry, I didn't mean to." He then opened the envelope and said, "No, that's your name on the check," and handed it back to her. She immediately broke down into tears. Why? The check was for over $2,100 in after-tax money, more money than she had ever received in one place in her life.

How did this happen? She was a contributing factor to profits above breakeven and that was her share of the profits, $.25

on the dollar. What was even more telling occurred two weeks later. The president came into the office in the morning, unlocked the door, turned on the lights and sat down, and did his morning e-mail and paperwork. He wandered out of the office to begin visiting various teams within the organization.

When he got back to his office, the doors were shut and the air-conditioning and lights were turned off. Wondering what had happened, he opened the doors, turned on the lights and air-conditioning and did a few more tasks. He then went to a lunch appointment.

When he returned from lunch, the doors were closed and the air-conditioning and lights were turned off. He asked the receptionist, "I am a little confused. Every time I come back to my office, the doors are shut and the air-conditioning and lights are turned off. Do you know who is doing this?"

The receptionist said, "Well, I am. Remember, those things are monthly fixed costs, and we want to reduce those expenses as much as possible. It does show up on our employee incentive program."

Summary

How do you create a work environment where people love what they are doing and work daily to improve efficiency, decrease costs, and increase revenue faster than expenses?

You create accurate job descriptions out of the Money Trail™ reflected in their Kolbe profile, hire people accordingly, and motivate them through employee incentives that reward them for increasing efficiency, revenue, and profitability.

The Kolbe Corporation has a number of powerful tools that can make the new-hire selection process much easier:

- *RightFit*™. When you are thinking about hiring a new employee, you and others in your organization can fill out a quick questionnaire. Then the corporation will provide you with a range in each of their four modes of what would be an appropriate hire in this particular position.

- *Kolbe B™*. This evaluates what an employee believes are the requirements of their position and shows if there is any stress between their true talents and their duties.
- *Kolbe C™*. This allows a manager to evaluate what abilities they think are appropriate in a particular position. It is one of the key pieces of information that is appropriate when determining the RightFit™.
- *Team Tactix®* This report looks at an entire team and predicts how efficient and profitable they are going to be.

Using Team Tactix® and RightFit™ requires working with a certified Kolbe advisor.

We recommend that you consider starting with Kolbe A™ profiles for you and everyone on your staff. You can take these tests on line, at http://www.kolbe.com/vestment.

Performance Reviews

Another critical factor in employee management is conducting periodic performance reviews. Although many financial advisors did conduct employee reviews, very few had well-documented, consistent performance review forms that evaluated elements of attitude, skills, efficiency, and relationships with other employees and customer-satisfaction level.

Multi-Million-Dollar Principle #21

Be more than fair to your employees.

We have designed employee evaluations with a weighting system that monitors all employees. These evaluations are also used to determine how the distribution of employee incentives and bonuses occurs. It allows those employees who have a great attitude and provide a lot of value to the business to reap a greater percentage of the profit sharing so that the incentives are not just a function of wage level.

The evaluation form we designed for our small business clients can be found in the Appendix. Electronic versions can be ordered at our Web site: VestmentAdvisors.com.

Another common issue we saw among financial advisors was the hiring of relatives. This usually started with a spouse and could extend to children, cousins, uncles, nieces, and nephews. We do not want to make a wholesale statement that all of these people are unqualified for their positions; however, many of them looked like charity hires to us. One firm's owners insisted on hiring their 30-year-old son to provide administrative skills. Unfortunately he had never really kicked his cocaine habit. Dad, the financial advisor, did not want to believe his son was still heavily into his addiction. It created havoc in the office as the other employees had to deal with an employee who was wildly emotional and frequently too strung out to work.

Hiring family members in a financial services practice comes fraught with many other dangers as well. It is difficult to establish professional business lines of authority when the relational dynamics of the family play over the practice. This always occurs and usually not for the better. Much of our initial time in working with clients is spent in helping them get the right person on the bus in the right seat and the wrong people off the bus. Naturally, this is extremely difficult when dealing with family.

No matter who you are hiring, it is important that their cognitive skills and their relational abilities, as well as their conative instincts as profiled on a Kolbe A™ index, match the job descriptions. Then treat your family members just as you would any other employee.

M ulti-Million-Dollar Principle #22

Hire based on the talent you need, not on family relationships.

OTHER PROBLEM PERSONNEL ISSUES

We have seen two other problems with personnel that can negatively impact any organization.

The first was an employee running an outside business within the practice. A few years ago we had a client in the hardwood floor industry who could not understand why her best salesperson's production had fallen off so dramatically. She did a little sleuthing and learned the ugly truth. He was managing his home-based business out of her office and on her time! This is great work if you can get it—getting paid by an employer to build your own business that you should be doing after hours. A survey of the salesperson's office revealed many products, inventory, and database all intermingled with the hardwood floor materials, his real job. Needless to say this employee did not remain long in their company.

The second thing we have found has been hard-core pornography on employee computers. We have also found employees using office time for inappropriate personal activities like computer dating services. Most people do not realize that with the right computer skills, you can easily trace who has been where on any computer, what they have been looking at, and what they have been storing—even when they think they have erased it.

There is no room for these types of behaviors within a financial services practice. The following will help you to avoid these problems:

- Make sure your employee manual references that this behavior is not tolerated and will be grounds for dismissal.

- Make sure your employees know you retain the right to review all the items on their computer, including e-mail and instant messages.
- Either through your own technology skills or through third-party service providers, review your employees' computers to make sure these things are not taking place in your practice.

Employee Performance Evaluation

The purpose of the standard employee evaluation process is to improve job performance and morale due to an atmosphere of continuous, objective feedback. Most employees want to do as good a job as possible. This does not always mean working harder but it does mean working more effectively. The objective employee evaluation, coupled with a coaching interview, is a means of achieving this goal.

Unfortunately, the use of an employee evaluation system can be intimidating to an employee. Most employees have a certain negative or fearful reaction to an evaluation. However, the intent should not be to find fault, but to use this method to develop better employees and a better corporate environment. In addition, many supervisors need help on working with employees and coaching them to better performance. The system, outlined below, is intended to be positive and constructive for each employee and their supervisor, as well as for the company. When followed correctly it can be effective in improving performance and morale, and even the bottom line.

We usually recommend a quarterly evaluation because it ties into the bonus system. At the very least, use a semiannual evaluation cycle. To wait longer can lead to misunderstandings becoming more pronounced and taking longer to resolve.

An effective evaluation procedure gives management a way to recognize a strong performance and to strive for improvements in a weak performance. The experience must always be positive and viewed as a benefit to the organization as a whole. Even a substandard review can be viewed as positive to the employee if it provides the means for them to improve their job performance.

The performance evaluation has the following main objectives:

1. To evaluate how the job is being performed and to determine what areas, if any, need improvement.
2. To evaluate short- and long-term potential for new duties and responsibilities.
3. To recognize weaknesses or limitations and turn them into strengths.

Performance evaluation is a continuous process and must not be restricted to the formal quarterly written evaluation. Supervisors should have regular, informal discussions with their subordinates throughout the year. This eliminates any "surprises" for the employee when they are formally reviewed.

The informal discussions establish:

- How the job is going.
- What problems, if any, there have been.
- What specifically is expected over the next three to six months.
- Short-term and long-term goals
- Status of key projects and initiatives

The formal review does the following:

- Informs the employee: 1) how their supervisor rates their job performance, and 2) the supervisor's performance expectations over the next quarter, six months to one year.
- Allows the employee to comment on their evaluation and their future with the organization.

- Provides a permanent record of review for purposes of career development, training, promotions, pay increases, and other potential human resource and employment issues.
- Establishes an objective criteria that is used for the employee incentive process.

Some suggested control systems you can use:

- Set up a database with the name of the employee, job title, supervisor's name, anniversary date, etc.
- Evaluate all new employees at the end of 45 days and 90 days, then on the anniversary date every quarter thereafter.
- The designated control person fills out the headings on an employee evaluation form along with the date the completed form is due back (usually one week). This form is then forwarded to the employee's supervisor.
- If the completed form is not returned within the week, the supervisor is notified that the evaluation is overdue.

Evaluation Ratings

Evaluations must be based on the supervisor's judgment of the employee's actual performance, not on the comments and opinions of fellow employees.

The overall employee evaluation must reflect the combination and culmination of events during the entire evaluation period. Single events of outstanding or faulty performance should be considered in the entire context of the rating period. The following tendencies need to be recognized and avoided to keep the ratings as objective as possible:

- *Halo effect.* Rating the employee the same in every category based on a general opinion of their job performance. Some employees do such a good job in one area, we want to give them better scores than they deserve in other categories. Each category must be evaluated separately and objectively.

- *Bias.* Rating the employee based on whether the supervisor likes or dislikes that individual.
- *Undue credit for length of service.* Rating an employee based on their tenure instead of the quality of work performed. In other words, thinking they must be doing an adequate job as they have worked here "X" years.
- *Personal projection and self-identifications.* Sometimes we have a tendency to over reward an employee because they are so much like us, and we identify with the employee's personality, appearance, work habits, etc. As a result, we may assign them a higher rating than would normally be deserved.
- *Ratings inflation.* Giving higher ratings out of a desire to please and remain in a positive light with the employee.
- *Tight ratings.* Rating all employees below standards because the supervisor is a "perfectionist."
- *Personal competitiveness.* Giving low ratings because the supervisor perceives that individual as a challenge or threat to their own job security.

The following notes offer an explanation of ratings and describe standards expected, rather than comprehensive definitions. Raters should use their judgment in determining other factors that should be taken into account for particular work situations.

Excellent–5

- Overall performance is characterized by exceptional high-quality and quantity of work in accomplishing tasks and projects. All duties and responsibilities are conducted in a professional manner. Performance is integrated very well with the overall activities of the corporation, and no direct assistance other than general guidance is necessary. This results in superior contributions on a regular basis.

Confident reaction under stress and sureness of approach at all times indicate a high order of mature judgment and initiative.

- Uses job-related skills in a superior way, and aggressively seeks out and assumes responsibilities that are above and beyond the position requirements. Contributes new ideas and ways to improve operational or procedural matters regularly.
- The employee has an excellent attitude and is cooperative both in team exercises and in individual projects.

Good–4

- Overall performance approached excellent in terms of completion of tasks and projects. Requires a degree of supervision that is typical for the employee's position and experience level. All responsibilities and duties are conducted in a professional and judicious manner.
- Makes a significant contribution to overall effectiveness of the company. Seeks out and assumes responsibilities that are beyond job requirements. Efficiently uses time and resources in carrying out assignments.

Average–3

- Performs all duties and responsibilities in an adequate and comprehensive manner. Little need for improvement. Generally works independently.
- Handles work in a professional manner and seeks out work in a related area.
- Makes contribution to the overall effectiveness of the organization.

Fair–2

- Performance of most duties is adequate and acceptable in quality and quantity of work necessary to accomplish tasks and responsibilities.

FIGURE 6.7 Employee Performance Evaluation Form

Name: Date:

Position: Supervisor:

Instructions: Indicate your rating of this employee by circling the number that best indicates or describes the employee's performance for the particular criteria. You may use a decimal (e.g., 3.5) to be more specific in the appropriate box, and in the score blank to the left. Total the score to evaluate the overall rating. Add comments where appropriate.

1. Attitude: Does the employee possess an acceptable attitude toward fellow employees, supervisors, and work assigned?

   Score 1.   2.   3.   4.   5.

2. Attendance: Is the employee at work on a regular basis?

   Score 1.   2.   3.   4.   5.

3. Appearance: Does the employee's appearance and personal grooming represent the image and standards of (Your Firm's Name Here) to its customers and stakeholders?

   Score 1.   2.   3.   4.   5.

4. Punctuality: Is the employee punctual and on time?

   Score 1.   2.   3.   4.   5.

5. Dependability: Is the employee's communication accurate and unbiased?

   Score 1.   2.   3.   4.   5.

6. Dependability: Does the employee fulfill assigned tasks and duties as directed?

   Score 1.   2.   3.   4.   5.

7. Adaptable/Flexible: Changes in job assignments or other issues are willingly accepted.

   Score 1.   2.   3.   4.   5.

8. Motivation: Is the employee self-motivated and willing to perform assigned tasks/duties?

   Score 1.   2.   3.   4.   5.

9. Decision Making: Does employee make timely and appropriate decisions when required without supervisor's assistance?

   Score 1.   2.   3.   4.   5.

(continued)

FIGURE 6.7 Employee Performance Evaluation Form, continued

10. Decision Making: Does the employee seek supervisory advice and decisions during appropriate situations?

    Score 1.   2.   3.   4.   5.

11. Job Knowledge: Does the employee possess adequate knowledge of their job?

    Score 1.   2.   3.   4.   5.

12. Productivity: Does the employee produce the volume of work at the speed and consistency expected by you?

    Score 1.   2.   3.   4.   5.

13. Quality: Does the employee's production quality consistently meet standards?

    Score 1.   2.   3.   4.   5.

14. Accuracy: Is work error-free with infrequent checks needed?

    Score 1.   2.   3.   4.   5.

15. Comprehension: Is employee able to understand and retain instructions satisfactorily?

    Score 1.   2.   3.   4.   5.

16. Communication: Is the employee able to express his/her thoughts effectively through either written or verbal communications with others on their work team?

    Score 1.   2.   3.   4.   5.

17. Communication: Is the employee able to express his/her thoughts effectively through either written or verbal communication with people on work teams in other departments of the company?

    Score 1.   2.   3.   4.   5.

18. Safety: Does the employee work safely and comply with current safety and legal policies?

    Score 1.   2.   3.   4.   5.

19. Housekeeping: The office and work areas kept organized and free from hazards.

    Score 1.   2.   3.   4.   5.

20. Bonus: An additional score of up to five points may be added for work above and beyond the call of duty.

    Score 1.   2.   3.   4.   5.

FIGURE 6.7 Employee Performance Evaluation Form, continued

Employee Evaluation Comments

Areas of strengths

Areas of weaknesses/limitations

Action plan for improvement

Employee comments

Employee signature   **Date:**

Supervisor's signature   **Date:**

Manager's signature   **Date:**

Evaluation Ratings
The evaluation of an employee is based on the total score arrived at by adding up the points for each of the categories rated. The total score will indicate the employee's overall evaluation as outlined below.

0–20   Employees scoring this low should probably be terminated. Their performance is far too low and chances for improvement are marginal.

20–40   Employees scoring in this range are considered marginal. They should be informed that if there is no improvement on their next evaluation, you will consider terminating their employment. Note: Be careful how this is worded. The employee may find other employment, and quit when you have not planned for a change in personnel.

40–60   This is the range for average performance. Most employees will score in this range. Improvement should be expected over several evaluations.

60–80   Evaluations in this range are very desirable. Employees who score in this range demonstrate above-average performance in their position.

80–100 This is the highest level of performance. Few employees will score consistently at this level. Only the top performers obtain it.

- Fulfills job description responsibilities.
- May hesitate to undertake work outside their defined area.
- Requires direction and review of major parts of assignments.

Poor–1

- Performance barely meets minimum acceptable standards in most instances, but is unsatisfactory in some cases.
- Improvement is necessary; assignments are occasionally completed late and/or are incomplete.
- Detailed direction and frequent progress checks are usually required.
- The employee is of questionable ability to meet job requirements and must be either reassigned to a position of lesser responsibilities or terminated.

Managing the Evaluation Process

Confidentiality is extremely important during the evaluation process. Keep the form in a secure place when not in use.

Circle the appropriate rating using the rating scale contained in this procedure.

Set aside the completed form for a day or two to allow you to reflect and ensure your objectivity. The supervisor's immediate superior may wish to review the evaluation before you discuss it with the employee.

Evaluation Interview

Select a place that is both private and without interruptions when meeting with the employee to review the evaluation. Several days prior to the evaluation, provide a copy to the employee so they can rate themselves on their copy of the form.

In conducting the evaluation interview, it is important for the supervisor to follow these guidelines:

- Never allow personal feelings to influence what is said to the employee.
- The discussion should be kept on a professional level, not a personal one. Personal comments are inappropriate.
- The employee should never be allowed to control the interview.

Discuss the evaluation form with the employee and explain how each category was rated. Specific examples should be cited whenever possible because an employee who does not understand their evaluation is less likely to try to improve their performance. Recognize an employee's strengths and reinforce good performance with praise, not just during the evaluation review but throughout the year.

When discussing weaknesses, be sure to have suggestions for improvements. This counseling is an integral part of the evaluation process because the objective is to improve the employee's overall performance and behavior patterns. Most employees want to know where they stand and how they can improve. Obtain a commitment from the employee to correct, or at least improve in, any of the problem areas noted. Let the employee realize that you will expect an improvement. In some cases, the employee will be required to receive further training or education.

Encourage the employee to make comments because the evaluation interview is a dialogue between the supervisor and the employee. Both the supervisor and the employee must sign the form upon completion. Give the employee a copy of the signature page. The original is forwarded to upper management to review and give final approval before it is placed in the employee's personnel file.

A supervisor should complete periodic informal progress reports following the performance review, carrying on a continuous exchange to identify and correct problems before they become serious.

Management Tips for Performance Reviews

- Do not wait until review time to let your staff know what is expected of them. Give them plenty of time to work on the specific goals, standards, and deadlines you expect them to meet. Explain how you plan to evaluate and reward their performance. You should also give them a copy of the evaluation questionnaire and let them evaluate themselves before you meet to review your evaluation.
- Keep a written record of each subordinate's performance throughout the period so that you can cite specific examples to support your criticisms, comments, or compliments during the review session.
- Keep the review focused on the particular individual's performance, showing that you care about them and their career. Otherwise, it will appear that you are just going through the motions.
- Whenever possible, try to base your judgments on observable behavior, not general opinions or impressions. Even when it involves rating personality or character traits, try to recall specific examples of such traits in actual practice on the job.
- Handling the interview of the failing individual:
  - There is a good chance that they are aware of their substandard work (or ineffectiveness) and may welcome the opportunity to discuss it with you.
  - Encourage the individual to talk and offer solutions. Do not solve the problem yourself. The employee has ownership of the problem; give them ownership for the solution. You can help guide them, but do not do it yourself.
  - Do not get involved in emotional problems. Refer them to the appropriate professionals.

Problem Areas to Avoid

- Avoid dwelling on the weaknesses of the employee.
- Do not use words that denote blame such as *guilty, fault, mistakes,* or *not logical.* These terms tend to degrade the employee rather than build them up.
- Do not compare them to others or yourself.

KEY POINTS

1. You cannot build the multi-million-dollar practice without help. Finding the right employees is important; delegating to them is paramount.
2. Most financial advisors hire someone they like and trust, someone like themselves. This creates problems in the organization.
3. Conation or drive is about the person's problem solving abilities and how they approach work. It is separate from intelligence, emotion, or personality type. It is our MO, measured by the Kolbe A™ index.
4. Leaders, managers, and supervisors—you can optimize individual and group performance by assigning jobs suited to the instinctive strengths of those reporting to you, or you can watch your company become stagnant. Doing it right results in
   - improving morale by allowing everyone the freedom to be themselves;
   - building synergistic, profitable, and efficient teams;
   - using time more effectively; and
   - allowing people to be rewarded for unique energy.
5. Everyone in an organization who has job responsibilities that include efforts from other people needs to learn how to delegate authority.

6. The organization's most valuable asset is its personnel. A key element in motivating an employee is a periodic, formal performance evaluation. It must assess the employee's value to the company in an equitable and objective manner.

7. An effective evaluation program will
   * indicate the organization's appreciation of good employees;
   * help improve average and substandard employees;
   * serve as a key element in any decision to eliminate marginal employees; and
   * serve as the basis for wage and salary increases.

8. Only the most recent evaluation should be the basis for any wage or salary increase. The main factor must be the improvement in either the overall score or in the individual categories.

9. The Kolbe System™ helps you find people with the right MO to complement you and others on the team.

10. Too many practices have a "here is the work, get it done" philosophy that can frustrate everyone and prevent efficiency.

11. What may be simple for one Kolbe profile may literally make another person with a different profile physically ill. When you are working within your natural instincts, you have increased productivity and reduced stress.

Chapter

7

DEFINED SALES SYSTEM THAT BECOMES THE "NO-SELL SALE™"

Prosperity Factor #7
Defined sales system—an orderly course of action
that naturally leads to an easy, painless sale

By Katherine

F. Scott Fitzgerald said, "The rich are different from you and me." Hemmingway, always quick on the uptake, responded, "Yes . . . they have money."

I have always felt the same way about superstars. Why would some people be easily making over a million dollars a year, while others, just as smart and just as dedicated, make only $50,000 or $200,000? I originally assumed that the superstars must be different from you and me. They must have some talent or gift that eludes the rest of us to make them so much more successful.

After sitting in on dozens of sales presentations made by numerous superstars, I discovered, just like the wealthy, there was one thing the superstar advisors had that set them apart: a system, a system so powerful they could not help but make money if they diligently followed it.

Each superstar had a clearly defined, orderly method that easily led to a simple, pain-free sale. The process was so successful that even inexperienced advisors who would join the superstar's firm could make a million-dollar income, just by sticking to the firm's established sales process.

We call this method the "No-Sell Sale™." It is a no-sell system, because the advisors are not involved in a hard-sell push to sell products. Advisors focus on building a relationship as a trusted consultant and friend whose goal is to help the client solve problems. It is a series of well-defined steps we call dominos, that when carefully choreographed, easily and effortlessly lead to closing the business.

WHY THE NO-SELL SYSTEM WORKS

A few years ago, we helped a broker/dealer implement our No-Sell Sale™ system throughout their entire sales force. This was crucial to the broker/dealer's turnaround, because they found that they had to be different to compete with other firms. In the process of rolling out the new system to the field, I was asked to give a number of presentations about the sales system we had created for them and elaborate on my personal experiences using this system to build my client base. Of course, all the audience wanted to know was how successful it was. I told them the truth—most superstar advisors' closing ratios are somewhere between 80 percent and 95 percent. My own personal closing ratios were no different.

Little did I realize what an uproar this would cause. I later discovered some naysayers were actually calling me the biggest liar in the world. After all, if my closing ratio was this high, why was I teaching these techniques? Why wasn't I working as a financial advisor?

As a person who strongly values the truth, I was cut to the quick when I realized they thought I was lying. It took me a long time to figure out why they had such a hard time believing I had actually closed more than 90 percent of my cases using this system. Finally, I realized that I had to put things into perspective for them. I had to give them the context, or a frame of reference, so they could understand the truth.

The reason this system worked so well is the dominos were lined up perfectly. Each and every domino was neatly in line so closing the sale became almost inevitable.

So here is the reality—I would love to take credit for creating this system, but the truth is we just discovered, refined, and enhanced this system. We did not create it.

As I stated in the opening pages of this book, you do not have to be brilliant or talented for this to work—you just have to stick to the system.

This is the inside scoop on why superstars close so many sales. First, a few of these superstars are natural salespeople. They were born that way. These were the kids who made a lot of money selling lemonade when they were eight years old. There were a few others who actually studied sales techniques with big trainers like Tom Hopkins or Zig Ziglar.

However, most of the superstars were very middle-of-the-road salespeople. The reason they were able to succeed was they had a great system, a superb foundation under them. They could not help but make money because the system, with all of its dominos, was so good. It was not that they were super salespeople, it was they were following a step-by-step program that worked. And they never deviated from the proven formula.

Nor did the system just work for a select few. I watched first-hand how midlevel financial advisors were turned into superstars just by following the system. One woman, who was previously with another brokerage firm, had been consistently making about $200,000 a year. She transferred to the superstar firm and in her first year with the new firm she made $1.2 million. She knew the system worked, and she never deviated from it. She did not try to reinvent the wheel. She just stuck to it. Another rep, a man less than 30 years old, was bringing down $750,000 by his second year with a superstar firm—and this was working with small accounts.

To be fair, not everyone fit the system. I can think of one advisor at American Dream.* Martin* was a super smart CPA/CFP®, with a lot of planning experience. In fact he was smarter and more experienced than their entire case-writing unit that created the financial plans the advisors used with the clients. Martin did not like the plans created by the planning team, did not trust the plans, and did not use the plans.

Martin created his own plans on an Excel spread sheet. They were probably great plans, but while Martin was spending a lot of time crafting the perfect financial plan, he was violating rule number one: American Dream financial advisors only meet with clients and close the sale—everything else is delegated.

The time Martin spent on creating his own plans took away valuable face time with clients. The end result? He only spent about one-half as much time meeting with clients as the other advisors and, as a consequence, his income was about half. It created so much consternation among the partners they asked Martin to leave the firm. Though he was a great planner, he just was not suited to American Dream's system. Martin had a process he

Sales System Report Card

A+

liked. However, Martin's process was not going to get him to a million dollars per year because it was too labor intensive. Martin moved to a firm whose system fit his personality.

Multi-Million-Dollar Principle #23

If you want to be wildly successful, follow a system that works.

Because the superstars were doing so many things right, we have combined their systems below along with the suggestions we made to make their great systems even better.

THE DOMINO EFFECT

The No-Sell Sale™ system is like setting up a series of dominos. This means the activities of the firm work so smoothly that all roads naturally lead to the same destination: a sale that looks on the surface to be almost effortless. We think of this as the domino effect. There may be hundreds of dominos to get the proper client experience and the right outcome. If lined up properly, leaning slightly on the first domino will eventually lead to the last domino falling over. The last domino is closing the sale. Taken individually, each step or domino may seem inconsequential, but taken as a whole, and lined up properly, it is quite easy to knock the last domino down by just tapping lightly on the first one.

In one sense, every tactic in this book, even behind the scenes operation strategies, are all dominos that lead to closing more sales. Although it would be impossible to list all the numerous dominos that need to line up to have an easy sale, here are some of the key ones that we create for our clients. Before we review these though, it would helpful to go back to Chapter 4 and review the model client experience. That model experience is what forms the framework for the No-Sell Sale™ system because once you have identified the kind of experience you want your clients to have at each step of the process, you have identified many of the dominoes that establish the foundation of your own No-Sell Sale™.

This particular sales process, outlined below, was designed for a two-meeting close that could be adapted by advisors all across the country. The first meeting was designed to build trust and to have the client move forward with a plan. The second meeting was to present the plan and close the product sales. We recognize there are other successful systems that use three or more meetings. We also clearly understand that even two-meeting closes can turn into three or four in certain circumstances. If you prefer to use more meetings in your sales system, just adapt these steps to fit your process.

To simplify, I have broken this system down to six major stages, in this chronological order:

1. Marketing and prospecting
2. First meeting
3. Analysis and preparation
4. Second meeting
5. Monitor and modify meeting
6. Retention program

1. Marketing and Prospecting

The compelling story or differentiation. There are a number of things that must be in place before a prospect ever walks in your door. As we discussed in the marketing chapter, every superstar had discovered something unique about their firm that made them stand out in the minds of the investor. We call this the compelling story. Once the firm identified their compelling story, it was presented to the clients and prospects in every possible way. It was on brochures, in ads, in seminars, and every other means used by the advisors to market themselves. Everyone in the firm, even the newest receptionist, understood the firm's differentiation and could recite it easily.

The financial advisors were constantly educating the client on the firm's point of differentiation and their investment style. This was done through seminars, radio shows, newsletters, face-to-face presentations, and any other available means. Once the financial advisor landed on a differentiation that worked, they used every possible chance to reinforce it with the client.

Mercury* had a big focus on improving retirement income by maximizing distribution strategies that reduced taxes. Some firms call this net planning, or planning from a net perspective. This became the focus of every seminar and client meeting. It was prominently displayed in all the corporate brochures.

Chicago Capital Investors* (CCI) had a different approach. Their differentiation was their "team of experts." CCI had developed talking points around their differentiation that went like this: "I do not know everything, after all I am just a farm boy from Iowa. It is easy to stump me. However I do know where to go to get more information. That is why I am glad I work for a firm where we have a whole team of experts. We have a team in our planning department to help us with the right strategies. We have a team in the tax department to help us with reducing your taxes, we have a team in the insurance department to help find the most cost-effective insurance alternatives, and we have a team in our investment department to help you get just the right investment for you."

This "team of experts" concept was so persuasive they were actually able to bring over investors who had been happy clients at other firms. CCI found the team concept raised the client's comfort level because the investor was not dealing with just one person—but a whole team is looking at their financial picture and making recommendations. That also meant if anything happened to Charlie, there would be a lot of people around to keep the plan moving on track.

Advance collateral. Any written materials received in advance by the prospect are professionally printed and designed. They reflect the right image and brand of the firm including their compelling story. For CCI, we helped them upgrade their collateral to reflect their differentiation. I recommended that they use pictures of people rowing or competing in crew competitions. If pictures are worth a thousand words, prospects saw a group of six people, in a boat, all rowing in harmony, with one person, the coxswain, bellowing out instructions over the bull-horn. Message: If we all pull together, we can win this race.

Bios. One piece of collateral is particularly helpful in making clients feel more comfortable—the full-page resume, or bio, on each financial advisor. Once again, there are well-written bios that help close the sale and there are run-of-the-mill bios that are so boring they may detract from closing the sale. Many firms do not bother with this crucial domino. For instance, one large broker/dealer I know created a bio for every rep. Unfortunately, they were cheaply printed in black and white on a third of an 8.5"×11" piece of paper. The photos of the advisors were difficult to see, about the size of a postage stamp, and not particularly good. The copy consisted of four paragraphs. Three of them were the same for every rep. One was slightly different telling how long the rep had been with the firm. There was nothing there that felt friendly or that encouraged the prospect to want to get to know the advisor. These bios were so bad, they would have been better off not using them at all.

Contrast that with a quality bio, like the one I used when I sat in front of investors testing out the No-Sell Sale™. A copy of it is in the Appendix. The photo is top quality, the piece is four-color and there is a lot of personal information about me, including my family and hobbies. These build connections with a prospect and are mailed to them prior to the first meeting. They can find something there they relate to. I know these bios were effective, because at the end of the first meeting with a new prospect, I would ask if they had any questions about me or my background. About 80 percent of the time they would say, "No, we read your bio." If they did not like what they had read, they would have stayed home.

A short fact finder is sent to the prospect to organize their information before the initial meeting. Most superstar firms sent the prospects a short paper form to fill out in advance of the meeting, which usually matched their software to make it easier to input the data and complete the final plan. Some clients had a difficult time completing the questionnaire. Either they did not have easy access to all their information or they just did not want to take the time to fill out the form. Filling out the form can be stressful for some clients, so stressful they will want to postpone their meeting with the financial advisor. Obviously this is the last thing the advisor wants. When that happened, clients were advised to just bring in copies of their statements and other key documents like tax returns and they were assured it would be no problem—the advisor would help them sort through the paperwork at the meeting.

Trust is built in advance of the first meeting. Before the prospect even set foot in the advisor's office for the first time, the firm had already reached a certain level of trust in the mind of the client. This trust helped eliminate fears, making it easier to close the sale.

There were numerous ways that trust could be built before the first office meeting. Some superstars built trust through a radio show, others used seminars. All recognized that even the person who answered a prospect's telephone calls could help make a prospect more comfortable and reduce their fears. Some firms did such a good job at this that they even created scripts for those answering the phones.

Marketing programs, including radio shows, ads, seminars, referrals, and events, all carry a consistent message that highlights the firm's differentiation. Charlie Chicago would frequently mention his team of experts on the radio show. They never missed an opportunity to maximize their difference. The mere fact that all marketing messages were consistent built trust.

Internal staff would promote the individual financial advisor with enthusiasm and excitement. Every person in the marketing department and anyone who might answer the phone should always be instructed on how important it is to be a cheerleader for the firm and for an individual financial advisor. The script might go like this:

> "I know you are going to enjoy working with Sarah Thompson.* We are so lucky to have her here. She is very experienced, a CFP®, and most of all she takes really good care of her clients. They all love her."

This simple third-party endorsement helps to set the stage for building trust and making it easier to close the relationship

Preclosed by the time they come into the office. Part of the reason these firms have such high closing ratios is the client was predisposed to make a purchase by the time they entered into the office. Unlike firms that are dependent on cold calling for appointments, these firms had the benefit of prospects calling in and requesting to meet with them. As the prospects are making the initial calls, they are already motivated to buy. This was accomplished through a marketing system designed to have the prospect call for an appointment—the exact opposite strategy of many firms who rely on the advisor making an outbound call to encourage the prospect to come into the office for a review.

2. First Meeting/Initial Interview

The purpose of the initial interview is simple: to build trust and close the prospect on creating a financial plan. Here are some of the dominos that help make that easier:

Predictable client experience. In Chapter 4 we discussed the model client experience. One of the key concepts is to make sure each client has a similar, predictable experience with the firm. Superstars did not change things—the materials sent to client number 450 were the same as those sent to client number 392. The mere fact that the experience is comfortably predictable in the client's mind, like going to Starbucks, helps build trust and reduces the client's fear of working with the advisor.

A good first impression. The superstars' offices reflected quality and made a good first impression. They were generally well appointed and tasteful, resembling a successful law firm. The offices were neat and tidy, and frequently had fireplaces, real wood paneling, and oriental rugs. High-quality artwork was also prominent along with fresh flowers. Nothing in the offices looked like the prospect might be facing a sales process.

There were no prospectuses sitting on the coffee table or ads on why the XYZ mutual fund can help fund your retirement. There were no brochures in the waiting area that promoted a particular product and there were no cutesy posters from the home office about maximizing your retirement income. Reading material fit the demographics of the firm's client base: it could be *O Magazine, Newsweek, Architectural Digest, National Geographic,* or the local paper. It never was *Money Magazine* or any do-it-yourself publication. They made sure the lighting was bright and cheerful.

Completely absent: any TVs. Some brokerage firms had trouble with this concept. They had TVs everywhere, including the advisor's office and the reception area. However, I have never seen a superstar firm with a TV blaring anywhere in their office (with the exception of the employee lunchroom and no clients ever ventured there). Having a TV does not create the quality, calm atmosphere that helps reduce stress in the mind of the client and helps close sales. It is distracting for clients and staff and does not further the message of the firm—we are high-quality advisors who take the long view with your finances.

Initial greeting. As every prospect or client walked into the office, the receptionist would greet them in a warm, friendly manner, no matter who was working the front desk. At American Dream's office, they offered each of the women a fresh rose to take home. The clients also would be offered a cold drink or coffee, always served in nice glasses or classy mugs—nothing with a product vendor's name or logo.

Not leaving anything to chance, even the receptionists were taught how to greet returning clients or new prospects. The receptionist was given a list of the clients and prospects that each advisor would be seeing that day and then the following script would be used for new prospects and adapted to existing clients: "You must be the Johnsons. We have been expecting you." That simple phrase starts to make the client feel like the most important client in the world. The subliminal message: They value me so much, they have been preparing for my visit.

Then the receptionist continued; "(name of financial advisor) asked that I bake some chocolate chip cookies for you. Or, if you prefer we have cheese and crackers. We also have juice, coffee, and bottled water. What would you like? Some firms took this so seriously they checked with the client in advance to find out what kind of drinks they preferred, made a note in their file, and always had them on hand for meetings.

The advisor's office. This sales system necessitates the financial advisor meeting with the client in a private office or conference room. Clients do not like to discuss personal matters around other people, so client meetings in a bullpen setting are out of the question. The office should also be neat and tidy with a few personal items, such as photos of the family on the desk. Artwork that reflects the advisor's taste is also used.

We counsel financial advisors to avoid meeting with clients in restaurants or the client's home. Of course there are exceptions, but most of the time you cannot control the environment when meeting in a prospect's kitchen. The phone is ringing, the kids are crying, and the dog is barking. It is hard to get the client's undivided attention and focus on your meeting. Also, financial advisors need to be doing three things: prospecting, meeting with clients, and closing the sale. The time spent driving across town does not produce income.

Most of the superstars we worked with had figured out that it was important to meet with clients over a round table, usually 48″ in diameter. Meeting with a client across from a large executive-style desk can be subconsciously intimidating. A round table, as King Arthur pointed out, puts everyone on the same equal status. It is another small piece of the process that helps build trust and remove barriers in the prospect's mind.

First meeting script. The initial meeting with a new prospect also followed a tried-and-true pattern. The financial advisor had a clearly defined agenda for the meeting. Before the agenda was disclosed, the financial advisor would ask the client what they wanted to accomplish in the meeting and then add it to the agenda. The talking points, questions, and format we designed for one broker/dealer are summarized in Figure 7.1. All the boldface writing is actual script—the rest is explanation.

FIGURE 7.1 The First Meeting Script

The financial advisor walks out to the reception area where there is a warm greeting with the prospects. ***Thanks for coming today. I am Katherine Vessenes; it is good to meet you. Did you have any trouble finding the offices?*** Offer them refreshments if they have not been offered one by someone else.

Before going to the financial advisor's office, the financial advisor would stop by the Client Service Manager's (CSM) desk for an introduction ***I would like you to meet Joe, your Client Service Manager. Joe's job is to take care of you and treat you right. If you have any trades, Joe can place those for you or any questions about your investments, he can answer them. Also, I can be hard to reach at times, so always try Joe first because he can usually handle most of your requests.*** The CSM smiles warmly and may even offer a business card.

Then the financial advisor escorts the prospects into the private office.

Start with a little small talk.

(continued)

FIGURE 7.1 The First Meeting Script, continued

AGENDA
- *Let me lay out what I had in mind for an agenda today.* (Write on whiteboard or flip chart: "Mary and John's agenda.") *First we want to talk about your financial goals and any concerns you may have.*
- *We will also review any questions you may have.*
- *We will review the information you brought in.*
- *We will review our philosophy of financial planning, which we call the four cornerstones.*
- *I want to describe some of the great changes that we are making here and how we work with our top clients.*
- *Our code of ethics.*
- *Finally, we will discuss some recommendations or next steps.*
- *Do you have anything else that you want to add to this list?*

On the board write:
AGENDA
 1) Goals
 2) Concerns
 3) Questions
 4) Info
 5) Expectations
 6) Philosophy
 7) Four cornerstones
 8) Good news
 9) Ethics
 10) Next steps

FOCUS ON CLIENT
Good. Let us start with talking about you.

What brought you in today? Or, **How can I help?** Note: never start out this meeting explaining how smart you are, how wonderful the firm is, or the importance of planning. We are like doctors or therapists—going into the long explanations makes us look like salespeople.

Listen, listen, listen, and take lots of notes. Some of the many questions you should ask to start:
- *What do you most want to accomplish in our meeting today?*
- *Tell me about your background and how you got to where you are.*
- *How did your family treat money growing up? Did you have a lot or was it scarce? How has that affected how you handle money now?*
- *What kind of questions do you have for me?* You may want to defer questions like "What products do you recommend?" and "How do you get paid?" until later.
- *What are your top three concerns about your financial future?*
- *Do you have any other concerns?*
- *What are your top three financial goals?*
- *What do you most want to accomplish in our relationship?*
- *What needs to happen over the next three years for you to be happy and satisfied with your progress?* This question must be asked in exactly this way because it sets up asking for referrals later.

FIGURE 7.1 The First Meeting Script, continued

Let us go through your questionnaire. We then review almost everything in the questionnaire line by line to make sure all the key data is included. This always brings up more questions.

EXPECTATIONS

We think the best relationships are based on each party clearly understanding the other's expectations. So tell me, what are the three most important things I can provide you as your financial advisor?

How would you define success in our relationship?

If we were going to treat you so well, you could not help but talk us up to your family and friends, what would need to happen?

OUR PHILOSOPHY

At this stage it would be good for me to explain a little about how we approach helping you fund your dreams and goals, because our process is different than many firms. Use the board to draw in the chart.

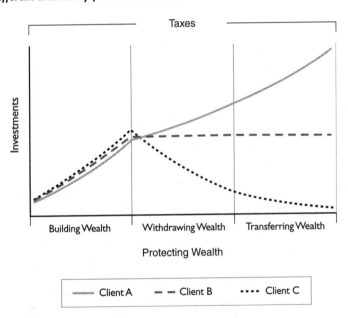

THE FOUR CORNERSTONES
This part is also done on the flip chart.

We believe there are four cornerstones that are essential in everyone's financial life. We call this BPDT™. This is shorthand for Building Wealth, Protecting Wealth, Distributing Wealth, and Transferring Wealth™. Have you ever heard of these terms? Pause for answer.

(continued)

FIGURE 7.1 The First Meeting Script, continued

• CORNERSTONE ONE: BUILDING WEALTH

Let's start with building wealth, or accumulation, first. This is the fun part, and it is what everybody talks about. It's increasing your net worth. In fact, this is where most brokerage houses and many planning firms focus most of their attention. How can we build or accumulate wealth?

Sometimes I think this is all the media is interested in. Every day they want us looking at whether the market is up or down. Unfortunately, this leaves a lot of people wondering "Why aren't I lucky?" They look at others who have made a lot of money, but they are feeling left out, particularly if their portfolio is dramatically down. Maybe you know some people who are feeling like that now. Pause for an answer.

The problem is most advisors are only focusing on one of the four very important cornerstones that are needed for people to become financially free. They have focused on accumulation, or building wealth.

Incidentally, any good accumulation strategy must take into account the taxes involved in investing because it can make a huge difference in the amount you have to spend in retirement.

• CORNERSTONE TWO: PROTECTING WEALTH

The second cornerstone means protecting your wealth, your lifestyle, and the wealth-generating machine, which is you. Protection can mean many things, including properly diversifying your investments or having emergency funds. Did you know there are certain types of insurance programs that provide exceptional tax advantages and protection at the same time? Pause

• CORNERSTONE THREE: DISTRIBUTING WEALTH

This second cornerstone means a strategy for withdrawing or distributing your money out of retirement accounts and other investments and spending it during retirement. Do you have a strategy for reducing taxes and optimizing your income at retirement? Pause for answer. *This is important because most people just think about building wealth and not about how to spend it in a tax-effective manner. Have you ever heard about how proper distribution or withdrawal strategies can increase your income in retirement?* Probe for depth of knowledge.

We have found there are three types of clients: Go through the chart and list the A clients, who want to run out of money at death; B clients, who want to live on interest during retirement and protect their principal; and C clients, who want to run out of money at death, live on interest, or have their money continue to grow during retirement.

> *A: Do you want to spend your last dime on the way to the mortuary?*
> *B: Do you want to just live off your interest in retirement?*
> *C: Do you want your investments to continue to grow during retirement?*

FIGURE 7.1 The First Meeting Script, continued

There are no wrong answers to this question. Your feelings about spending your money usually depend on whether you want Uncle Sam to be your senior partner in retirement—have you properly managed your investments so that you can withdraw money in a tax-advantaged way?

Tax-Control Triangle

Let me share with you a strategy to help you with your goals and investments. We have had a lot of success approaching the financial process this way, and there is no reason it shouldn't work for you.

All of your investments fit into three tax categories or pockets. We call this the Tax Triangle. Draw a triangle.

Fully taxable. These would include your passbook savings account, stocks, bonds, annuities, CDs, or a mutual fund that you own in your own name. The gains on these investments are taxed as you earn them.

The next is the tax deferred. They usually accumulate without paying income taxes, but the principal and the gains are taxable upon withdrawal. These include: IRAs, 401(k)s, SEPs, TSAs, and other pension plans.

The best is the tax advantaged. These generally grow tax-free and have income that is tax-advantaged. Examples here would be municipal bonds where the interest is free from income taxes and certain kinds of cash-value life insurance; 529 plans for college; and Roth IRAs.

Most of our clients come to us with too much in the fully taxable pocket; not enough in the tax-deferred pocket; and almost nothing in the tax-advantaged pocket.

According to the information you have given me, this is how your investments would roughly fill your pockets or where you stand on the tax triangle: Fill in the rough percentages of the client's portfolio into each of the three categories.

Why is this a concern to us? For a number of reasons:

First, the goal is to have control over your money no matter what happens to taxes. We know over time:
tax rates change,
tax brackets change, and
tax laws are constantly changing.

We have never yet had a client who wanted to make Uncle Sam their senior partner in retirement. If you have all your investments

(continued)

FIGURE 7.1 The First Meeting Script, continued

---

in one pocket, you won't be able to take advantage of tax changes. Just the way we diversify your portfolio to reduce risk, we believe in diversifying a portfolio to reduce tax risk.

By having some funds in each pocket you will have more control over the tax you pay, and ultimately more money to live on. How does that sound to you?

Retirement myths

When financial planning first gained credibility about 30 years ago, all the software and the gurus had two assumptions that formed the basis of all of their advice: one was that you would be in a lower tax bracket when you retired, and the second was that you would not need as much money in retirement as you need now.

Recently though, a few experts have discovered a startling truth— What if these basic assumptions were not correct? What if all of retirement and accumulation plans and strategies have been based on faulty assumptions? How soon would you want to find out about it? Right away, of course!

The first assumption was you would need less money during your retirement years than you do now. A common assumption was: 75 percent of your current salary was needed during retirement. For most people, this assumption doesn't work either. Why do you think that is? (Pause)

Who wants to reduce their standard of living during retirement? In fact, if you are planning to travel, golf, or get involved with charities, you could potentially be spending more money in retirement than you do now. This problem is magnified when you consider that inflation is doubling the cost of living every 15–18 years or so. So have you thought about how much money you would like in retirement? Do you want the same amount of spending power you have now, more or less? Pause for response.

The second assumption was that tax brackets would be lower in retirement, so the thought was you should push as much income into retirement because you would be paying less in taxes then. This assumption, too, may be flawed. Why? The only way you will be paying less taxes in retirement is if one of these two things happen:
   1. **Tax rates are dramatically reduced. What do you think the chances are that that will happen?**
   2. **Your portfolio declines and it throws off less in income. Who wants that to happen?**

When we talk about a distribution or withdrawal strategy, we are talking about acquiring and preserving wealth in a way that is tax-efficient so you can retire with dignity without making Uncle Sam a beneficiary of your retirement plan.

FIGURE 7.1 The First Meeting Script, continued

I have an important question to ask. Would it be beneficial for us to review your entire financial situation to see if you are properly positioned to avoid the devastating effects of taxes and inflation? Pause.

A key concern of many of my clients is that they may run out of money in retirement. Is that of concern to you? Pause.

If you had a major problem with your retirement strategy, how soon would you want to know about it? Right away, of course!

• CORNERSTONE FOUR: TRANSFERRING WEALTH

The final cornerstone is what we call transferring wealth, or leaving a legacy. For some people, it is important to make sure their spouse or loved ones are well provided for. Or they may want to establish a legacy by gifting money to their favorite charity. Once again, they want to do it without overpaying taxes and reducing the size of their estate. Is it important for you to provide for a spouse, children, grandchildren, or even a favorite charity? Pause.

TAXES
That is why the umbrella for our four cornerstones is solid tax planning, because in this country, it impacts all of our finances. Taxes are a vital overriding component that many people overlook. It seems most people keep their eyes on the stock market, but taxation and inflation can have a far more devastating impact on your finances than any downturns in the stock market. Did you know that the average American labors 1 hour 55 minutes each working day just to pay federal taxes, and an additional 55 minutes to pay various other taxes? How many hours do you think you are spending every day to pay taxes?

We think the four cornerstones—building wealth, protecting wealth, distributing wealth, and transferring wealth—all handled in a tax-efficient manner, are critical for every American. Even the youngest of our clients, who are fresh out of school with no assets, have a need for a plan that includes all four cornerstones.

If you are just getting started, you should save something every week. That's accumulation. You should put money away in a tax-deferred program for retirement or plan your assets to avoid taxation. That's distribution. Everyone needs to protect themselves, even if it is an inexpensive policy and an emergency fund. And everyone should have a will so that their children and their charities become their beneficiaries, not Uncle Sam. That is legacy. Does that make sense? Pause.

Most of our clients come to us just thinking about accumulation or building wealth, but can you see that all the cornerstones can have a huge impact on your lifestyle in retirement?

(continued)

FIGURE 7.1 The First Meeting Script, continued

GOOD NEWS

Let's shift gears, because in the past year, we have made some very exciting and bold changes here that are going to be very positive for clients like you. I think it would help frame our discussion if I could explain them first, and why we don't operate the way other firms do, before we start talking about possible solutions for you. Would that be okay with you?

CODE OF ETHICS

First of all, like any responsible, dedicated financial services company, we always do what is best for our clients. However, there is a distinct point of difference between us and the rest of the industry. We believe the trust of our clients is so important that every advisor is asked to commit to a code of ethics. Here is a copy of our Code of Ethics. Basically it says that we will always put your interests and needs ahead of our own.

We believe:
- *Your needs, as an investor, should always come first.*
- *You should be treated fairly, ethically, and respectfully.*
- *You have a right to competent and courteous service and advice at a fair price.*

In fact, every person working here must sign this pledge before we can even start working with clients.

Does that make sense?

This trust is so important to us that I want you to promise me if something ever happens that breaks that trust, that you will call me personally and give me a chance to make it right before you talk to your neighbor or your brother-in-law. Would you be willing to do that?

TEAM OF EXPERTS

Another reason we are different from other firms is we use a team approach. This team concept is crucial to us here. As you can see by reviewing the four cornerstones of BPDT, proper financial management is complicated. I don't know anyone who is an expert in all four areas, do you? (Wait for response.) *That is the reason the very wealthy have always had an entire team helping them manage their money. The fortunate few have always used a team approach, including a tax expert, an insurance specialist, an estate planning attorney, and an investment professional—sitting around the table, they can cost thousands of dollars an hour!*

Our philosophy is different from many firms. We believe that every American needs and deserves the same type of comprehensive team of experts that previously have only be available to the very wealthy. And that is exactly what we provide, a team of experts to each and every client, from tax professionals to financial advisors. That's why I am considered the team leader. To assist us, we have expert tax help, a top-notch planning department, and insurance and investment experts. That has been very successful for wealthy Americans.

FIGURE 7.1 The First Meeting Script, continued

You can imagine how excited we are to help all Americans get the advice and service that has previously been unavailable to them. This is a mission that is important to each and every one of us. We see it as a lifetime process.

What do we mean by "for life?" We believe we can best serve our clients if we take the long perspective. So we do not look at the next five weeks, or months, or even years. We are looking at the next five decades.

How does this philosophy sound to you? How does it compare with your current financial strategy? Pause

NEXT STEPS (THE CLOSE)
So what I would like to do next is review your worksheet in more detail, address any other concerns you may have, focus on your hopes and dreams, and see if there is a way we can help you pursue your dreams and retire with dignity.

Then I will review the plan with you and make some recommendations on ways you might be able to better achieve your goals and objectives. How does that sound?

If they are not sure: *Would you like to see what a sample plan looks like?* Walk the client through the sample and explain.

HOW I GET PAID
Now, you may be wondering how I get paid. Basically, I get compensated in three ways:
  1. Our plans are $____. But you should know they come with a guarantee. Although we cannot guarantee an investment's success, we can guarantee that you will like your plan. If not, we refund the money you paid for the plan, no questions asked.
  2. Some of the companies that we recommend pay us a commission, much like a travel agent, for recommending their products. Those relationships are disclosed to you.

SET UP REFERRALS
  3. Finally, and most important, the best way you can thank me is this: If you are happy with our service, you will recommend me to other successful clients just like you.

ADVISOR'S EXPECTATIONS
Now that we have talked a lot about your expectations, I should tell you I have expectations of my clients, too. I have found that in order for this process to work well for you and for us, there are certain things we need to agree on:
  1. The first is open communication. If we need to get in touch with you, it is usually very important. Can you agree to get back to us within 24 hours?

(continued)

FIGURE 7.1 The First Meeting Script, continued

---

2. *I cannot promise you investment results. No one can. It is impossible, because we do not know what the market will do, and in fact there is always a risk that an investment may lose money.*

However, there is one promise I can make you: great service. Will that work for you?

THE RECAP
Now if I can, Work backwards through the flip charts focusing on what is most important to them. For example:
- *Help you transfer your estate to your loved ones without making Uncle Sam your chief beneficiary*
- *Help you keep more money in your pocket during retirement*
- *Help you accumulate and protect your wealth in a tax-efficient manner*
- *Help you put your children through college and retire with confidence*
- *Help you find the funds to finance your new business*
- *Communicate with you on a regular basis*

COMMITMENT
Would this be what you are looking for in a financial advisor? Pause.

CONFIRM DATE FOR NEXT MEETING
Great! Then let us take the first step of developing your plan. It will take us about two weeks to prepare the plan, so we can set up the next meeting now to review it. Set up date and time. *Do you have any questions?*

I will invite our Client Service Manager in to review the paperwork while I prepare for you the notes from our meeting.

Use a template to create notes. The CSM reviews RIA forms and anything else that is important. You return to the table with the clients.

Let us take just a minute to review my notes, to make sure I clearly heard what you wanted to accomplish. Read through the notes template. *If this is accurate, go ahead and initial the bottom of the page. The copy is for your files. Do you have any other questions?*

I look forward to seeing you on date/time. Walk them out the door.

Key dominos that improve success in the first meeting:

- Using the flip chart or whiteboard keeps the meeting focused and the clients' attention on you solving their problems.
- Standing while writing on the chart creates authority. Like a teacher, you command attention. It is very powerful.
- The flip chart is a written reminder to simplify your note taking, to make sure no important information is lost. It creates trust because the client knows you understand them.
- The written notes the client takes home after the meeting also increase trust.
- The biggest win is a commitment to the planning process.
- The sale is made in this meeting. If the client agrees to go forward, you have an 80 percent to 90 percent chance of closing the business.

The first meeting's goals are:

- Build trust.
- Get commitment for the second meeting.
- Lay out the compelling story—why team of experts.
- Explain BPDT™.
- Educate the client.
- Disturb the client. Contented clients don't need advice.
- Provide hope for solutions.
- Set expectations.
- Explain code of ethics.
- Uncover key issues that are important to move forward.

3. Analysis and Preparation

During this stage, the financial advisor will pass off the analysis and prep to the team of experts or the junior planner and the CSM. The financial advisor will make brief notes about the type of products that would be appropriate and the team will take over the rest of the process and do the following:

- *Planning department.* Creates the plan, including meeting with the client if necessary to get additional information.
- *Investment expert.* Current investments are reviewed for buy, sell, and hold recommendations.
- *Tax expert.* Reviews plan for tax savings and strategies, particularly distribution strategies in retirement.
- *Insurance expert.* Reviews current policies and makes recommendations for holding current and/or purchasing new ones.
- *Estate planning expert.* Looks at transfer issues and how to minimize taxes; also whether trusts would be appropriate.
- *CSM.* Makes sure the process stays on time and all the necessary work is completed before the next meeting. The CSM also completes all subscription agreements and paperwork prior to the meeting.

4. Solutions Meeting

The second meeting with the client had the financial advisor presenting a written financial plan and product recommendations, including precompleted subscription agreements. These meetings refer to the goals and objectives set by the prospect in the first meeting.

Plan meetings are highly individualized, depending on the client's goals and how the plan turned out.

An outline of a typical script is shown in Figure 7.2.

Going through the plan depended a lot on the prospect. Some wanted details, others quick overviews. In any case, particular attention should be paid to their hot buttons and concerns.

FIGURE 7.2 Solutions Meeting Script

Great to see you again. Have you thought of anything that could have an important bearing on your plan since our last meeting?

Here is my agenda for today (write on flip chart or whiteboard):

1. *Briefly review your goals from our last meeting.*
2. *Review your plan in more detail, looking at both the strengths and weaknesses of your current situation.*
3. *Take a look at the specific recommendations we are going to make.*
4. *Answer any questions.*
5. *Take the next steps.*

Is there anything else we should discuss?

Your top three goals were:

1. *Educating your children.*
2. *Retiring with confidence.*
3. *Saving enough money to buy your dad's business.*

Have you thought of any other goals since our last meeting?

Tell me, do you like a lot of details or do you prefer the executive summary and then we can dig deeper if you have any questions?

When discussing the new purchases, keep it simple. Use a couple of sentences to explain the investment in general terms and then two or three sentences on why you like the one you recommended.

Then the financial advisor (or sometimes the CSM) reviewed the paperwork. This process goes very quickly because all the forms were filled out prior to the meeting.

The last thing was to set up the next meeting—it may be a delivery meeting or a monitor and modify meeting.

After the meeting, the CSMs maintained a high-touch follow-up with the prospects to make sure that the business stayed on the books. This included handwritten notes, phone calls, and invitations to lunch or seminars.

Key points of the plan presentation meeting:

- Find out if any major problems could sabotage your plans by asking if they thought of anything that could have a bearing on the plan since the last meeting.
- Refresh their memory of the last meeting by reviewing their goals and objectives.
- Match your delivery to their style. Go slow for the detailed-minded and fast for those who just want the big picture.
- Have all subscription agreements completed in full prior to the meeting. Any time a client has to wait while forms are being completed, they are subconsciously talking themselves out of a sale. The longer the process takes, the more likely they are to back out.
- Assume the sale—there are no special closing phrases here except, "How does that sound to you?" Going through the plan, the products are a natural flow. We assume the client will go forward with all of our recommendations.
- Sometimes there is just too much information to review before they sign the paperwork. When that is the case, give the clients the plan and a red pen. Ask them to read it and mark any places where they have questions. Make them promise that they will come back in within ten days, so you both do not forget what you talked about. When they come back you can move into the products that will solve their problems.

5. Monitor and Modify

Depending on the size of the client's assets, follow-up meetings are crucial. Larger clients will need more frequent meetings. These meetings would focus on comparing current status with the original plan, reviewing any necessary changes prompted by the market or the client's lives.

Some of the superstars we coached did not have much of a background in insurance. They found it easier to sell investments during the first pass and save the insurance for the monitor and modify or the review meeting.

Key points of the monitor and modfiy/review meeting:

- Renew the relationship.
- Ask about changes in their lives.
- Ask whether they are happy with the service they have been getting.
- Close the gaps on any action items that were not implemented the first time around.
- Bring clarity to their current situation by reviewing their investments and comparing them to the plan.
- Ask for referrals.

6. Retention Program or Client Happiness Plan

No sales process would be complete without attention to keeping clients. It is much cheaper to keep an existing client than it is to get a new one. Therefore, keeping current clients on the books and keeping them happy is crucial to the success of the firm. Client retention plans are discussed in detail in Chapter 4.

However, the most important part of a client retention program is the least expensive: personally written thank-you notes after every meeting. Taking the time to write a personal note on good quality stationery has never been more important than in this age of impersonal mass e-mails. One realtor, who is the top producer in his city, told us that he had forgotten how important personal thank-you notes were. He started writing them to current clients, old clients, anyone he could think of. When I asked him how it was working, he said he had so much new business that after 60 days he had to stop—he could not take on any more new clients.

CONCLUSION

This defined sales system works like an assembly line. Every client is faced with the same model client experience and the results are very predictable.

One of the best exercises you can do is take your staff through every step of your sales process, starting with your clients parking in your lot. Ask yourself at each step of the way, How would a client rate this part of their experience? If you have clients who would give you and 8, 9, or 10 on a scale of 1 to 10, you will have an easy time closing your sales and you will have your own No-Sell Sale™ process.

A SUCCESS STORY

Meet Jim Watson,* branch office manager of North Star Financial Advisors. Here is Jim's story in his own words:

I joined a discount brokerage firm right out of college. Later, it was acquired by North Star. At the discount firm we built our business via the telephone. We prospected for clients by phone and also sold stocks to those same clients over the phone. Through persistence and hard work I was able to build a successful book of business. In 2000, I had my best year in the business hitting $500,000 in gross production. What I did not realize at the time was this was the year my business would plateau and subsequently drop. In 2001, 2002, and 2003, I was unable to reach my previous peak in production. My income had decreased and it seemed that the way I had always done my business, via the telephone, was not as effective anymore. When Guy Nelson became president in 2002, the business model had to change because the market had changed. It went from selling stocks over the phone to a face-to-face consultative selling using financial planning—a huge leap for us.

I lived in Omaha at that time, had about 350 clients, and was generating $350,000 per year in production. Later that year I moved to Minnesota to take the branch office manager position. Although I did not know a single person, I was able to take most of my transactional clients with me. However, by the summer of 2003 I was struggling. My BOM duties were taking a lot of time and not allowing me the time to meet with my clients and generate income. I was not able to penetrate the new market the way I wanted and my income had declined.

Everything changed dramatically in June 2003. That is when Katherine Vessenes, as part of her assignment of transitioning us into a consultative sales process, started assisting our branch as our personal sales coach. She spent one day a week in our offices for about 12 weeks, working with every rep in the office, teaching us the same system she used to turn average advisors into superstars. About one-third of her time was spent with me, helping me sort through my new duties as a branch office manager and, more important, how to work with clients on a face-to-face basis, instead of over the phone.

Katherine gave us numerous practical tools to help us close more business and increase the average commission per case. We spent a lot of time rehearsing the first meeting, because that is where Katherine says the sale is really made. During this time we also mastered our own compelling story and learned how to close more business.

In addition to completely restructuring my approach to conducting business, I also formed a team with two other advisors in the office. We felt that each of us had complementary skill sets and as a team we could collectively accomplish more for our clients. The results were beyond my wildest expectations. Our team saw an immediate increase in sales. By the end of 2003, I closed $400,000 in sales, and by the end of 2004, I closed $828,000, making me the top broker in all of North Star! In fact, I am confident I will be the first million-dollar advisor ever at this firm.

Katherine's help changed our office completely. Not just the physical structure, but the type of reps we hire. Some of the reps here in 2003 did not buy into the new sales process. They all left, some voluntarily, some not. Some of the remaining reps only adapted 10 to 20 percent of Katherine's suggestions—but they still had huge bumps in their income—some as much at $100,000 per year.

Here are my big takeaways and suggestions for anyone who wants to double their income:

- *Meet face-to-face with the clients.* I think I knew subconsciously that this was a good idea, but at the discount firm, all of our work was done over the phone. We never put any emphasis on meeting in person. Katherine made this our top priority. It became an absolute must. I went from seeing one client face to face per month to seeing 20 to 25 clients per month. The selling process became so much easier and less stressful because I am building rapport with these clients. They trust me now because they know me. I am more than a voice on the phone.
- *Do not sell a product. Sell a solution, a process, and a relationship.* Unlike our old system, we never lead with a product or even the solution out of the box. We take

the time to build a relationship, really understand the client's concerns, then craft solutions that solve their problems. The product sale falls naturally into the No-Sell Sale™ and is just one small part of the entire process. The client does not feel like they are being sold a product, but they are given a solution.

- *Use a comprehensive planning process to capture all the assets.* We use the BPDT™ system that Katherine and Peter created to get clients thinking about issues other than accumulation. We do not want clients' eyes on the market every day, because we cannot control the market. Unfortunately, clients who are sold an accumulation philosophy to investing just look at the up and down tics. We like using the comprehensive approach of BWPT because it covers all the clients' issues and gets clients thinking about something much more satisfying to them—living the life they want in retirement and leaving a legacy.

My final recommendation is simple: If you want to become a million-dollar advisor, do what I did. Everything Katherine says to do, just do it!

KEY POINTS

1. Even middle-of-the-road salespeople can be successful if they have a great system—a superb foundation under them.
2. The first meeting with a prospective client is a time to build trust and get a commitment for the next step.
3. The No-Sell Sale™ is about numerous different steps, which when properly aligned lead to an easy, effortless sale.
4. Have a defined sales process and stick to it.

5. The four cornerstones essential in everyone's financial life are what we call BPDT™: Building Wealth, Protecting Wealth, Distributing Wealth, and Transferring Wealth™.

6. Using a flip chart or whiteboard in your client meetings keeps the meeting focused, and the client's attention on you.

7. Follow-up meetings and ongoing marketing or contacts are crucial. Your CSM can help with these.

8. Keeping current clients happy is more productive and cheaper than getting new clients.

8

ETHICS AND COMPLIANCE SYSTEMS

Prosperity Factor #8
Superstars integrate high-integrity ethics and
compliance systems into all aspects of the practice.

By Katherine

There has never been a greater
need for ethics in the securities industry. With daily notices
from the SEC advising consumers of the latest securities fraud
and CEOs heading to jail or paying multi-million-dollar fines,
consumers are becoming more and more distrustful of the industry. Frightened consumers worry that they will be ripped off
or lose money. Worried consumers do not place trades.

Superstar financial advisors are even more exposed to regulatory sanctions and lawsuits than the average advisor. The
reasons? First, regulators target them when performing examinations. It is common for regulators to examine the books and
records of a broker/dealer by focusing on the trades of the top-
producing reps. Little do the big guys know, but regulators are

scrutinizing every trade. Naturally, the sheer volume of trades makes it more likely the superstar will make a mistake. Finally, some investors target the large superstar financial advisors. Investors know their success means they have deeper pockets for judgments and are concerned about their reputation. These two factors make it easier to settle a case in favor of the investor.

Savvy financial advisors who want to be superstars will incorporate a system of good ethics and tight compliance that covers the entire organization. The message is very powerful: We treat all of our clients fairly and with respect because we put the investors' needs above our own. That philosophy needs to be such an integral part of the organization—even the newest receptionist or file clerk should be able to recite it easily.

This focus on ethics and good compliance is good for business. It increases a client's level of trust and leads to more business. Ethics and tight compliance is just plain smart because it will add up to more business.

Superstars need compliance systems that are easy to follow. In fact, their systems need to be automatic because the superstars do not want to take any extra time creating or maintaining the systems, and they certainly do not want to spend any time defending lawsuits or responding to regulators.

We have found that a superstar's attitude toward compliance varied between thinking of it as a necessary evil, and arrogance that they were "beyond" those regulations. Some firms scrupulously stuck to every detail of the regulations. Others ignored certain regulations with impunity.

Certain broker/dealers might be tempted to look past a top-producer's compliance record as long as they were continually bringing in big dollars. I have often said that even the cleanest firm cannot skate through a serious compliance examination. The rules and regulation governing our industry are so complex that it is almost impossible to dot every "*i*" and cross every "*t*."

The superstars, the multi-million-dollar financial advisors, were no exception. Although most of them had a desire to take compliance seriously, they all had areas that needed additional improvement.

Some of the larger firms had hired their own on-staff compliance personnel to serve as a Series 24 supervisor. Others relied completely on outside help from a compliance-consulting firm. In most offices that we have visited, if the superstars could tighten up their compliance procedures in a number of ways, it could help them reduce the chances for a lawsuit or deficiency letter from regulators.

Although they were doing many things right, for our purposes, it would be more helpful to list their weaknesses and how to avoid them. Below are some of the major problems we found in the superstar's compliance programs, listed in no particular order.

Compliance Report Card

B−

FINANCIAL PLANNING SOFTWARE

Many of the firms we have worked with were using financial planning software that was outdated, or even inaccurate. Unfortunately, this is not just a problem with superstars. I have also seen broker/dealers use software that could not pass a basic due-diligence test.

One of our financial planning clients refused to believe that their software was outdated and did not even do the calculations correctly. The advisors had no motivation to change because they were making so much money on the old system, they felt no need to invest into something new.

I also noticed that older systems were time-consuming and laborious to create a financial plan. Newer programs were more integrated and much faster at compiling the necessary reports.

In case you are tempted to skip over this section because your broker/dealer has provided you with some software, think again. A few years ago, I helped a broker/dealer select a new

financial planning software for its reps. Part of this project included looking at the popular brands. I found one that I really
liked—it looked pretty and is very well known. Before I put it
on my short list, I called their references. Much to my surprise,
a large firm advised me not to touch the program. Why? The
methodologies were incorrect and the numbers did not calculate properly. This broker/dealer had even sent two experts to
the software company for several months to try and fix the
problems. Think about the thousands of advisors using their
software, relying on its conclusions, not knowing how exposed
they are to lawsuits!

At the other extreme, I have seen some advisors believe their
own Excel spreadsheets were far superior to a tried and true
software package. These advisors never used planning software
and always relied on their own number crunching. By chance I
happened on one of these homemade plans when I took over
for a planner who had moved to another firm and I assumed
all of his existing files. I will never forget my shock at looking at
Ms. Fielding's* case file. She was a 54-year-old single executive
at a local company who wanted to retire in three years. Her
question to Mr. Do It Yourself Planner was, could she afford to
retire and not run out of money in retirement? Her assets consisted of company stock and a pension plan that was not yet
vested, totalling about $300,000 in taxable investments. Her cur-
rent income of $120,000 was to be maintained during retire-
ment at an inflation rate of 3 percent.

Fortunately there were a few notes in the file: Mr. Planner
had advised Ms. Fielding she would not run out of money in retirement and that it was perfectly safe for her to retire at any
time during the next three years.

Inside her file was a simple spread sheet that Mr. Planner had
used to make his recommendation. It only took me two minutes to find two major fallacies with Mr. Planner's analysis. First,
he started depleting her assets from a starting point today of

$300,000. The problem? No matter how many times I added up her liquid assets, I could not come up with more than $250,000. He was 20 percent off on his calculations before he even got started. Second fallacy: He assumed her company stock would grow at 8 percent—another assumption that would come back to haunt him, because during the six months that transpired from his evaluation to the time I looked at the file, the company stock had tanked and had little chance of ever recovering.

Bottom line: Ms. Fielding had no business retiring with so few assets unless she wanted to reduce her standard of living to $30,000 per year and take on a job at Barnes and Noble to pay most of her bills. Mr. Planner's advice was dead wrong and very scary.

Solution: Do your own due diligence on all software you use. Check out the program carefully and see if it comes to logical conclusions. Many of the problems I saw did not require a math background to spot them. If the program is being used by a nationally-known and well-respected planner, you breathe a sigh of relief. Ask about who created the methodologies. One well-known, widely used software program I reviewed was created by a mutual-fund wholesaler. He had no background in planning, and to an experienced planner, it really showed.

FILES

When reviewing a financial advisor's files, I like to look at them from two different perspectives. One is from the eyes of a regulator and the other is from the eyes of a plaintiff's attorney. Most of the firms had retained an outside compliance consulting firm, sometimes ours, to help them get their files in order to withstand an internal audit from their broker/dealer or external audit from state or federal regulators.

We advised them to think like a Boy Scout and "be prepared." Advisors knew that sooner or later regulators would be looking through their file drawers, and sooner or later, they were likely to be sued.

The files varied greatly from firm to firm. Some firms had well-organized files, while others did not. Here are some common problems:

- *Loose papers.* Sometimes we found scraps with notes or messages, without any notes on who made the memos.
- *Undated notes, memos.* If you cannot prove when they were written, they are worthless.
- *No organization.* Because there was no standardized procedure for filing certain types of documents, key information became difficult to find.
- *No notes on suitability.* This was a huge omission, as discussed below.
- *No notes on why a particular investment was chosen or the due diligence on selecting the investment.*
- *Few notes in the file at all.* These cases are almost impossible to defend.

Solution:

- *Get organized.* Take good notes after every interaction, and document, document, and document. Be systematic in filing so every file is treated the same.
- *Establish procedures that are followed on every case.* Every file should have the same format (i.e., a special file for correspondence, another one for client data gathering including tax returns and wills). Handwritten notes should always be in the same place and dated and initialed.

E-MAILS ARE A HOT ISSUE
WITH REGULATORS

This problem seems to have escalated among large corporations. One of our clients, who had hundreds of employees, routinely used e-mails to handle most of the company's business. Unfortunately, no one had taught them e-mail etiquette. Sometimes included in the e-mails were disparaging comments about other employees or associates. Inevitably, the damaging e-mails got back to the person who was being defamed. I do not believe this kind of information ever belongs in e-mail. If you have a problem with a fellow employee, you need to talk about it face-to-face, and not send them a "nasty-gram." Many interoffice communication problems could easily be squelched by picking up the phone or meeting personally with that person.

Here are a few of the problems that can get a financial advisor in trouble:

- Financial advisors are required to keep e-mails just like other correspondence. Five large broker/dealers were each fined $1.65 million dollars when they could not retrieve e-mails. Sometimes the e-mails are not stored in a single location, or there is no backup. Sometimes they are stored on an employee's computer. When that employee leaves the firm, the e-mails are destroyed in violation of the regulations. Other firms would write over e-mails, destroying the original version.

- It is not enough to just save e-mails, they must be searchable and retrievable. This can be an expensive proposition as USB Warburg discovered *(Zubulake v. USB Warburg)* when the plaintiff, a former employee, requested e-mails from the defendant, USB. USB sought a ruling that they would not be required to provide them because it would cost them about $175,000 to produce the requested e-mails. After appeals, USB was ordered to pay 75 percent of the cost of retrieval.

- No policies on e-mails? Make sure your compliance manual includes a section on e-mails, how to store them and how to search and retrieve.
- Set the standards. Clearly state what can or cannot be included in an e-mail.
- Delete does not mean gone. Some people think just because they hit the delete button, the e-mail is erased. In many cases it can still be retrieved and used against you.
- Incriminating statements in e-mails are common fodder for lawsuits. One case sealed the defendant broker/dealer's fate when it was discovered internal e-mails were contrary to what their analysts were recommending. Stocks that were being touted by the analysts were being described in internal e-mails as "dogs."
- Ferris Baker Watts (broker/dealer) was fined $100,000 for having policies that reps must submit e-mails for review, but they had no procedures for making sure they were enforced.
- All issues with email also apply to instant messaging.

Solution: Set e-mail policies and procedures on how they are to be enforced. Be careful, and think of a front-page story on the *Wall Street Journal.* If you do not think your e-mail would look good in the *Journal,* do not write it. Train your entire staff on what good e-mails are, what you can say, and what you cannot.

CONTACT MANAGEMENT

We counsel our clients to be very careful what they put into file notes and into their contact management software. I always look at this information as whether I would be embarrassed if my mother was watching it read on national TV. One financial advisor had a habit of writing very disparaging remarks about his clients in his contact management system. It was not unusual for his notes, which could be read by anyone in the firm, to say that the client was a "turkey," or "an absolute idiot." Or worse, "this client is a cash cow." First, I think name-calling is an extremely bad precedent, as any third-grade teacher will tell you. It also sets the example that this kind of behavior is appropriate if their firm's top people are doing it. Take a look at each of the notes in your files. Would you be embarrassed to see them in print? If the answer is yes, it is time to rethink what you are putting in your file notes.

REGULATORY EXAMINATIONS

We advise our clients to obtain a copy from their broker/ dealer or regulator of the required files and documents they are obligated to keep. Or, if they are a fee-only registered investment advisor, they should check the appropriate statutes. Once they know exactly what can be examined, the next step is to plan for a system that allows quick retrieval. The last thing you want is for an examiner to be in your office for a lengthy period of time. The longer they are there, the more likely they are to find trouble.

We recommend a dual set of files. For instance, registered investment advisors are required to keep copies of client correspondence, the firm's checkbooks, all advertising materials, and numerous other documents. We suggest that filing a copy of a client correspondence in the client's file is perfectly appropriate and certainly the right thing to do. We advise making a separate copy of all relevant correspondence and file it chronologically in a separate file cabinet reserved for examinations. This way, should examiners come into the office and request all copies of correspondence between May 1 and July 31 of last year, instead of having to rifle through each client's file, they could go to the file cabinet for the duplicate file. Likewise, when the examiners ask for a copy of their advertising, it would all be neatly labeled in an advertising file folder.

Looking at the files from the plaintiff's counsel point of view can be more problematic. Financial advisors can be sued on numerous different theories. Once again, an ounce of prevention can prevent thousands of dollars of fines or restitution. For instance, alleging that an investment was unsuitable is one of the most common causes of complaint by unhappy investors. The good news is that it is one of the easiest ones to defend. The bad news is that you can go broke defending it. Because we know that suitability is a likely claim, it makes sense to make sure that every file has a carefully documented record of why each investment is suitable.

I always recommend the *two-by-two suitability rule*. By that I mean whenever a financial advisor is making a recommendation to a client (buy, sell, or hold), I suggest taking two minutes and writing two sentences about why this recommendation was suitable, or why the investment was appropriate. This helpful practice can save you hundreds of thousands of dollars. Regrettably, it is a little harder than it looks. When I was working as a financial advisor, I took the two-by-two test to heart and added another component to it. I wanted each of my sentences to be unique. I found it was fairly difficult to put in two unique sentences why an investment was suitable at this time. If a client was thinking of a variable annuity purchase, the first set of two-by-two notes would look something like this:

Client is interested in obtaining tax-deferred growth on his investment, and is concerned about market fluctuations and the impact the investment losses will have on his heirs. The client liked the idea of a "guaranteed death benefit."

That worked great the first time, but because I did not want every recommendation to be exactly the same, it became more difficult to change it as time went on.

LAWSUITS/ARBITRATION

As I reviewed clients' files from a defense attorney's perspective, I found numerous gaping holes that could make it difficult to defend a complaint. In all likelihood, the super producer's files were probably in better shape than a midrange financial advisor. Some of the items I noticed that would cause them trouble if they were sued overlap with problems in an examination:

- *An appalling lack of file notes.* If they did have notes, they were incomplete, undated, and not initialed. It was difficult to tell who had actually made the notes and when. None of that would be very helpful if they ever had to be on a witness stand to defend their actions against an unhappy investor. Many attorneys have looked at hopeless cases and found good file notes actually saved them.
- *Lack of investment justification.* As I mentioned to one financial advisor, "I think you've done a great job choosing investments for clients, however, nothing in your files states why you chose them." This was an important distinction. Although the investments may have been perfectly appropriate and suitable for his client, he could not prove it. He had not one scrap of paper in his files that could prove why this investment was appropriate. With every investment, think, "It is not just the 'what,' it is the 'why.'"
- *Breach of fiduciary duty* is another common violation. A fiduciary must always do what is in the client's best interest, not the financial advisor's. Although I never saw any blatant violations of their breach of fiduciary duty, there were plenty of gray areas. Financial advisors who are going to work in the gray area should have even more carefully documented files to justify their actions.

Solution: To help financial advisors become more systematic about their files and documentation, we created file checklists for them. The idea behind the checklist is that they could open up each file, review the checklist, and see if all the necessary documents were in place.

UNREALISTIC PERFORMANCE PROJECTIONS

Promising performance always seemed to me like a prescription for disaster. Why promise something that you cannot control? We had one broker/dealer client who wanted me to work with their top producers to create a series of drip-marketing letters. In the process, I interviewed one of their top producers about how they sold mutual funds during the euphoric dot-com market frenzy. His style with clients was, "We have been averaging 25 percent or more per year with our mutual funds. What is not to like about that? How much more would you like to invest?"

One great thing about having been in the business for almost 20 years, I have seen it all. I knew the euphoria was not going to last, and clients who had been sold based on performance were going to be very unhappy when the market suffered a downturn as it did a few years later.

Another subtle way that advisors will promise performance is by using insurance illustrations that show an unlikely rate of return. Even during the boom years of the market, the 12 percent rate of return on a VUL policy can be difficult to obtain after fees and expenses. Although we know that a hypothetical illustration is not a promise or a guarantee, the client may not understand that. They tend to think that anything in writing is carved in granite. This creates unrealistic expectations of performance and unhappy clients. Unhappy clients lead to expensive lawsuits.

The better approach is to get the client's eyes on service, not performance, and to make sure that their performance expectations are reasonable. Here are some scripts you might be able to use in your next meeting:

You know, Mary, I can't promise you performance, in fact, nobody can because none of us knows what the market is going to do. However, we can promise you great service.

Or,

Sooner or later there is a good chance that something we do may lose money.

Getting clients to have reasonable expectations up front greatly reduces the chances of an unhappy investor filing a claim with their local regulator.

ILLEGAL REFERRAL SYSTEMS

Twice we have seen multi-million-dollar producers pay out referral fees in violation of the regulations. The financial advisor rewarded the referrer handsomely by paying him a full 25 percent of every commission and fee that the financial advisor received. The problem with this system is it gets both the financial advisor and the referral source into trouble. Under this kind of arrangement, the referral source would have to be registered or the financial advisor and the referral source would both be violating NASD, NYSE, and broker/dealer rules. Of course, most of the referrers would not take the time required to study and sit for the securities exams.

Solution: Get registered; operate as a solicitor or do not accept or pay referral fees.

M *ulti-Million-Dollar Principle #24*

Unrealistic expectations lead to unhappy clients. Unhappy clients lead to expensive lawsuits.

AN OVERLY FOCUSED PRODUCTS LIST

Many superstars have a tendency to fall in love with a particular investment product. It could be a variable annuity, a real estate program, a B share fund, a variable universal life, or even a particular money-management firm. It seems that inevitably they fall into a groove and almost all of the investments they sell are their personal favorites. Some of them truly believe that these are the most appropriate and best investments for their clients.

However, I often wondered if the commissions were not coloring their judgment. Placing the bulk of one's production with a particular product sponsor can provide numerous benefits for the financial advisor, including increased commissions and a lot of financial assistance from wholesalers.

One firm worked with a broker/dealer that had thousands of different investments on their approved list. However, for their financial advisors, they limited it to 12 products. The reason? When all of their financial advisors were selling the same 12 products, they were able to cut special deals with the vendors. Now is this in the best interest of the client? It can be, but it certainly looks suspect on the surface. Cover yourself by making sure these products are in your client's best interests so you do not breach your duty.

This issue has escalated recently as many broker/dealers have faced stiff fines for selling "shelf space," a practice where the broker/dealer is given extra compensation from the product provider for putting their investments on a short list of

---

Multi-Million-Dollar Principle #25

Treat your product list just like a manufacturing company would—do your due diligence and diversify.

"preferred vendors." Morgan Stanley was fined $50 million for failing to disclose the conflict of interest that certain mutual funds paid $100,000 per year to be their preferred vendor, and they then offered special trips to reps for selling these funds. Reps were pressured to sell the preferred products.

INVESTMENT POLICY STATEMENTS

Many of the superstar firms did not use investment policy statements. Shockingly, some of them did not even know what an investment policy statement was. Investment policy statements are great tools for helping to solidify reasonable client expectations and getting them in writing. It makes for much happier relationships in the long run.

I had great difficulty getting this concept across to one particular firm. They were used to having investment policy statements from their portfolio managers, but they had never done one from a client's perspective. I maintained that a client needed to state what they are expecting from the managers, not just the other way around.

Investment Policy Handbook, the best book on this subject, was written by Norm Boone and Linda Lubitz. You can get more information on it at http://www.ipsadvisorpro.com.

VARIABLE ANNUITIES

To a firm, superstars love variable annuities. Some really thought they were a good investment and others, I am sure, just loved the higher commissions. Here are some of the ways this good investment can go wrong:

- *Improper exchanges.* Another hot spot with regulators, improper exchanges, those motivated primarily by additional compensation for the rep, are under additional scrutiny. This was a lesson Prudential learned the hard way. They were ordered to pay $9.5 million to customers and a $2 million fine for improper exchanges. Home office personnel also are not excluded from the scrutiny. Waddell and Reed's two senior executives were charged with recommending 6,700 variable annuity exchanges without determining if they were suitable.

- *Weak disclosures, particularly about bonus products.* Many of the firms had not done a good job of making the proper disclosures, particularly about no additional tax savings, for putting a variable annuity into a retirement account.

Solution: Do not "switch for the commish." It is acceptable to switch for a better product, improved features, and different accounts, but not for the commission. Make sure you document your file on why this was in the client's best interest.

MUTUAL FUND ABUSES: B SHARES AND BREAKPOINTS

What I once thought of as a "sleepy investment" has proven to be another product that can keep all of us up at night—mutual funds.

An additional hot area with regulators is A shares, B shares, and C shares. There have been a number of cases where financial advisors were sanctioned or fined for improperly placing

---

M*ulti-Million-Dollar Principle #26*

Do not "switch for the commish."

clients into B shares, or for not disclosing the breakpoints on the A shares. These fines can be substantial. A few years back, two financial advisors from one firm were fined $50,000 for improper mutual fund switching. Recently a large broker/dealer was fined $600,000 for a similar offense. Clearly the fines are escalating.

Even with the fervor over improper use of B shares and failing to disclose breakpoints, some of the superstars still put a lot of their clients' assets into B shares. I am reminded of a conversation I had with a financial advisor who looked me straight in the eye and tried to explain why a million dollars in B shares in one year was the proper thing to do for his client. He may have felt strongly about it, but I bet the regulators would have an entirely different point of view. Because this area is so hot now, why take chances? Always err on the side of being conservative, keeping in mind that it is important to do what is in the client's best interest.

To show how serious this issue is, I have reproduced the charts in Figure 8.1 listing the major firms and their recent settlements with regulators for breakpoint violations. The percentages reflect the percent of mutual fund trades regulators found that ran afoul of the breakpoint rules.

Many firms were found to have an appalling 30 percent of their mutual fund trades violate the breakpoint rulings. Some firms were over 80 percent.

Solution: Now is the time to look at your own practices in this area, before regulators come knocking on your door. Also, make sure new purchases comply with the breakpoints. You might even consider extra disclosures in this area. When it comes to B shares, I recommend these guidelines: avoid B shares for amounts over $100,000 without supervisor approval, and avoid over $250,000 like the plague.

FIGURE 8.1 Settlements for Breakpoint Violations

The firms settling with the SEC and NASD in separate actions are:

	Amount settled for	% of mutual fund trade
Wachovia Securities, LLC	$4,844,465	28.77%
UBS Financial Services Inc.	4,621,768	30.03
American Express Financial Advisors Inc.	3,706,693	29.70
Raymond James Financial Services, Inc.	2,595,129	31.78
Legg Mason Wood Walker, Inc.	2,315,467	34.61
Linsco/Private Ledger Corp.	2,232,805	35.64
H.D. Vest Investment Securities, Inc.	725,216	33.39

The firms settling with the NASD only are:

	Amount settled for	% of mutual fund trade
Bear, Stearns & Co. Inc.	$280,469	52.00%
Lehman Brothers Inc.	123,882	59.96
Cresap, Inc.	99,458	88.48
SWS Financial Services	66,468	89.69
Kirkpatrick, Pettis, Smith, Polian Inc.	39,935	53.56
Southwest Securities, Inc.	36,971	89.02
David Lerner Associates, Inc.	32,711	64.88
Brecek & Young Advisors, Inc.	31,224	53.74

Source: NASD, 2004

FUNKY INVESTMENTS

Although I did not see this often with our clients, it is a major problem in the industry. I call them funky investments, those risky and hard-to-understand new offerings. They appeal to Mr. Marketing because the commissions are usually higher than traditional investments. The general rationale is that the market is not doing well, so maybe my clients would do better in a nontraditional investment vehicle. This reasoning is faulty, of course, because if the market is not doing well, why would these do any better? Here are some of the problem issues:

- Hedge funds
- Notes
- Limited partnerships
- Viaticals
- Anything exotic

The problems with using these are many:

- Generally these exotic investments have little or no oversight and regulation. It is impossible to tell if you are getting the straight story from the management or if their financials are even accurate.
- Usually there is no transparency. You do not know what is going on and you do not have any way to find out.
- With no secondary market, there is no place to liquidate these if your client needs to cash out.
- Sometimes there are undisclosed compensation arrangements between partners and affiliates that make the investment suspect.
- Rarely are these investments included in an "E and O" policy. So if you are sued on them, you are on your own.
- Finally, they are usually not on a broker/dealer's approved list. Selling them is considered selling away, a serious rule violation.

Solution: If it is not on the approved product list—do not sell it. If you are fee-only, be very careful about oddball products.

FAILURE TO SUPERVISE

Many home office staff members think their securities licenses are relatively safe—after all it is the rep or salespeople who get into trouble, not the group with the steady jobs in the home office. Unfortunately, even home office personnel are not immune in today's environment.

Going up the chain of command is now a common occurrence. At Morgan Stanley, the head of retail sales was fined substantially for failure to supervise branch offices for illegal mutual fund contests. If anything, supervisors may be hit harder in the future because regulators reason they should have known better.

USING A MORTGAGE TO PURCHASE INVESTMENTS

At the 2004 SIA conference, one senior person from the NASD went on record as saying 99 percent of the time it is unsuitable to recommend an investor borrow money on their home and invest it. The NASD and other regulators will be bringing more actions in this area. The risks are many because large amounts of money are usually involved, investors risk more than just their savings—they could lose their homes, and the investments must return more than the loan in order to succeed.

Solution: Given the attention of regulators, it is best to avoid these entirely.

ADVERTISING

Even rookie reps know they need to file their advertising with the proper supervisor. However, this area is becoming more filled with land mines. Regulators recently reported on a case where the rep filed her ad with the compliance department, just as her policies and procedures demanded. The compliance department approved it. Unfortunately for the rep, she still was sanctioned for the offending ad. The rep's defense that she relied on the compliance person did not cut any slack with the regulators. The rep was fined and suspended even though she had relied on her compliance department.

Solution: Learn what you can and cannot say in ads, correspondence, and sales literature, because you will be held responsible.

FLAKY CLIENTS

One of the biggest dangers in the business is the flaky client. They could be the alcoholic or the compulsive gambler—whatever the cause they can be a lot more trouble than their commissions are worth. Take the case of a small broker/dealer in Denver. One of their newer reps had a client walk in one day with millions to invest on margin. The rep did not properly complete all the margin documents or do his own due diligence on the new client. He did not even ask the obvious question: "If you have made so much money, why are you now wanting to do business with me?" The rep just looked at the dollar signs. It turned out to be a stock manipulation scheme. When the stock went south dramatically two days later, and the client had not put up the proper security for the margin calls, the broker/dealer found itself in the dreadful position of violating net capital requirements. The NASD and the SEC showed up to close the doors in short order. This one flaky client brought down an entire company.

Solution: Do not ignore the warning signs in favor of the big check. Good questions to ask:

- Why are you coming to me?
- Why are you changing advisors?
- Have you ever sued anyone?

TRADING ERRORS

Trading errors can be common with some superstars because they are doing so many trades. The typical situation involves failing to invest the client's money and not discovering it until after the market has moved adversely to the client's interest. These will always cost you the price of the error. One rep managed to lose his biggest client's check. By the time he discovered it, there was $65,000 in lost interest. Fortunately for the rep, he had errors and omissions insurance.

Solution: Set up procedures to double-check trades; match the confirms with the trades and do a daily accounting check, like a bank would do, to make sure nothing falls through the cracks.

LIVING ON THE EDGE

Although this has never happened to one of our clients, the situation is so common, it is good to discuss it here. Sometimes superstars let the money go to their head and they start living on the edge. I am reminded of one well-known advisor who was frequently in the top three producers of his broker/dealer. I was in the home office of the broker/dealer when they let me in on a little secret: They were planning to terminate Mr. Superstar. I was flabbergasted because he added a huge amount of commissions to their bottom line.

I asked if he had committed some heinous violation. "Not yet," they replied, "but it is only a matter of time. Mr. Superstar was so overextended they knew it was only a matter of time before at the least he started to push inappropriate products for the commissions, or in the worst case, started stealing from clients. The broker/dealer did not want to take chances, so they terminated him.

Solution: If you are in financial trouble yourself, get help before your clients suffer.

In conclusion, sometimes financial advisors become discouraged with the plethora of rules and regulations in our industry. It is true, it is a very complex industry; however, I believe we can keep it very simple. If it is good for the client, it is likely regulators are going to think it is good, too.

MORAL OF THE STORIES

Take these steps to help you sleep better at night:

- Be your own chief compliance officer. Do not solely rely on your broker/dealer to save you—you might know more than they do.
- Stay away from funky investments.
- Disclose, disclose, disclose.
- If you make a lot of money at the expense of a client, it is wrong and you are in trouble.
- Watch what you say in e-mails and instant messaging.

KEY POINTS

1. Focusing on good ethics is good for your business.
2. Rules and regulations covering the financial industry are so complex even the cleanest or most reputable firm may not escape a serious compliance examination.
3. Superstars should tighten up compliance procedures and reduce the chances for a lawsuit or deficiency letter from regulators.
4. Files—be prepared and always have them in good order.

5. Examinations—know what you are required to keep and what could be examined in a surprise audit. Then set up a system that allows quick retrieval:
   - Have a dual set of files.
   - Keep thorough notes on your recommendations.
   - Always do what is in the best interest of the client.
6. Do not promise something you cannot be sure will be delivered, such as investment performance.
7. Paying referral fees without proper registration violates regulations, no matter your motive.
8. Do not let your commissions influence what products you recommend.
9. A written investment policy statement helps solidify reasonable client expectations.
10. Create the right forms for proper disclosure to clients.
11. Developing an easy-to-follow compliance system will save you time and trouble.
12. Everyone in your firm needs to understand the importance of good ethics.
13. All the rules and regulations can be discouraging. Keep it simple: If it is good for your client, it is likely regulators are going to think it is good, too.

9

PULLING IT
ALL TOGETHER

By Katherine and Peter

WHERE TO START?

We recognize there is a lot of information here and you may be wondering how to get started creating your own multi-million-dollar practice. There are two kinds of firms that will want to start implementing these principles right away: The first is the stressed-out entrepreneur who is working harder and making less money. This person does not want to sell his practice, but he wants to make a whole lot more money with a lot less effort. The stressed-out entrepreneur, or group of advisors, needs to focus on increasing profitability. It is the increased profits, methodically saved and invested, that will allow him to reach his financial dreams.

The second firm is one that wants to maximize their return on investment (ROI). These folks see the business as an asset, that when properly positioned, leveraged, and sold will return a large sum of cash, enabling the owners to live the life of their dreams. This group needs to focus on building the valuation of their firm, so when the time comes to sell it, they can get top dollar.

The good news: Most of the principles in this book will work in both types of practices.

We are well aware that implementing the principles in this book can feel like eating an elephant. How do you do that? One bite at a time. Sometimes it can be difficult to determine which bite to take first. Take this test to see how your practice measures up. The results will let you know where you need to start.

1. Team-based business

___ We have a written plan in place to transfer loyalty from our star to the team. (Strong yes = 5 points, Weak yes = 3 points, No = 0)

___ New prospects are easily and happily transferred from the star to another member of the team. (Strong yes = 5 points, Weak yes = 3 points, No = 0)

___ Our company is set up to have the financial advisors do what they do best—everything else is delegated. (Strong yes = 10 points, Weak yes = 5 points, No = 0)

Total points _____ divided by 20 = _____ percent

2. Strategic planning

___ We have a written document that lists our company's goals and objectives over the next five years. (Strong yes = 20 points, Weak yes = 10 points, No = 10)

___ We have a written tactical plan for how we are going to accomplish our goals over the next five years. (Strong yes = 10 points, Weak yes = 5 points, No = 10)

___ We have a written exit strategy that includes transferring the practice to a new buyer, employees, or appropriate relatives. (Strong yes = 10 points, Weak yes = 5 points, No = 10)

Total _____ divided by 40 = _____ percent

3. Fiscal and asset management

___ We have mapped our own Money Trail™ and have listed all the steps necessary in our business process. Each step has been assigned to an employee. (Strong yes = 20 points, Weak yes = 10 points, No = 0)

___ We know what our true breakeven is and we are profitable 10 months out of every 12. (Strong yes = 20 points, Weak yes = 10 points, No = 0)

___ We have a written plan for profits allocating them to reserves, growth, risk, incentives, and dividends. (Strong yes = 20 points, Weak yes = 10 points, No = 0)

___ We are so profitable we do not know what to do with all of our profits! (Strong yes = 20 points, Weak yes = 10 points, No = 0)

Total _____ divided by 80 = _____ percent

4. Marketing

___ We have a written marketing plan that covers the next 12 months. (Strong yes = 10 points, Weak yes = 5 points, No = 0)

___ We track our leads and know precisely how much each prospect costs and which methods are working. (Strong yes = 5 points, Weak yes = 3 points, No = 0)

___ We have a steady stream of new business coming in the door and are confident our marketing techniques are working. (Strong yes = 10 points, Weak yes = 5 points, No = 0)

___ We have thought through our model client experience and compared it to each step of our process, making changes according to the model where necessary. (Strong yes = 5 points, Weak yes = 3 points, No = 0)

___ We have an elevator statement and short commercial about our firm. And everyone in the firm, including all support staff, can recite it easily. (Strong yes = 5 points, Weak yes = 3 points, No = 0)

___ We have identified our compelling story and differentiation—it is included on all of our materials, ads, and promotions. (Strong yes = 5 points, Weak yes = 3 points, No = 0)

Total _____ divided by 40 = _____ percent

5. Operations and support

___ We use registered assistants to process paperwork, handle service requests, and free up the financial advisor's time. (Strong yes = 20 points, Weak yes = 10 points, No = 0)

___ Financial advisors in our firm spend an average of 25 hours per week meeting face-to-face with clients. (Strong yes = 20 points, Weak yes = 10 points, No = 0)

___ We use other experts to assist us with areas beyond our expertise, such as estate planning, tax, etc. (Strong yes = 5 points, Weak yes = 3 points, No = 0)

Total _____ divided by 45 = _____ percent

6. Employees

___ Each of our employees has a job description and clearly understands what their duties and responsibilities are. (Strong yes = 10 points, Weak yes = 5 points, No = 0)

___ We have a system for delegating to our employees that takes into account the five levels of delegation. (Strong yes = 10 points, Weak yes = 5 points, No = 0)

___ We have a warm, friendly, affirming culture at our company. (Strong yes = 10 points, Weak yes = 5 points, No = 0)
___ We focus on everyone working in areas of their strengths. (Strong yes = 10 points, Weak yes = 5 points, No = 0)
___ We have an employee incentive program. (Strong yes = 10 points, Weak yes = 5 points, No = 0)
___ We review our employees quarterly. (Strong yes = 10 points, Weak yes = 5 points, No = 0)
___ We never hire an employee without them taking the Kolbe A™ index to see if they are a good fit. (Strong yes = 10 points, Weak yes = 5 points, No = 0)

Total _____ divided by 70 = _____ percent

7. Sales system

___ We have an effective, documented sales system that allows us to close more than 60 percent of our prospects. (Strong yes = 10 points, Weak yes = 5 points, No = 0) (5 bonus points if your closing ratio is above 90 percent.)
___ Our system is low key, respectful, and focuses on the client's needs and goals. We do not push products. (Strong yes = 5 points, Weak yes = 3 points, No = 0)
___ Our entire staff clearly understands each and every domino in our sales system and all the dominos are in place. (Strong yes = 5 points, Weak yes = 3 points, No = 0)
___ We carefully explore and document our client's expectations of us before we take a new case. (Strong yes = 5 points, Weak yes = 3 points, No = 0)
___ We advise clients of the importance of referrals early in our relationship. (Strong yes = 5 points, Weak yes = 3 points, No = 0)

Total _____ divided by 35 = _____ percent

8. Compliance

___ We have a person in our office who is our internal compliance officer. They are responsible for keeping us up to speed on the latest rules and regulations and for making sure we have the proper policies and procedures in place. (Strong yes = 10 points, Weak yes = 5 points, No = 0)

___ We are especially careful when selling products that are on the regulator's hot list, such as variable annuities. We use the proper disclosure forms in every case. (Strong yes = 5 points, Weak yes = 3 points, No = 0)

___ All of our files are carefully documented. There are no loose papers. All notes are signed and dated. (Strong yes = 10 points, Weak yes = 5 points, No = 0)

___ If required, we could easily produce e-mails from all clients who bought a particular investment three years ago. (Strong yes = 10 points, Weak yes = 5 points, No = 0)

Total ___ divided by 35 = ___ percent

Scoring: Take your points in each section and divide by the maximum in that section for a percentage. We found many entrepreneurs could be making a great deal of money just averaging a 60 percent score on all of these factors. The problem was they were very stressed, sometimes unhappy, and they did not have a business to sell. If you want to sell your business, or just increase profits and reduce stress, you will need at least an 80 percent in each section. The higher the number, the more likely you will be wildly profitable. No one ever scores 100 percent!

Knowing where to start can be a challenge. In fact, in every firm we have ever assisted, we started in a different spot. The reason was complex. First we looked at the hopes and dreams of the owners, and then we looked at their greatest area of pain. We would usually work on fixing the most pressing pain, so long as it moved us closer to the ultimate goal.

Frequently, the most pressing problem was a combination of employee issues with the superstar doing a great deal of work that was draining and not adding to the bottom line. For these people, we looked at the Kolbe indexes of the owner and all the staff to see if they were working within their strengths. We realigned job duties to fit strengths or hired appropriate people to fill in with the right talents when necessary. One of the main goals was always to free up the financial advisor's time to spend more time meeting with clients and making money.

Another common occurrence was lots of income, with little-to-no profit, leading to high levels of financial stress with the owners. Here we would get a handle on their cash management with a FlexBudget™, and create a plan for increasing profits. Whenever possible, we put the owner on a salary, augmented with bonuses based on profits. This helped balance the cash flow and made it easier to compute employee bonuses. We usually beefed up the marketing efforts to make sure there were enough derrieres in chairs.

You should look at your scores above. Circle every one that is below 60 percent. Then go back and number the categories in the areas of greatest pain. Number one is the area of greatest pain; number eight should be running pretty smoothly. This analysis should help you identify which area to start improving on first, or as we say, where to start eating the elephant.

VALUATION

Here are Peter's suggestions for those who want to sell their business for top dollar.

The key element to building valuation of the company is to create a sustainable business that can continue to service its clients when you, the owner, are no longer there. What are the core elements in accomplishing this?

1. Become a team-based company, not a star-based company.
2. Define your systems through the Money Trail™ so they become your business's actual day-to-day practices, and occur as part of the routine of running the store, whether or not you are there.
3. Pay yourself a salary and collect your profitability on the practice through dividends. This is critical as an accounting practice because it displays to potential buyers or people who may wish to merge with your firm what the true performance benefit of the practice becomes.
4. Document your strategic plan year by year and keep the history. Show how you have been able to migrate through your growth tactics and strategies, learning along the way, while increasing revenues, profitability, and dividends to both employees as well as shareholders. This becomes an important factor in establishing a growing valuation of your practice.
5. Utilize good accounting practices both in reports you generate through accounting software as well as through tools like the FlexBudget™.
6. Understand that the sale of your practice is a transition. Clients have come to trust you as well as your team on a personal basis. Make sure that the acquiring party is integrated initially into meetings and gradually takes over the relationships with clients. This can be done through events and actual planning reviews.
7. Build marketing strategies that regularly generate strong customer service and support, as well as a steady stream of new clients through referrals, marketing campaigns, and education. This can include contact with your clients and prospects through the Internet, the media, and public relations efforts.
8. Finally, if you are truly curious, invest the money to have a professional organization, such as Moss Adams, do a true valuation of your practice.

Follow these guidelines and you will see your financial services practice steadily grow in valuation. Most of all, you will know the satisfaction of having contributed great things to all the people connected with your life.

We are well aware that moving your company to the next level can seem a daunting task. Here are a few thoughts that can help you through your transition to building the business of your dreams:

- First, cut yourself some slack—there was a reason Rome was not built in a day, and building a world-class practice takes time, too. Even taking just one area and making steps to improve it will reduce your stress and add to your bottom line. We had one advisor who was making about $275,000 per year. He only followed about 10 percent of our advice and he increased his income by more than $100,000 in just one year. Sometimes even minor changes can bring big results.

- Second, get some outside help. One thing about the superstars—they are willing to do whatever it takes to become a star and stay a star. Superstars are willing to do what the average advisor is not willing to do. They are not afraid to spend money on marketing, coaching, and business consulting because they know it will all add up to a much more profitable business.

- Finally, the first place we start with every one of our clients is a thorough Kolbe review. If we clearly understand the strengths and weaknesses of the superstars and their support staff, it is much easier to design a system that will plug their gaps, reduce their stress, and make them a lot more money. It is crucial to getting the right people on the bus in the right seats.

KEY POINTS

1. There are two types of advisors: those who create a team-based practice and will sell their business for top dollar and live on the proceeds, and those who want to stay the star. The stars must have a serious savings plan in place to fund their retirement because they will be unable to sell their practice for top dollar.

2. The principles in this book will help both types of advisors.

3. Score your business using our test, and then pick the area with the lowest percentage score and the highest pain factor to start working your strategic plan.

4. Early in your business makeover, use the Kolbe System™ to get the right people on your bus in the right seats.

5. Commit to yourself that you will do whatever it takes to become a superstar.

6. Superstars are not afraid to spend money on coaching, marketing, or business consulting because they know it will help them make more money.

By Katherine and Peter

One person who has had an impact on our business thinking is Napoleon Hill, author of the classic *Think and Grow Rich*. You probably know the story. Hill was a young reporter/investigator when he was sent to interview Andrew Carnegie. Carnegie challenged him to interview the wealthiest Americans and discover the common traits that led them to create vast sums of wealth and become industry leaders. Hill took the challenge and interviewed hundreds of America's best businessmen and leaders, including Teddy Roosevelt, Henry Ford, George Eastman, John D. Rockefeller, Thomas Edison, and F. W. Woolworth. Unfortunately, there were no women on his list.

Based on his interviews he came up with 13 steps to creating wealth. Five of them are important success factors for the multi-million-dollar advisor.

KEY FACTORS FOR THE MULTI-MILLION-DOLLAR ADVISOR

1. A burning desire to succeed
2. Faith they would succeed
3. A written plan for success
4. Using an accountability group to stay focused on success
5. A plan for overcoming the fears that prevent success

A Burning Desire to Succeed

We do not believe financial advisors, wealth managers, and financial planners lackadaisically fall into making a million dollars a year. In order to be a wild success in this business you need a burning desire—a desire that is so strong nothing will stop you from achieving your goal. That is why superstar financial advisors, like the wealthiest self-made Americans, are willing to do what average advisors are not willing to do.

Faith They Would Succeed

Superstars have a great level of confidence. They strongly believe they have what it takes to make a million dollars a year or even more in this business. Once again they never let in any thoughts to the contrary; they never entertain any doubts that they can achieve the goals they set. Locking on this belief, and never letting go, is an essential part of the emotional mind-set necessary to achieve superstar status.

A Written Plan for Success

As we mentioned, few financial advisors had created a formal, written strategic business plan. However, even taking a single piece of paper and writing down your goals and then putting down your strategies and tactics for reaching those goals can be a big part of achieving the success you desire. Keep this document in a place where you can review it every day to keep you focused.

Using an Accountability Group to Stay Focused on Success

Napoleon Hill originated the Master Mind Group for getting input into the entrepreneur's business and for staying accountable. Most superstars must be held responsible to someone besides themselves to get to the levels they desire. Some advisors have their own Master Mind Groups. Others have created a board of advisors from their best clients. A few have personal coaches.

We sometimes become the accountability partner for our clients. This seems to be a big part of keeping the advisor on track and focused toward the ultimate prize. One thing we discovered is that financial advisors who stop using an accountability partner quickly fall back into old patterns that keep them from becoming or remaining a multi-million-dollar advisor. Their success can evaporate if they are not answerable to someone.

A Plan for Overcoming the Fears That Prevent Success

We saved this for last because it is the number one reason advisors fail to build a multi-million-dollar practice—their fears. Frankly, there is no end to the list of fears that can stymie a good business plan. However, the two big ones are fears of spending money and fears of hiring staff.

Many ideas we have outlined in this book to help you succeed are either no-cost or low-cost strategies for helping you make more money. Eventually, though, if you have a burning desire to be a multi-million-dollar advisor, you have the faith to believe you can succeed as a multi-million-dollar advisor, and you have your written plan and accountability partners, you will be faced with a choice: spending money to help you get to the next level, or giving in to your fears, and staying where you are.

The expenditures might be for a coaching program, for training on how to close more business, or even money for a high-touch marketing plan or hiring a needed assistant. This is where you will be faced with a crossroads—can you overcome your fears to make the investment your future needs to get to the next level, or will you stay in your comfort zone? Only you can make that decision, but let us give you a little encouragement: Go for it. If you don't, you will always have regrets about what you could have achieved had you just taken the plunge.

You must overcome your fears in order to succeed.

PARTING THOUGHTS

Your role as an entrepreneur and advisor can dramatically impact not only all the people who work for you, but the hundreds or even thousands of clients you will serve in your career. In many cases, by showing them the way to prosperity and financial security, you are impacting their lives forever. It is an awesome responsibility. More than teachers, counselors, pastors, or lawyers, you can have a dramatic impact on your clients' lives and the lives of your employees. You can help them live the life of their dreams.

We think the true way to prosperity is to take this responsibility seriously and strive to create a business that allows all your stakeholders to prosper, including your employees, your family, and your clients.

We wish you and all your stakeholders health and prosperity.

VESTMENT ADVISORS FORMS

Electronic versions of the following forms are available at http://www.vestmenstadvisors.com/docmate/.

First Meeting

- Agenda letter for first meeting   277
- Interview questions for first interview   279
- First meeting summary letter   280
- Engagement letter   283
- First meeting follow-up letter #1   285
- First meeting follow-up letter #2   286

Second Meeting

- Agenda letter for second meeting   287
- Follow-up letter after recommendations   288
- Second meeting follow-up letter   292

Product

- Agenda letter for delivery meeting   293
- Additional information letter (VA, VUL, MF)   294
- Variable universal life summary description   296
- Letter of product recommendations   298
- Variable annuity suitability checklist   299

Marketing (Drip-Marketing Letters and Response Notes)

- Children letter   303
- Children response note   304
- Social Security letter   305
- Social Security response note   307
- Small business retirement plan letter   308
- Small business retirement plan response note   310
- Stock funds letter   311
- Stock funds response note   313
- Self-employed letter   314
- Self-employed response note   316
- Retirement planning letter   317
- Retirement planning response note   319
- Referral letter   320
- Client satisfaction letter   322
- Client satisfaction survey   323
- Sample bio/professional profile   325

Employment (Job Descriptions)

- Chief operating officer   326
- Client service coordinator   328

Miscellaneous

- Money Trail™   330

AGENDA LETTER FOR FIRST MEETING

Enter Date

Enter Client's Name(s)
Enter Client's Address
Enter Client's City, State, and Zip Code

Dear *Enter Client's Name(s):*

Re: Courtesy Interview Agenda

I look forward to meeting with you next *Enter date and time* AM/PM. To help our meeting run smoothly and ensure we cover all your areas of concern, an agenda is listed below. Be sure to bring any documents you want reviewed.

Courtesy Interview Agenda

1. Overview

   a. Brief review of the seminar you attended, the financial planning process, and why planning from a tax perspective is important.
   b. Discuss confidentiality of information.

2. Discuss or Review Data-Gathering Forms and Documents

   a. Personal information booklet
   b. Investment policy and objective-setting questionnaire
   c. Employee benefits and career path
   d. Investment attitudes and risk tolerance
   e. Current will and estate arrangements
   f. Attitude on gifts to children/grandchildren
   g. Current attitude toward charitable bequests
   h. Any additional documents and information necessary for planning

3. Review of Notes and Personal Objectives

   a. Anticipated retirement date, location, and philosophy.
   b. Prioritize the personal objectives.
   c. Determine education goals for self/children/grandchildren.
   d. List other personal goals.

4. Our Next Steps and Your Next Steps

Please call me right away at *(phone number)* if you have any questions or wish to make any changes to the agenda.

With warmest personal regards,

Your Company Name

Your Name
Title

INTERVIEW QUESTIONS
FOR FIRST INTERVIEW

Name: *Enter Name*

Date: *Enter Date*

Questions

1. What are your top three concerns about your finances, your future, and the future of your loved ones?
2. What are the three most important things we can do for you?
3. What are the three most important reasons for working with *Your Company Name* as your financial advisor?
4. What should we do in an emergency if we cannot reach you?
5. What is the best and worst investment you ever made, and why?
6. How would you describe a successful relationship with a financial planner?
7. One year from now, what needs to happen for you to be happy and satisfied with your financial progress?
8. Three years from now, what needs to happen?
9. What can we do to make this relationship better for you?
10. Have you had any previous financial advisors? If so, how many? Why did you terminate the relationship(s)?
11. What did you like about the previous relationships? What would you have wanted to change?
12. Have you ever been involved in litigation and/or arbitration? With a financial advisor? Please elaborate.
13. If there were one thing that I would do that would cause you to terminate our relationship and move your assets to a competitor, what would it be?
14. What did you learn in the last workshop that had the most positive affect on you?

FIRST MEETING SUMMARY LETTER

Enter Date

Enter Client's Name(s)
Enter Client's Address
Enter Client's City, State, and Zip Code

Dear *Enter Client's Name(s):*

It was a great pleasure to meet with you last *Enter date and time* AM/PM in our offices to review the classes *Enter name of classes* that you attended.

Our last visit was very productive and therefore a good beginning. Although compiling this data is somewhat tedious, its accuracy is essential to proper comprehensive planning. I would now like to recap that meeting and outline what is ahead. We have gathered a great deal of factual and subjective financial information from you. We determined your goals, timing parameters, and risk temperament. We also know what assets, discretionary income, and other potential resources we have to work with. If I understood you correctly, your current major areas of concern are: *(LIST CONCERNS)*

1. <u>Your Goals and Values</u>
    During the courtesy interview, we reviewed what is important to you about your money. After working through your own personal financial road map, you came up with the following goals and values that are critically important to you:

    a. _____
    b. _____
    c. _____
    d. _____
    e. _____

2. We discussed the need for income for your survivors, should the head of your family die. At this time, it appears that you would need approximately *Enter appropriate lump sum needed* dollars in a lump sum to provide the necessary monthly income if *Enter client's name* should predecease *Enter spouse's name*.

We also discussed how the devastating effect of taxes and inflation can impact the amount most working Americans need to retire with dignity.

Based on the information you provided us, you agreed that the following asset mix seemed appropriate to you: *Describe new recommendations.*

3. <u>Assumptions</u>
   As you know, it is absolutely impossible to predict the future with any degree of certainty. This is particularly true when it comes to financial planning. Generally, there are no guarantees in this business, unless specifically stated in the prospectus. It is important to realize that any investments will fluctuate in value. Although we can make projections and educated "guesses," it is crucially important that we continue to work together over the next few years. We will constantly reassess your situation and make changes as necessary.

   For your information, we are currently using the following assumptions:

   - For inflation, we assume a 4 percent rate. In fact, inflation has actually averaged 4.6 percent over the past 20 years.
   - For tax brackets, we generally use a 35 percent figure, which we have found to be typical for clients in this area. It usually covers federal, state, and local income taxes, but your actual tax bracket may be higher or lower based on your income.

4. <u>Documents</u>
   Before we concluded our meeting, we provided you with a copy of our ADV, Part II, which describes our registered investment advisory services. You also signed a receipt for this form. We left you a copy of our engagement letter for future services. We would like you to take it home, review it, and bring it to our next meeting.

5. <u>Confidentiality</u>
   To put your mind at ease, be assured that we treat all personal information and conversations with the strictest confidence. In fact, outside of a court order, we cannot release this information to anyone without your permission.

Optional. However, you did indicate that we would be free to discuss your situation with *List the names of the people: attorney, CPAs, or children.*

6. Next Meeting
   Our next meeting is scheduled for *Enter date, time, and location,* or (we will call to schedule the next meeting). The purpose of the next meeting will be to review your personal financial situation, and at that time, we will be making specific financial recommendations.

7. Our Goals
   At *Your firm name here* we have a number of goals. We particularly enjoy helping working Americans retire with dignity. We also believe strongly in planning from a NET perspective. That means that although returns are important, of course, it is probably more important to look at tax consequences. Our goals also include helping you design a more tax-efficient planning strategy.

Remember, we are in the business of happy, satisfied clients. We do ask that you make us one promise. If, for any reason, you are ever unhappy with our products or services, come and talk to one of us immediately. Please give us a chance to rectify the situation before you discuss it with your neighbor or your brother-in-law.

We look forward to our next meeting. In the meantime, if you have any questions at all, feel free to call me at *Enter your phone number.*

With warmest personal regards,

Your Firm Name Here

Your Name
Title

   P.S. Do not forget to bring your engagement letter and *(Enter other information needed)* **to the next meeting.**

ENGAGEMENT LETTER

Enter Date

Enter Client's Name(s)
Enter Client's Address
Enter City, State, and Zip Code

Re: Engagement Letter

Dear *Enter Client's Name(s):*

It was a pleasure to meet with you last *Enter day*. You have already completed the most difficult part of the financial process, gathering the necessary data and making the commitment to improve your financial future. Congratulations! I am looking forward to helping you reach all of your financial goals.

Let me take a few minutes to summarize our relationship and to make sure I clearly understand what you want to achieve.

Goals and Objectives: You indicated you wanted to retire in *(Enter number)* years on the equivalent of $_____ per month, pretax, in today's dollars. You have also indicated the desire to *(Fill in goals and objectives)*.

Investment Temperament: Based on our conversations, it appears you are fairly *(Choose One: a) conservative, b) willing to take moderate risk, c) willing to take some risk to reach your goal.)*

Capital Available: You have indicated you are able to invest $_____ per month this year toward reaching all of your goals. You also anticipate you should be able to increase that amount by ___ percent per year between now and retirement. You also have an additional lump sum of $___ that is available for investing.

Expectations: We reviewed a number of expectations that you had of our relationship. Briefly, they are: _____. *(Do not include anything about returns.)*

My Role in Insurance and Security Sales: As your financial advisor, I am involved in the sales of securities and insurance products on a commission basis. All recommendations made for the purchase of insurance and securities products would then be made in my capacity as a salesperson for your account. There will be no additional fees and compensation received on my part. The only compensation I will then receive would be commissions on the products I recommend.

What I Will Not Do: As I mentioned to you in our interview, I will not be giving you legal or tax advice. If we determine legal advice would be appropriate, we will meet with your personal attorney. Furthermore, I will not review any of your property or casualty policies, including your homeowner and automobile policies. However, these are important areas, and I strongly recommend you review them with your property and casualty insurance agent to make sure you have adequate coverage. I will not be preparing a written financial plan.

Next Meeting: Our next meeting is scheduled for *(Enter date* at *Enter time)*. I will be presenting some investments for you to review at that time. The meeting should take approximately ___ hours.

No Guarantees: Due to the fluctuating markets, it is important to remember that your investments, at any point in time, may be worth more or less than the original purchase price.

Misunderstandings: I believe open communications are the key to a successful relationship. If at any time you feel I am not meeting your expectations, or worse, have done something that is upsetting to you, please contact me immediately! I want the chance to make it right. This is extremely important to me, because I want to make sure you are happy and satisfied with our relationship.

Action: If this letter accurately reflects your understanding of our relationship, please sign below and return the original to me. The copy is for your files. If I have misunderstood something, please call me immediately at *your phone here.*

Once again, I know I am going to enjoy working with you, *Enter client's name(s),* and getting to know you better.

Warmest personal regards,

Your Company's Name

Enter Your Name
Title

_____   _____
Enter Client's Name   *Enter Client's Name*

Date _____   *Date* _____

Reprinted with permission of Bloomberg Press.

FIRST MEETING FOLLOW-UP LETTER #1

Enter Date

Enter Client's Name(s)
Enter Client's Address
Enter City, State, and Zip Code

> *"I think this is the beginning of a beautiful friendship. . . ."*
> **—Humphrey Bogart, *Casablanca***

Dear *Enter Client's Name(s):*

It was a pleasure meeting with you last *Enter day* at *Enter date* and reviewing your goals, objectives, and concerns. We are honored that you want to work with our firm, and we look forward to a long-term relationship.

Enter client's name, enclosed are the notes from our last meeting. Please review them carefully and call us if we have misunderstood anything.

Our next meeting is scheduled on *Enter date and time.* At that time, we will *"fill in purpose of meeting."* Feel free to call if you have any questions. Once again, thank you for choosing us.

Sincerely,

Your Company Name Here

Your Name
Title

FIRST MEETING FOLLOW-UP LETTER #2

Enter Date

Enter Client's Name(s)
Enter Client's Address
Enter City, State, and Zip Code

Dear *Enter Client's Name(s):*

Our last visit was very productive and a good beginning. Let me recap that meeting and outline what is ahead. We have gathered a great deal of factual and subjective financial information from you. We determined your goals, timing parameters, and risk temperament. We also know what assets, discretionary income, and other potential resources we have to address. *Enter client's name,* if I understood you correctly, your current major areas of concern are:

1. *Enter primary area of concern.*
2. *Enter secondary area of concern.*
3. *Enter third area of concern.*

I am now in a position to assess your personal financial profile. I will also determine what areas need to be addressed first and prioritize them for you. Our next meeting is scheduled for *Enter day and time* and will take approximately *Enter time.* At that time, we will review your profile and I will make specific recommendations.

Enter client's name, I am pleased with the opportunity to work with you because I believe we work well together. I am also confident we can provide the needed strategies required to reach your financial goals. I look forward to seeing you again soon *(or at our next meeting, scheduled . . .).*

Sincerely,

Your Company Name Here

Your Name
Title

PS. We are planning a golf clinic next month. Would you like to come and bring your favorite four-some?

AGENDA LETTER FOR SECOND MEETING

Enter Date

Enter Client's Name(s)
Enter Client's Address
Enter Client's City, State, and Zip Code

Dear *Enter Client's Name(s):*

Re: _____

We are looking forward to visiting with you again on *Enter date and time* in our offices. At that time, we will be taking the next steps toward helping you reach your financial goals. In order for the meeting to run more smoothly, we have prepared an agenda.

Agenda for second meeting where we will discuss:

1) Your goals and objectives again
2) Growing your money, including your current positions and recommendations for repositioning your assets in a more tax-efficient manner
3) The issue of sufficient emergency funds
4) Risk management, particularly in the areas of long-term care, long-term disability, and umbrella coverage
5) Estate planning recommendations.

We look forward to our next meeting. Please call if you have any questions.

Very truly yours,

Your Firm's Name Here

Your Name
Title

FOLLOW-UP LETTER AFTER RECOMMENDATIONS SECOND INTERVIEW (WRITTEN FINANCIAL PLAN)

Enter Date

Enter Client's Name(s)
Enter Client's Address
Enter Client's City, State, and Zip Code

Dear *Enter Client's Name(s):*

It was good to meet with you again in our offices on *Enter last meeting date and time.* Let me congratulate you on your taking the most important steps to reaching your financial goals; you are not only getting organized, you are making the commitments necessary to achieve what is important to you.

This letter will recap our last meeting and cover the financial planning recommendations that we made.

1. **Review Goals and Objectives**
   At our last meeting, we began by reviewing your goals and objectives. They included the following:

   1._____

   2._____

   3._____

   4._____

   Your personal risk tolerance and your Risk Tolerance/Investment Policy-Setting Questionnaire were also discussed.

2. **How You Are Growing Your Money**
   We next looked at your current investments to assess how you are growing your money.
   a. Matrix

At that time, your investments were put in our *Your firm's name here* Net Tax Planning Matrix to review how you were currently positioned. We then determined that you have the following distribution:

You have approximately $_____ ___% in guaranteed funds.

You have approximately $ _____ ___% in fixed income.

You have approximately $_____ ___% in equities.

"Or insert matrix"

b. Tax Efficiency

The tax efficiency of your current portfolio was reviewed. We determined that you currently have your investments distributed as follows:

$_____ Thousands of dollars ___% in taxable

$_____ Thousands of dollars ___% in tax deferred

$_____ Thousands of dollars ___% in income tax avoidance.

3. **Recommendations**

In order to have the potential for a greater return and more tax-efficient earnings, we recommend the following repositioning:

$_____ _____% in guaranteed funds

$_____ _____% in fixed income

$_____ _____% in equities

"Or insert new matrix"

4. **Emergency Funds**

Most of our clients find that they can pass the sleep test if they have three to six months in savings. For you we would recommend: (Money Market Accounts, Pass Book Savings, CDs, Line of Credit, amounts, etc.).

5. **Risk Management**

A number of different areas where you might have exposure to risk were reviewed, and we made the following recommendations:

a. Long-Term Care
We recommended a long-term care policy that will provide
$___ to $___ per day and would have lifetime benefits with a
5 percent inflation. It would also have an assisted-living
clause in addition to home health care. Based on your age,
we recommend *(Choose one: 1) wait until you become 40 to
50 to start long-term health care benefits, 2) start now, or 3) unfortunately, due to your health and age, long-term health care would be
too expensive for you at this time)*.

b. Long-Term Disability
We also discussed that your greatest asset is not your portfolio,
but your ability to earn money. Consequently, we recommend
a long-term disability policy. *Describe*

c. Umbrella Coverage
Finally, one of the most catastrophic things that can happen
to a family is an accident either in your car, your home, or
at some other location. Although it can be tragic if one of
your family members is injured in an accident, it can be
equally as tragic if your actions caused the injury of another.
Consequently, we recommend that you purchase, through
your property and casualty agent, a $1,000,000 to $2,000,000
umbrella policy to reduce exposure in lawsuits. Incidentally,
because our firm does not review property and casualty insurance, this is a good time to have your agent review all of your
property and casualty coverage to make sure that it is up-to-
date and sufficient.

6. **Estate Planning Recommendations**
Please see an attorney to review the status of your wills and
trusts. Based on our preliminary review, it is possible that you
might need an A-B Trust, an Irrevocable Trust, or even an
Irrevocable Living Trust. A good attorney should be able to
advise you on these matters, and I will be happy to work with them.

7. **Investment Policy Statement**
To clarify our thinking on how you want to handle your investments, we prepared a draft of an Investment Policy Statement
for you. We will review it with you at our next meeting.

8. **No Guarantees**
As we have discussed, past performance is not a guarantee of
future success. This is because the markets will never be exactly

the same as they are on any given day. Regrettably, we can make absolutely no guarantees about performance. However, we can guarantee top-quality service. If for any reason we are not meeting your needs, please let us know so that we may address them immediately.

9. **Your Expectations**
Finally, we discussed your expectations of us. You said you most wanted an advisor who *(Refer to document #___, question # ___)*. We will work diligently to meet your needs. Thanks again for the confidence you have expressed in our firm, and please let us know if there is anything we can do to make your experience better.

Very truly yours,

Your Firm's Name Here

Your Name
Title

P.S. You and your family will be glad you took these important steps in financial planning for the future—yours and theirs.

SECOND MEETING FOLLOW-UP LETTER

Enter Date

Enter Client's Name(s)
Enter Client's Address
Enter City, State, and Zip Code

Dear *Enter Client's Name(s):*

Thank you for your expression of confidence in me as your financial consultant and congratulations on your progress thus far! It was good to see you again.

Enter client's name, I would like to recap the decisions put in motion at our last meeting, list any further items for consideration, and outline what is ahead:

1. *Decision*
2. *Decision*
3. *List further items/outline*
4. *List further items/outline*

It is now important for you to follow through with the recommendations, or if necessary, seek sound alternatives. The most valuable ingredient in successful investing is time. The sooner you begin, the greater your chances for success. The more time you have, the less money and risk required. The decisions you make now can mean financial independence and security for your future.

Developing financial strategies is a methodical procedure. It is a process that will change in both speed and direction as income and objectives change during your lifetime. Our relationship is therefore a potentially long-term one. We are determined to work hard to help you achieve your goals, and look forward to being of service to you for many successful years.

I will contact you to set a convenient time for our next visit. In the meantime, *Enter client's name,* please review the materials I have provided and come prepared to implement the ideas we agree are suitable. If you have any questions, please call me at any time.

Sincerely,

Your Company's Name Here

Your Name
Title

AGENDA LETTER FOR DELIVERY MEETING

Enter Date

Enter Client's Name(s)
Enter Client's Address
Enter Client's City, State, and Zip Code

Dear *Enter Client's Name(s):*

We look forward to meeting you on *Enter date and time* AM/PM in our offices. At that time, we will be delivering the following to you:

1. *(List product by company name, and amounts where necessary (e.g., $250,000 term policy with ABC, etc.)*
2.
3.
4.

In the meantime, if you should have any questions, do not hesitate to contact us.

With warmest personal regards,

Your Company's Name Here

Your Name
Title

P.S. Just a reminder: Our next client dinner is scheduled for *date, time, place*. If you have a friend who would like to attend with you, please let us know and we will be happy to send them an invitation.

ADDITIONAL INFORMATION LETTER
(VA, VUL, MF)

Enter Date

Enter Client's Name(s)
Enter Client's Address
Enter Client's City, State, and Zip Code

> *"Wisdom is knowing what to do next,*
> *skill is knowing how to do it, and virtue is doing it."*
> **—David Star Jordan**

Dear *Enter Client's Name(s):*

At *Your firm name here,* we would like to congratulate you on having the wisdom to know what to do next and the virtue of doing it. For you that meant taking a number of steps to create a better future for you and your family. You may recall some of those steps were selecting a variable annuity with _____, a variable universal life with _____, and mutual funds with

_____.

As we are in the process of updating the kinds of information we provide clients, it came to our attention that you might be interested in some of the new information we have regarding Variable Annuities, Mutual Funds, and Variable Universal Life. Consequently, we have attached descriptions of them. Please review each one and insert them in your binder.

Although there is nothing new in these letters, we thought you might like to have something in writing for your files.

By all means, if you have any questions at all about your investments, or if we could serve you in a better way, do not hesitate to call me at *Your direct number here* or via e-mail at *Your e-mail address here.*

Looking forward to seeing you at our annual barbeque on either *date* or *date.*

With warmest personal regards,

Your Firm's Name Here

Your Name
Title

P.S. **Our next dinner seminar is on *Enter date and time* AM/PM.**
Would you like to bring a friend?

VARIABLE UNIVERSAL LIFE SUMMARY DESCRIPTION

Enter Date

Enter Client's Name(s)
Enter Client's Address
Enter Client's City, State, and Zip Code

Dear *Enter Client's Name(s):*

RE: Variable Universal Life Policy

Today, we also recommended a Variable Universal Life policy in the amount of $_____. In the simplest terms, the Variable Universal Life policy provides life insurance and a chance to participate in the market. We recommended this policy for a number of reasons:

1. The *name of the policy* provides protection in the case of a premature death. It is one of the few things we can do in life that can benefit people we love or charities we care about when we are no longer here to protect and provide for them.
2. The policy provides tax-deferred growth.
3. It can provide income tax–advantaged withdrawals and income tax–free loans during your lifetime.
4. The death benefit, if structured properly, is income tax free to your beneficiaries.
5. It can also be estate tax free if it is put inside a proper life insurance trust.
6. With spendthrift provisions, in most states, the proceeds can be protected against creditors.
7. You can also use this as collateral should you need a loan.
8. The premium payments can be flexible.
9. You can move between subaccounts 12 times a year at no cost. This can help facilitate rebalancing.
10. It provides diversification between as many as 32 subaccounts in International Growth, Growth, Growth and Income, Balance, Bond, Money Market, Fixed Income, and Aggressive Growth.

11. Costs

The costs of this insurance policy fall into the following areas:

a. Premium taxes generally run between 2 percent and 3 percent.
b. Sales charges are generally 2 percent to 3 percent.
c. Administrative fees run between $8 to $12 per month.
d. Cost of insurance varies depending on the death benefit.
e. Mortality charges and expenses are approximately .9 percent.
f. Fund operating costs are currently between .35 percent to 1.5 percent.
g. In addition, there is a surrender charge for the first 15 years.

Consequently, it is important to realize this is an intermediate to long-term product. It is designed for a minimum 5- to 10-year holding period and it is not good for short-term liquidity.

During our meeting, we provided you with a prospectus and illustrations, and suggested that you review them carefully.

We thought this product was a particularly good choice for you because _____
_____
_____

If you have any questions about your policy, please feel free to call at any time.

Warmest personal regards,

Your Company's Name Here

Your Name
Title

P.S. **As I mentioned in out last meeting, I would be happy to meet with your children to review your plan with them. Just let me know what will work for you.**

LETTER OF PRODUCT RECOMMENDATIONS

Enter Date

Enter Client's Name(s)
Enter Client's Address
Enter Client's City, State, and Zip Code

Dear *Enter Client's Name(s):*

Once again, *Enter client's name* it has been a pleasure working with you and meeting together in our offices on *Enter date and time.* Let us recap the specific product recommendations we made. They include:

1. **Emergency Funds:** We recommend placing $_____ in *Name of specific product or investment.* We made this recommendation because _____.

2. **Taxable Equities**: We recommend placing $_____ in the *Name of mutual fund* for the following reasons:
   a. Mutual funds are a good way to diversify risk and get the advice of a professional money manager.
   b. _____.
   c. _____.
   We made this recommendation for the following reasons:
   _____.

3. **Tax-Deferred Money:** We recommend $_____ be invested in _____ Retirement Plan or _____ Qualified Plan because _____.

4. **Tax Free/Tax Avoidance:** We recommend placing $_____ in *Name of specific product or investment.* We made this recommendation because _____.

Separate letters are attached that describe variable annuities and variable universal life. Included also is a disclosure form about mutual funds. Please take time to read them because they summarize all our comments today.

Once again, it is a pleasure doing business with you.

Very truly yours,

Your Firm's Name Here

Your Name
Title

VARIABLE ANNUITY SUITABILITY CHECKLIST

Enter Date

Enter Client's Name(s)
Enter Client's Address
Enter Client's City, State, and Zip Code

Dear *Enter Client's Name(s):*

RE: *Name of Variable Annuity*

Recommendation
Based on the recent information that you provided us regarding your income, investable assets, liquid assets, financial objectives, age, and other data, we recommended a $_____ purchase into the *Name of annuity.*

Information Summary
To summarize the information that you gave us, you stated that:

Your annual income range is $ _____.
Your investable assets are $ _____.
Your estimated top tax bracket is % _____.
Your liquid assets are $ _____.

We also reviewed your financial information, tax status, investment objectives, and risk tolerance questionnaire before making a recommendation to purchase this variable annuity.

Experience
Your past investment experience includes the following types of investments:
    List

Variable Annuity Features
Variable annuities utilize private money managers and money managers from mutual fund companies to manage their subaccounts. A variable annuity offers three basic features that are not available in mutual funds:
  1. Tax-deferred treatment of earnings
  2. A death benefit
  3. Annuity options that can provide guaranteed income for life

Information about Variable Annuities

This letter will review various features about variable annuities that we discussed during our meeting today.

a. Insurance contract. We explained that a variable annuity was a contract with an insurance company with a securities component. This security is offered by *Name of broker/dealer*, our registered broker/dealer.

b. Returns not guaranteed. We also explained that the principal, dividend, yields, and return on this particular variable annuity's subaccounts may fluctuate with the market and other factors and **are not guaranteed.**

c. Prospectus provided. We provided you with a current prospectus for this annuity and encouraged you to read it, because it provides complete information about fees and expenses.

d. Features reviewed. We also reviewed all the product features of the variable annuity, which are also outlined in the prospectus in greater detail.

e. Surrender charges. The purchase of a variable annuity is a long-term investment product that not only lacks liquidity, but will have penalties for early withdrawal. This annuity includes a surrender charge of _____ percent, declining to _____ percent, over _____ years as outlined in the prospectus. Withdrawals from the annuity prior to age 59½ may be subject to a tax penalty.

f. 1035 exchange. (Optional. As we are doing a 1035 tax-free exchange, or qualified transfer from an existing annuity, it could be that the new annuity will provide a lower interest rate than the annuity you currently own. The current annuity may be free of surrender charges that the new annuity may have.)

g. Qualified plans. Purchasing a variable annuity in a qualified plan is purchasing a tax-deferred investment for a tax-deferred account, and there are no additional tax deferments available outside of those originally available in the tax-deferred account. As such, this variable annuity does not provide any additional tax treatment of earnings beyond the treatment provided by the tax-qualified retirement plan itself.

Why Did We Recommend a Variable Annuity?

There are a number of reasons we thought a variable annuity was appropriate for you and suitable at this particular time:

a. <u>Guaranteed death benefit in case of a down market</u>. At death, your beneficiaries will be protected and receive the greater of the balance in the subaccounts or $ _____ × $_____ . This benefit is also described in greater detail in the prospectus.

b. <u>Guaranteed annuitization option at retirement</u>. Unlike other investments, an annuity is valuable because it offers a guaranteed income for life, even if the market goes down. This is not available with other investments and it is the only product with a guaranteed income for life in retirement.

c. <u>You have access to different fund groups under one umbrella</u>. This allows you many different fund groups from the same investment vehicle.

d. <u>Diversification.</u> Using a variable annuity not only allows you to diversify by asset classes, but also by company style and manager.

e. <u>Simplicity.</u> A variable annuity allows you one statement even though you may have been invested with a number of different companies. We find many of our clients particularly like the simplicity this provides them in managing their finances.

f. <u>Simplicity</u>. A variable annuity also can simplify your affairs by providing you with one check when you either use systematic withdrawal or annuitization options.

g. <u>Money manager</u>. You are able to get some money managers who are not available outside of these investments.

h. <u>Rebalancing</u>. Finally, you can do automatic asset rebalancing at no additional charge, or if you prefer, we can advise you on a periodic basis on how to rebalance your portfolio.

i. We thought this was a particularly good choice for you because _____.

Costs

This variable annuity has the following charges:

a. There are mortality expense charges, administrative charges, and state and local government premium taxes of approximately _____ percent. Part of this fee goes to us to pay for our services and assisting you with this investment. Most clients agree to this because this is a long-term, tax-deferred vehicle.

b. Actual management fees on the subaccounts average about .8 percent. They can range from a low of .3 percent to a high of 1.5 percent.

c. Total costs usually range between 2.1 percent and 2.2 percent annually.

    d. You can move between subaccounts 12 times per year at no cost and with no tax consequences.

If this information is clear and understandable, please sign below indicating that you received a copy of this letter and understand the contents. Return it to us in the attached envelope. The copy is for your files.

If for any reason you have any questions, please contact me personally.

Very truly yours,

Your Company's Name Here

Your Name
Title

_____   _____
Client's Name   Date

_____   _____
Client's Name   Date

CHILDREN LETTER

Enter Date

Enter Client's Name(s)
Enter Client's Address
Enter City, State, and Zip Code

> *"Children have never been very good at listening to their elders,*
> *but they have never failed to imitate them."*
> **—James Baldwin**

Dear *Enter Client's Name(s):*

Your children and grandchildren have big dreams for the future. Will they have planned well enough to enjoy their hard work?

Maybe your children have expressed an interest in investing, but do not know where to start. I would like to meet with them to discuss their financial futures. I take pride in the service I give my clients, and want to extend that same level of service to their families.

Helping our children be financially secure should be the emotional legacy of every parent. This does not necessarily mean money, but education, opportunity, and a strong encouragement that they focus every day on their financial future. Too many people wait until nearing retirement age—do not let your children be in that group. Now is the best time for them to start saving and investing for the future.

> *When we are gone . . . we cannot help them, but we can today!*
> *We can be part of their "peace of mind"!*

Please fill out the enclosed form and fax it back to me.

If there is anything I can do for you, or your family, do not hesitate to call me at *Enter phone number.*

Sincerely,

Your Company's Name Here

Your Name
Title

Enclosure: Children Response Note

CHILDREN RESPONSE NOTE

Enter Date

Enter Your Name
Enter Your Address
Enter Your City, State, Zip Code

Dear *Enter Your Name*:

_____ Sounds interesting! My children do want to see some additional information on *investing*. Please drop it in the mail right away.

_____ Today, our children are not interested in *investing*, but I would like some information on how to encourage them to start planning now.

_____ Please contact my family member. They are expecting to hear from you.

Name

Relationship

Address

City/State/Zip Code

Phone Number

Best time to call is:

Sincerely,

Enter Client's Name(s)
Enter Client's Address
Enter Client's City, State, and Zip Code

For faster service, please fax to *Enter your fax number.*

SOCIAL SECURITY LETTER

Enter Date

Enter Client's Name(s)
Enter Client's Address
Enter City, State, and Zip Code

> *"You must know for which harbor you are headed if you are*
> *to catch the right wind to take you there."*
> **—Seneca**

Dear *Enter Client's Name(s):*

Many people are becoming more and more aware that Social Security may not have enough "wind" to help them reach their retirement harbor.

If you are concerned about the future of the Social Security program, *Enter client's name*, I can help you learn more about the role it may play in your retirement years, including:

- The future of Social Security

- When you become eligible to receive Social Security benefits

- What your annual Social Security benefits may be

Not knowing what lies ahead can be unsettling. However, you do not have to rely on Social Security alone for retirement, *Enter client's name*. You can take control of your retirement future. One way to save for a secure financial future is to invest in a diversified portfolio of mutual funds.

Call me today at *Your phone number here or* return the enclosed informaton request to discover what role Social Security plays in your retirement planning and how mutual funds may provide additional income for you. I can provide prospectuses containing more complete information, including a description of all charges and expenses, for any of the funds we discuss. You should read the prospectuses carefully before investing or sending money. I look forward to hearing from you.

Sincerely,

Your Company's Name Here

Your Name
Title

Enclosure: Social Security Response Note

P.S. **This is an opportunity to let me help you plan to reach your retirement dreams.**

SOCIAL SECURITY RESPONSE NOTE

Enter Date

Enter Your Name
Enter Your Address
Enter Your City, State, Zip Code

Dear *Enter Your Name:*

_____ Sounds interesting! I want to see some additional information on *Social Security's role.* Please drop it in the mail right away.

_____ I am not interested in *Social Security's role,* but I would like some information on:

_____

_____ I am not interested in anything now, but a friend might be. Please give me a call at _____. Best time to call is: _____.

Sincerely,

Enter Client's Name(s)
Enter Client's Address
Enter Client's City, State, and Zip Code

For faster service, please fax to *Enter your fax number.*

SMALL BUSINESS RETIREMENT PLAN LETTER

Enter Date

Enter Client's Name(s)
Enter Client's Address
Enter City, State, and Zip Code

> *"A journey of a thousand leagues begins with a single step."*
> **—Lao-tzu**

Dear *Enter Client's Name(s):*

Many small business owners like yourself would like to offer their employees a 401(k) retirement plan but feel overwhelmed by the process. You might think it is too complicated, too time consuming, and too costly. I can make that journey as easy as a single step for you.

Now, there is a 401(k) retirement savings plan that allows you to serve your employees in a special way. It is easy to understand, simple to administer, and affordable to install and maintain—the *Your broker/dealer name* 401(k) retirement savings plan.

This plan offers you and your company the opportunity for:

- Expert investment management

- A wide selection of investment options

- Simplified administration and recordkeeping

- Employee education and communication programs

- Affordable costs

And a *Your broker/dealer name* 401(k) provides you with the expertise of experienced portfolio managers.

If you would like more information on how easily and inexpensively you can offer your employees a 401(k) plan, please return the enclosed information request. As always, if you have immediate questions or concerns, please contact me at *Enter your phone number.* I look forward to hearing from you, *Enter client's name.*

Sincerely,

Your Firm Name Here

Your Name
Title

Enclosure: Small Business Retirement Plan Response Note

P.S. Let me make reviewing your 401(k) options seem like a single step instead of a long, hard journey.

SMALL BUSINESS RETIREMENT PLAN
RESPONSE NOTE

Enter Date

Enter Your Name
Enter Your Address
Enter Your City, State, Zip Code

Dear *Enter Your Name:*

_____ Sounds interesting! I want to see some additional information on *retirement 401(k) plans*. Please drop it in the mail right away.

_____ I am not interested in *retirement 401(k) plans,* but I would like some information on:
_____

_____ I am not interested in anything now, but a friend might be. Please give me a call at _____. Best time to call is: _____.

Sincerely,

Enter Client's Name(s)
Enter Client's Address
Enter Client's City, State, and Zip Code

For faster service, please fax to *Enter your fax number.*

STOCK FUNDS LETTER

Enter Date

Enter Client's Name(s)
Enter Client's Address
Enter City, State, and Zip Code

> *"Goals are not only absolutely necessary to motivate us.*
> *They are essential to really keep us alive."*
> **—Rev. Robert Schuller**

Dear *Enter Client's Name(s):*

Like many investors, you know the value of goals, but you may be facing the uncertainty of not having enough money to reach your goals—such as buying a home, paying for college, or preparing for comfortable retirement years.

One solution may be a stock mutual fund. Though subject to greater market fluctuations, over the long term, stocks have provided the opportunity for more capital appreciation than fixed-income alternatives and can help you stay ahead of inflation.

Mutual funds are an easy way to invest in stocks. As your financial advisor, I can offer you a wide range of portfolios. *Enter client's name,* consider these benefits:

- **Growth potential:** Investing in stocks of established or growing companies could help you build capital and keep ahead of inflation.

- **Diversification:** Shareholders are part owners of companies of many sizes, industries, and geographical locations.

- **Full-time professional management:** Portfolio managers have extensive experience and vast resources for daily analysis of the global stock markets.

- **Access to your money:** Shares may be redeemed on any business day at the then-current net asset value, which may be more or less than the price you paid.

Enter client's name, I can help you determine how a stock fund can fit into your investment portfolio. Call me at *Enter phone number* or return the enclosed information request for more complete information. I look forward to helping you reach your financial goals.

Sincerely,

Your Company's Name Here

Your Name
Title

Enclosure: Stock Funds Response Note

P.S. **If you are thinking "I don't know . . . ," I want to assure you there is no obligation or pressure at all, just an opportunity to learn more about planning for your essential goals.**

STOCK FUNDS RESPONSE NOTE

Enter Date

Enter Your Name
Enter Your Address
Enter Your City, State, Zip Code

Dear *Enter Your Name:*

____ Sounds interesting! I want to see some additional information on *stock funds*. Please drop it in the mail right away.

____ I am not interested in *stock funds*, but I would like some information on:

_____

____ I am not interested in anything now, but a friend might be. Please give me a call at _____. Best time to call is: _____.

Sincerely,

Enter Client's Name
Enter Client's Address
Enter Client's City, State, and Zip Code

For faster service, please fax to *Enter your fax number.*

SELF-EMPLOYED LETTER

Enter Date

Enter Client's Name(s)
Enter Client's Address
Enter City, State, and Zip Code

> *"Vision is the art of seeing the invisible."*
> **—Jonathan Swift**

Dear *Enter Client's Name(s):*

Certainly, being in business for yourself has its rewards: independence, and the ability to call the shots and be the visionary of your own destiny. At the same time, it means that you are the one with responsibility for seeing the invisible . . . including your retirement security. Unfortunately, unlike those who work for someone else, you cannot rely on an employer to provide you with a nest egg for your old age.

Today, there are a number of retirement programs designed specifically for the self-employed that make building a pool of money for retirement easy, convenient, and relatively painless. These plans feature:

- *Tax-deductible plan contributions,* meaning you reduce your tax bill each year you put money into the plan

- The *deferral of taxes* on your contributions and investment earnings until you withdraw them at retirement, when you are likely to be in a lower tax bracket.

- A *wide choice of mutual funds*

- A *toll-free phone number* for account inquiries and convenient account transactions

- *Regular reports* that make it easy to track the growth of your nest egg

As a financial advisor, I have been counseling individuals on retirement planning issues for more than __ years. If retirement is a nagging worry for you—and it probably is—I would like to help you get some peace of mind. Return the enclosed information request to receive additional information. As always, if you would like to speak with me immediately, do not hesitate to contact me at *Enter your phone number.* I look forward to talking with you.

Sincerely,

Your Company's Name Here

Your Name
Title

Enclosure: Self-Employed Response Note

P.S. Let *me* take the time to help you plan for your retirement, so you can keep your vision on your business, not on planning for your retirement.

SELF-EMPLOYED RESPONSE NOTE

Enter Date

Enter Your Name
Enter Your Address
Enter Your City, State, Zip Code

Dear *Enter Your Name:*

_____ Sounds interesting! I want to see some additional information on *retirement programs for the self-employed.* Please drop it in the mail right away.

_____ I am not interested in *retirement programs for the self-employed,* but I would like some information on:

_____

_____ I am not interested in anything now, but a friend might be. Please give me a call at _____. Best time to call is: _____.

Sincerely,

Enter Client's Name
Enter Client's Address
Enter Client's City, State, and Zip Code

For faster service, please fax to *Enter your fax number.*

RETIREMENT PLANNING LETTER

Enter Date

Enter Client's Name(s)
Enter Client's Address
Enter City, State, and Zip Code

> *"Eighty percent of success is showing up."*
> **—Woody Allen**

Dear *Enter Client's Name(s):*

Sometimes, investors put off investing because they are looking for the perfect investment. As your financial advisor, I have learned there is no such thing as the single perfect investment. In fact, 80 percent of successful investing is just "showing up" or doing something.

Take the case of the Jones triplets.
- In 1978, Jan Jones started investing $200 a month. At an average interest rate of 12 percent over 20 years, her investment would grow to over $197,000.
- Her sister Jean waited five years to invest at $200 per month at the same interest rate, but only for 15 years. Jean had almost $100,000 at the end of 15 years. Waiting five years cost Jean almost $100,000.
- Jenny waited even longer to start her investment program. She, too, invested $200 a month at 12 percent, but she only invested for ten years. At the end of ten years, her investment was worth $46,000, more than $50,000 less than Jean and almost $150,00 less than Jan.

Monthly Investment	Interest Rate	Years	Future Value (tax consequences are not considered)
$200	12%	10	$46,008
$200	12%	15	$99,916
$200	12%	20	$197,851

Projections do not guarantee future results.

It seems the Jones triplets were interested in the Johnson boys—Jimmy, Joe, and Jay. The Johnson boys also believed in investing, but started out with a one-time lump sum each.

- Jimmy started with $20,000 at a 12 percent average return for 20 years and accumulated over $217,000.
- Joe waited five years, and also invested $20,000 and also received an average return of 12 percent. He managed to accumulate almost $120,000, roughly $100,000 less than his brother Jimmy.
- The last to start, Jay invested his over a ten-year period with the same return rate. He accumulated $66,000, approximately $150,000 less than Jimmy and $54,000 less than Joe.

Lump Sum	Interest Rate	Years	Future Value (tax consequences are not considered)
$20,000	12%	10	$66,008
$20,000	12%	15	$119,916
$20,000	12%	20	$217,851

Projections do not guarantee future results.

There is no time like the present to get started on your investment program. Let me now show you how easy and painless it can be.

If you are interested in learning more about systematic investment programs, please call me today at *Enter your phone number* or return the enclosed information request. I will be happy to discuss your investment goals and to provide you with a prospectus detailing investment policies, expenses, and risk considerations. Please read it carefully before you invest. I look forward to hearing from you, *Enter client's name.*

Sincerely,

Your Company's Name Here

Your Name

Enclosure: Retirement Planning Response Note

P.S. If you are about to set this aside to think (or worry) about later, I promise you will be better able to think about this issue with the information at hand. This is an opportunity to learn more about your future.

RETIREMENT PLANNING RESPONSE NOTE

Enter Date

Enter Your Name
Enter Your Address
Enter Your City, State, Zip Code

Dear *Enter Your Name:*

____ Sounds interesting! I want to see some additional information on *retirement planning.* Please drop it in the mail right away.

____ I am not interested in *retirement planning,* but I would like some information on:

_____

____ I am not interested in anything now, but a friend might be. Please give me a call at _____. Best time to call is: _____.

Sincerely,

Enter Client's Name
Enter Client's Address
Enter Client's City, State, and Zip Code

For faster service, please fax to *Enter your fax number.*

REFERRAL LETTER

Enter Date

Enter Client's Name(s)
Enter Client's Address
Enter Client's City, State, and Zip Code

Dear *Enter Client's Name(s):*

As your financial advisor, it is very rewarding to help you reach your financial goals. A good financial advisor is a combination of outstanding service, attention to detail, and delivering products that help meet your objectives—all based on your specific needs. Please call me if you require additional financial advice or have questions. I am here to help.

When clients ask, I tell them, "Yes, I am accepting referrals." Each time we talk, you will find it easier to think of names of friends, family, or neighbors who would like to learn about becoming more financially educated and secure, like you have. They will receive the same high level of attention you received. As a satisfied client, when you give me referrals, it is the best compliment I can receive.

Those you refer will receive a free, personalized analysis reviewing their situation. Sometimes they already have a financial plan. In that case, I work like a doctor and give them a second opinion. Maybe I can make suggestions that might benefit them.

Do you know people who wish to become more educated about their financial choices and feel assured from a second opinion? I will work closely with them to ensure they will soon feel the same level of trust you do. Together we can help them have a brighter financial future, and they will be glad you referred their name.

Sincerely,

Your Firm's Name Here

Your Name
Title

P.S. Imagine . . . being the person who refers someone and they become more financially secure. I will be calling you soon for those names. For personal referrals or any questions you may have, I can be reached at *Enter your phone number.*

<u>NOTE:</u> *In the P.S. we state you will call them (it is a good excuse to say hi and talk business with present clients). However, if you wish them to call you with the referred names, change that line.*

CLIENT SATISFACTION LETTER

Enter Date

Enter Client's Name(s)
Enter Client's Address
Enter City, State, and Zip Code

> *"A frog has a wonderful advantage in life:*
> *he can eat everything that bugs him."*
> **—Anonymous**

Dear *Enter Client's Name(s):*

Your happiness and satisfaction with our firm is our number one priority.

So . . . if anything is "bugging" you, I would like to know. To better serve you, I have enclosed a client satisfaction survey. Please mail it back to me, or fax it to *Enter your fax number.*

Let me know not only what I could be doing better, but what you value about our relationship. *Enter client name,* I appreciate your business. As always, if there is anything you have questions or concerns about, please do not hesitate to call me at *Enter your phone number.*

Sincerely,

Your Firm's Name Here

Your Name
Title

Enclosure: Client Satisfaction Survey

CLIENT SATISFACTION SURVEY

Client Satisfaction Survey for _____
Name of Client

Rate the following on a scale of 1 to 5, with 5 being completely satisfactory and 1 being completely unsatisfactory.

Completely Unsatisfactory   *Completely Satisfactory*

My advisor carefully and accurately explained all investments and confirmation statements.

☐ 1   ☐ 2   ☐ 3   ☐ 4   ☐ 5

My advisor took the time to thoroughly understand my financial goals and temperament.

☐ 1   ☐ 2   ☐ 3   ☐ 4   ☐ 5

My advisor is accessible to answer questions.

☐ 1   ☐ 2   ☐ 3   ☐ 4   ☐ 5

My advisor handles my affairs in a timely manner.

☐ 1   ☐ 2   ☐ 3   ☐ 4   ☐ 5

I feel comfortable with my planner's/advisor's recommendations.

☐ 1   ☐ 2   ☐ 3   ☐ 4   ☐ 5

My advisor did a good job making recommendations that fit my goals and my investment temperament.

☐ 1   ☐ 2   ☐ 3   ☐ 4   ☐ 5

- Do you have any comments about our service?

_____

- Is there anything we can do to serve you better?

_____

- Is there someone we should thank for taking good care of you?

_____

- If you have not received the service you think you should have, please let me know personally so we can address your concerns immediately.

Thank you for your time. As always, please contact us with any questions or concerns.

Client's Name(s) (optional): _____
Please fax this to *your fax number.*

Reprinted with permission of Bloomberg Press.

SAMPLE BIO/PROFESSIONAL PROFILE

"To help you live the life
of your choice through
the accumulation and
conservation of your
financial resources."

Katherine Vessenes, J.D., C.F.P®
Senior Financial Advisor

Since 1990, Katherine has been working with broker/dealers, financial advisors, and large insurance companies, teaching them how to do *the right thing by their clients.* "My mission has been to make sure every advisor puts the needs of their client first," says Katherine. A popular keynote speaker, she has written two books and almost 100 articles. Bloomberg Press said she is **"America's best-known authority on the legal and ethical issues facing financial advisors today."** Blue Bonnet Advisors is delighted that Katherine will now put all that sound advice and counsel into practice, working directly with our clients as a financial advisor.

Katherine knows that most clients have concerns about two things: their financial future and selecting the right advisor. Choosing a financial advisor with ethics and integrity is a vital part of getting a sense of peace about their financial future. She says, "I have two goals for every client. First, I want to be the kind of financial advisor whose integrity and character would be good enough for my own mother. And, second, I want to help each client create enough wealth so that they have the resources to live a life with no regrets—the life they have always dreamed about."

Between 1989 and 1991, Katherine was Vice President and Officer of the IDS Mutual Fund Group, now American Express, where she was legal counsel to the independent directors, including President Gerald Ford. She has also served on the CFP Board of Ethics and Professional Review. She is currently Of Counsel with a St. Paul law firm. Her previous business development clients included: American Express Planners, Jefferson Pilot, SunAmerica Securities, Financial Planning Association, Institute for Certified Financial Planners, Charles Schwab, and many others.

Katherine and her husband Peter live in Shorewood, Minnesota. They have three adult children. Katherine loves to antique, especially for Japanese prints, and has recently taken up cross-country skiing.

(Broker/dealer information and address here.)

JOB DESCRIPTION
Chief Operating Officer

The purpose of this Job Description is to define the position of Chief Operating Officer (COO).

Goals and Objectives

To manage the day-to-day activities of the company in a way that meets or exceeds revenue objectives, establishes a quality system that increases efficiency at all levels of the company, and stays at or below allocated budgets. The position will also free up time for the CEO and the President so they can pursue activities that ensure the future growth and profitability of the company. The position will maintain and strengthen the culture of the company as defined by the CEO. The COO will reflect the mission, values, and ideology of the practice in all communication that takes place through this position.

Responsibilities

- Improve the efficiency of all operations of the company.
- Minimize the legal and ethical liabilities of the company.
- Ensure that the company follows all OSHA and other work-related laws and regulations.
- Assist in optimizing profitability and advise the President and the CEO on issues and factors that affect it.
- Assist the CEO in maximizing his time in appointments, referrals, and growth opportunities through the activities of the rest of the company.
- Implement, create, and manage training in the company. Help employees grow and develop skills and abilities that help them and the company reach the mission of *Your company name.*
- Create and maintain "raving fans" in both clients and employees.
- Evaluate and manage new product, service, and business opportunities for the company.
- Assist in creating and manage a quality system for the company.

Duties

- Monitor the hours worked by employees.
- Master the use of Gorilla Systems. Manage its use in the company.
- Conduct meetings at least monthly with employees that report to the COO.
- Monitor and manage expenditures under the position's authority.

- Create a monthly report that reviews the current status of employees and the company on personal growth, corporate culture, operational bottlenecks, budgets, process and procedures, and quality systems.
- Participate in a manager's meeting twice a month with the CEO and the President.
- Manage all employees reporting under the position.
- Conduct employee reviews.
- Assist in developing strategies and planning for the company.

Position Requirements
- To use computer systems, including word processing, marketing software, and data entry.
- To use courteous and professional communication skills with employees, clients, and others.
- To evaluate financial reports.
- To manage resources as assets in the efforts of the company.

Level of Authority
- All responsibilities and duties are Level 4 authority.

Reporting
- The COO reports to the President.
- All positions in the company, other than the CEO, the assistant to the CEO, the President, and the assistant to the President, report to the COO.

JOB DESCRIPTION
Client Service Coordinator

The purpose of this Job Description is to define the position of Client Service Coordinator.

Goals and Objectives
To help clients of the company reach their personal financial objectives while minimizing their future tax liabilities. To effectively reflect the mission, values, and ideology of the practice in all communication that takes place through this position.

Responsibilities
- To deal honestly and ethically with all clients.
- To make all clients feel as if their needs are the most important thing in the world to the Client Service Coordinator.
- To accurately record all information required for investments by clients in the forms and paperwork.
- To maintain long-term relationships with clients that turn them into "raving fans."
- To monitor future needs of clients.
- To effectively manage their time to ensure sufficient meetings with clients in order to meet and exceed their quantitative performance objectives.

Duties
- Fill out paperwork with clients. Complete paperwork after client's portion is finished.
- Send thank-you notes to clients.
- Stay in contact with clients weekly until the delivery of a product or policy.
- Request medical evaluations for VUL products.
- Use Gorilla Jr. for all aspects of their client responsibilities.
- Fill in the daily stat sheet. Review and evaluate the daily and weekly stat sheet.
- Process letters associated with their activities.
- Review client folders prior to meetings.
- Send paperwork and money to the receptionist for delivery to the appropriate product provider.
- Follow up with clients according to the duty lists generated by Gorilla Systems.

Position Requirements

- The ability to use computer systems, including word processing, marketing software, and data entry and services research.
- To be courteous and professional in the use of the telephone in communicating with clients and others.
- The ability to write legibly and professionally.
- The ability to communicate with clients and others in a professional and meaningful manner.
- The ability to drive during the work day, to occasionally lift objects weighing up to 25 lbs., to sit for extended periods of time (five to eight hours per day) in using the telephone and the computer systems.

Level of Authority

- All responsibilities and duties are Level 4 authority.

Reporting

- The Client Service Coordinator reports to the COO.
- The Client Service Coordinator works laterally with all other positions in the company including the President, CEO, and all staff that report to these positions.

MONEY TRAIL™

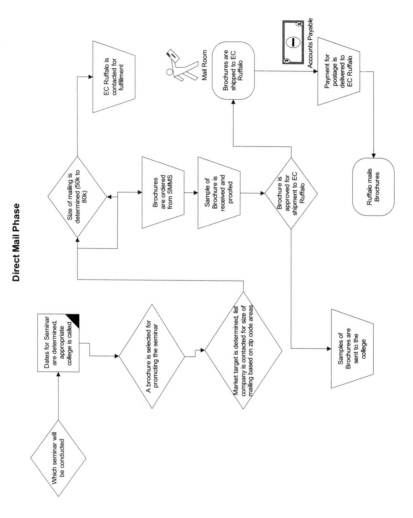

Response to Direct Mail Phase

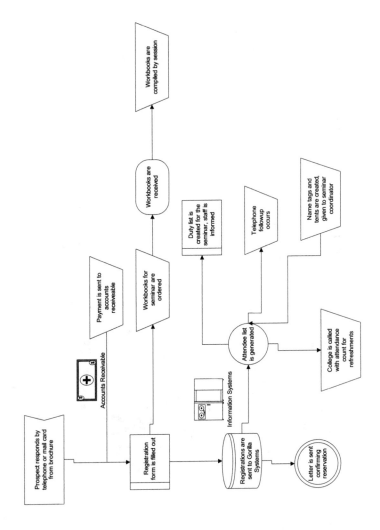

Preparation for the Seminars

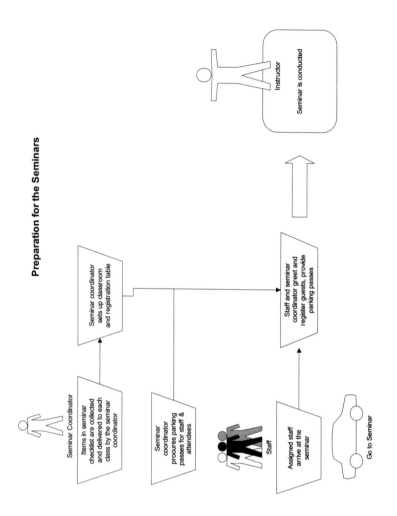

Followup with Seminar Students

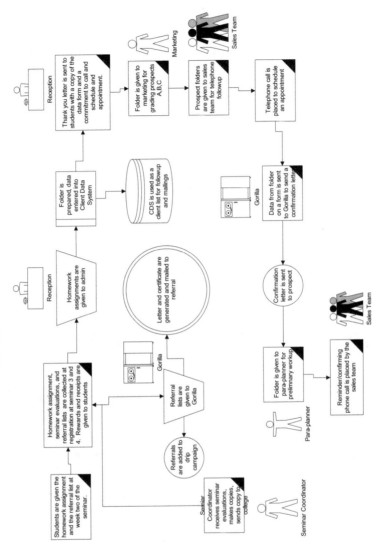

The Appointment with the Prospect

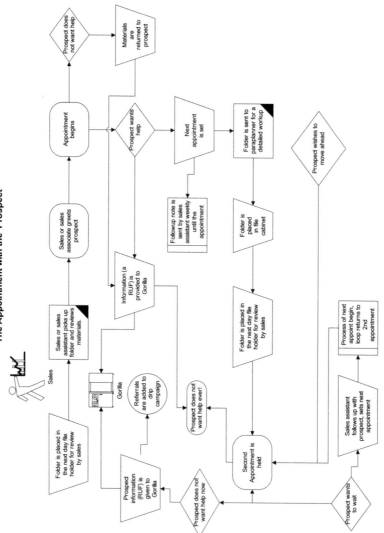

The Delivery of the Investments

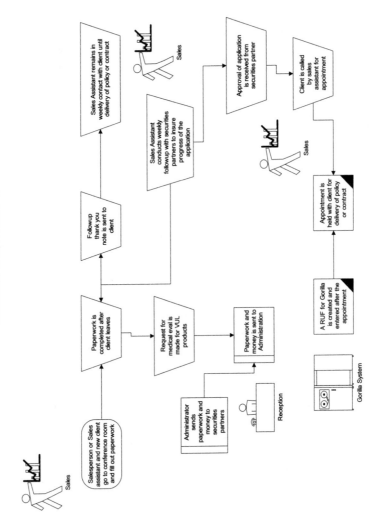

Legend

Manual Process

An internal and external paper event

An external paper event

Decision

Computer disk storage

Event

Tagged Process

A message from

Pre-defined process

For more tips and resources to help you **increase your income** while **reducing stress,** visit the authors' website at **www.vestmentadvisors.com**

TAKE ADVANTAGE OF THESE EXCLUSIVE OFFERS FOR READERS OF *BUILDING YOUR MULTI-MILLION-DOLLAR PRACTICE:*

DocuMate – The digital companion to *Building Your Multi-Million-Dollar Practice*. Offers contracts, letters, surveys and the forms from this book, already entered into Microsoft Word™! Absolutely indispensable! Save time and money with these crucial practice management tools. Regularly $175.00, go to **www.vestmentadvisors.com/bookoffers** to save $50.00 and get DocuMate for only $125.00!

Touch Tone Talks – Be part of a live conference call on topics of importance to financial advisors! Visit **www. touchtonetalks.com/bookoffers** for a list of our upcoming calls and how to get $15.00 discount off the regular price!

Vestment Advisors Workshops – Be a part of a powerful two-day workshop that can supercharge changes in your practice! Visit **www.vestmentadvisors.com/workshops/ bookoffers** for a listing of upcoming events and how to get a $200.00 discount off the regular price!

VESTMENT ▼◣
A D V I S O R S

952-401-1045   FAX 952-470-7989
www.vestmentadvisors.com

Share the message!

Bulk discounts
Discounts start at only 10 copies and range from 30% to 55% off retail price based on quantity.

Custom publishing
Private label a cover with your organization's name and logo. Or, tailor information to your needs with a custom pamphlet that highlights specific chapters.

Ancillaries
Workshop outlines, videos, and other products are available on select titles.

Dynamic speakers
Engaging authors are available to share their expertise and insight at your event.

Call Dearborn Trade Special Sales at 1-800-621-9621, ext. 4444, or e-mail trade@dearborn.com.

Dearborn™
Trade Publishing
A **Kaplan Professional** Company